WONDERLANDSCAPE

WONDERLANDSCAPE

YELLOWSTONE NATIONAL PARK
AND THE EVOLUTION
OF AN AMERICAN
CULTURAL
ICON

JOHN CLAYTON

PEGASUS BOOKS
NEW YORK LONDON

WONDERLANDSCAPE

Pegasus Books Ltd.
148 W. 37th Street, 13th Floor
New York, NY 10018

Copyright © 2017 John Clayton

First Pegasus Books edition August 2017

Interior design by Maria Fernandez

Library of Congress Cataloging-in-Publication Data is available.

ISBN: 978-1-68177-457-2

10 9 8 7 6 5 4 3 2 1

Printed in the United States of America
Distributed by W. W. Norton & Company

To my parents, Paul and Jackie Clayton,
who raised me with abundant love, curiosity, and national parks

CONTENTS

PROLOGUE

On a crisp sunny morning after a spring snowstorm, I drove along an empty road that snaked through thick lodgepole pines. I came across a bison, quiet if obstinate, standing almost in the road. I stopped the car, killed the motor, stepped out. Keeping the car between me and potential danger, I snapped a photograph. The whir of the advancing film highlighted the surrounding silence: no noise of humans or their vehicles, instead the muffled drips of melting snow. I was so close to the bison that I could hear the air huffing out of its nostrils. I took a deep breath. I gazed at the animal. Then I glanced up and down the road to confirm that I was alone with one of the wonders of Yellowstone National Park.

It was May 1, 1988, my first visit to Yellowstone, and like any first-time visitor I wanted to understand this place. Why was

Yellowstone famous? Why did so many people—including me—feel compelled to make this pilgrimage? The encounter with the bison pointed me toward one answer: here one could find unique and incredible wildlife.

Later that day I walked the rim of the Grand Canyon of the Yellowstone River, with its extraordinary colors etched in snow. I also felt the *whoosh* of the Old Faithful geyser, right on time. I heard the gurgle and smelled the sulfur of nearby hotpots. The answer to my question broadened: here one could also find rare geological marvels. Combining wildlife and geology, Yellowstone stood for pure, rich nature.

I knew this answer had to be incomplete. I'd spent less than a day in this landscape of two million acres. I hadn't read any books, watched only a quick introductory film at a visitor center. I missed several of the park's famous destinations, including the terraces at Mammoth Hot Springs, more geysers and thermal features at Norris and Midway, a waterfall at Tower, and views from atop Mount Washburn. Furthermore, I spent most of my time in the car rather than out in that natural world. But I was satisfied that I'd gotten a start. I didn't realize how that single day would expand to a twenty-nine-year quest.

In 1990 I moved to a small town a couple of hours away. Although I didn't move *to Yellowstone*—I never worked in the park and spent much of my time in my own vibrant community—I did experience it regularly, in all seasons. And although I sometimes went alone, I eventually realized that many of my lasting, significant memories involved *people*. For example, one November afternoon, K— asked me to stop the car alongside Soda Butte Creek to watch what she thought was a wolf, although I thought it was a coyote. Several miles later, four grand animals suddenly swaggered in front of us. These were obviously wolves: bigger, darker, and far more regal than the coyote. I'll never forget them, but the stronger memory of that moment is my experience of K—'s amazement. Likewise, one September evening, G—, J—, and I stood at the edge of a meadow deep in the Pelican Valley, watching the deer, elk, and other creatures materialize as the dusk faded, like vampires no longer threatened by daylight. The sighs of delight from my companions were as fascinating and rewarding to me as the meadow's lively hush. A different experience: one August afternoon, C— and I sat in the lobby of the Lake Yellowstone Hotel, sipping cocktails. We admired the architecture, the well-heeled patrons, and glimpses of the broad lake out the window. C—, a former working-class kid from Long Island, the first in his family to go to college, didn't speak about amassing the sensibilities to appreciate this upper-class activity, but I sensed his triumph and found it as valuable as the activity itself. Likewise, one June evening my parents and I shared a meal in a cafeteria near Old Faithful with a tableful of chatty international travelers. To me that meal was as memorable as the geyser, because that instant community was full of happy noises, comparing notes and sharing stories, everyone friendly and open like they could never be at home. I climbed Mount Washburn with D—, soaked in a remote hot spring with M— and the R—s, and watched a contented grin overtake L— as she promenaded around the terraces at Mammoth Hot Springs.

As magical as Yellowstone's natural features were, to me their chief significance became the way they prompted experiences that I shared with other people. I had to admit that I was not Henry David Thoreau, immersing himself in nature for its solitude. Then again, once I accepted that "flaw" in my character, I realized that it probably held for other people too. Once I spent an hour at Artist Point overlook, as waves of tourists disembarked from buses and swarmed around in small groups. I noticed that they didn't spend much time pondering the views in silence. Instead, they valued the *sharing* of the experience. As groups posed in front of the best panoramas, they gazed at the camera—at the world back home, because what mattered most was their engagement with their loved ones.

A friend who spent a few summers leading smaller, more intimate tours reported similar behaviors. He'd prepared for his job through lengthy study of the region's science and history, but was surprised at how many guests simply asked for his life story. They valued the opportunity to get to know Yellowstone through biography rather than facts. It's great to understand a natural wonder, but it's more accessible, and perhaps even more satisfying, to approach that understanding through personal story.

So I started paying attention to people's stories about how they experienced Yellowstone. It was usually in the context of relationships, such as a honeymoon, a family vacation, or a tour. They remembered their connections to other people: roasting marshmallows, singing campfire songs, telling stories, or rejoicing in the opportunity to share an emotional reaction. To many people, Yellowstone's meaning arises from its function as a social place.

Although this notion surprised me, the more I thought about it, the more true it felt. I realized that often, when people (including myself) think we're reacting to nature in Yellowstone, we really do so in the context of how *other people* have reacted. Maybe our reaction is *shaped* by the comments of a tour guide, the content of a Ken Burns documentary, or our previous history with religion or spirituality. Or maybe the reaction is in a class by itself, but in trying to *express* it we find ourselves quoting or paraphrasing Thoreau, Theodore Roosevelt, or Edward Abbey. Either way, our response to Yellowstone is framed by the accumulation of our experiences and values and social interactions—by our *culture.*

"The national park is nature that has been made culture, while claiming to be pure nature," wrote scholar Lynn Ross-Bryant.[1] At first I resisted this conclusion. After all, Yellowstone boasted *so much* nature. It had a gigantic lake, tall mountains, and travertine terraces; it had waterfalls and endless forests; it had wildflowers and rare plants; it had wolves and grizzlies and black bears and a huge, delicate web of processes and life-forms to support those wonders. It was all so unique, so overwhelming. Lacking skyscrapers or junkyards, lacking the bustle of workaday life, it felt like a place where people were—or at least *should be*—irrelevant.

But culture is all-encompassing. Culture affects the way we view nature—even the way we define it. Today we often define nature as *wilderness*, separate from humans, unspoiled by people's activities. But that definition is itself a cultural belief; other cultures have seen people and nature as inseparable.[2] Indeed over the past 150 years our own culture has changed its view of what nature means in Yellowstone. At first it was a set of resources, and the question was how best to exploit them. Then it functioned as a glorified zoo, where we granted sanctuary to wild animals. Later people came to define nature as a symbol of the bygone frontier, or of the explanatory power of blossoming scientific knowledge, or of spiritual purity unsullied by commerce. Each of these ideas was a cultural construction. In each case a shift in American culture as a whole shifted the features of nature that Americans chose to highlight in Yellowstone.

So, I concluded, our conception of Yellowstone's "nature" was in many ways subordinate to our conception of its culture. Ultimately Yellowstone was a cultural place. So the key to understanding Yellowstone—to appreciating it, to knowing it—would be to engage its cultural history. My first step didn't require political or administrative history, a chronicle of laws or superintendents. Nor—although it would be fascinating—did I need *indigenous* history, a history of the worthy cultures that preceded my own in this place. First I wanted to understand Yellowstone in the context of my own culture, to know why Yellowstone was important to previous generations of people like me. Why it was famous, and why that fame endures.

Culture is always layered, with new meanings piling atop old ones, adding to them rather than eradicating them. In 1870, the earliest white explorers didn't see much more than a geological freak show, and that still matters, even though today Yellowstone's meaning encompasses much more—including wildlife, architecture, frontier history, and environmental politics. These newer layers merely add to the geological significance, like additional layers of deposition atop old rocks. Indeed, one reason Yellowstone today feels so central to our culture is that it has accumulated so many varied and compelling layers of meaning. Those early explorers called it Wonderland after the weird place in Lewis Carroll's just-published *Alice in Wonderland*. But it has since shown itself to be home to uncountable diverse wonders—a wonder-landscape.

In this book I tell stories of Yellowstone's cultural history since 1870. We proceed chronologically, with a series of individuals pursuing their passions in the park. As they accomplish their goals, they illustrate what Yellowstone meant to the culture of their era. You can compare their stories to that of the blind men and the elephant: each chapter describes a different way to portray this huge thing. On their own the portrayals are compelling and wondrous, but in the big picture the hero is the elephant itself—such a grand beast that it can be seen in so many different ways.

The book contains ten stories. The first story shows Yellowstone as special, full of unique wonder and power, just like the American self-image—and it shows that specialness being discovered at a moment when the nation was in desperate need of unifying traits after its wrenching civil war. Second, amid the vanishing of bison, elk, and other once-abundant creatures, Yellowstone is portrayed as a refuge from industrialization, a sanctuary that humans could create on behalf of wildlife. Third, the rustic style of Yellowstone's

Old Faithful Inn forms the architectural expression of a desire for an informal, classless society that arises from and complements the surrounding bounty of nature.

Fourth, Yellowstone serves as a sample of the mystique of the romantic frontier. Founded on frontier nostalgia, the dude ranching industry revolves around the national park, with a trip to Wonderland as the centerpiece of an experience that seeks to capture the West as rugged adventure. Fifth, Yellowstone acquires associations with democracy and patriotism as the so-called birthplace of the National Park Idea. This founding mythology of the National Park Service is given a very specific setting on the banks of the Madison River, and thus adds new layers of symbolism onto those peaceful meadows. Sixth, the automobile helps transform Yellowstone from an upper-class leisure destination to a middle-class learning expedition. People in their cars seek the empowerment of knowledge, and roadside exhibits and museums arise to provide it. Seventh, Yellowstone gets honored for its vast unpeopled landscapes. Photographer Ansel Adams exemplifies a new set of Thoreau-style idealists who seek more than recreation or education from a national park—they seek, and find, the wonder of spirituality. Eighth, Yellowstone becomes a place where scientists research the natural world, a sort of gigantic natural laboratory. The scientific advances lead to political battles about how humans can best manage and interact with that natural world. Ninth, as the mythical home of a famous cartoon bear, Yellowstone becomes an icon of popular culture with a deep reach into childhood fantasy.

Then in chapter 10 we see this set of accumulated values nearly crash and burn. The 1988 wildfires tore across one-third of the park's acreage and threatened most of its tourist developments. But what they were really burning, in many people's minds, was the notion that Yellowstone was an unchanging paradise capable of holding so many ideals. The fires were burning a sanctuary and patriotic symbol; they were destroying representations of American exceptionalism, can-do frontier spirit, and naïve sense of benevolent control over nature. On the ground, firefighters were valiantly saving buildings. In the world of theory, ecologists were coming to see fires as essential to the natural processes that create wildlife habitat, processes that represented the true purpose of the park. But in the wider culture the fires were far bigger and more devastating, because their threat felt existential.

The park survived that threat, as attested by its four million visitors per year today. In three decades since the fires, Yellowstone has continued to serve as an icon of accumulated cultural heritage, as well as an ecological wonder. For example, Yellowstone today serves as a focal point in national debates about how wolves complete an ecosystem, what to do about climate change, which role public lands should play in a democracy, and whether a supervolcano will usher in an apocalypse.

As I put this story together—as I chose which characters and narratives to use to illustrate these points—I found that my ambition had changed. I started out wanting to understand the uniqueness of Yellowstone National Park. I pictured the moment I shared with the huffing bison as special and impossible to duplicate in any other place. I thus imagined that moment as opening a door to somewhere different from the rest of America. But my quest ended up taking me to a place that's at the very heart of America. The story of Yellowstone is the story of what America *wants* from Yellowstone. As Americans, we keep changing our minds about what we want our country to be. And because we have national parks to embody those ideals in the form of landscapes, with every such wider cultural change, we have to change what we want from a national park. Thus Yellowstone's cultural history is the nation's cultural history. And what's truly amazing about Yellowstone, what makes it America's wonderlandscape, is how it can continually meet those demands.

In ways I hadn't initially expected, the story thus matters not only to people visiting Yellowstone, or living nearby, but also to people who have only vaguely heard of it. The story of Yellowstone is the story of a place gifted with natural wonders and cultural force, and with powerful yet ever-changing ways to harness those gifts for the greater good. It is, in other words, the story of America. It's a story Americans tell about ourselves, hear about ourselves, and come to see as a description of who and what we are.

1
SPECIAL

When you go to Yellowstone today, you receive repeated signals that it's special. You have to pay to get in. Most of the signs are painted a distinctive brown. The area is printed a different color on the map. You can't escape knowing that you're in a national park, and even if you've never been to a *national park* before, the signals tell you that you have entered a distinctively different space. They prepare you to experience life differently than you would even a half mile outside the gate.

Yellowstone, as effectively as any place in the country, fulfills your expectations. If you experience nothing else—if the animals are hiding, and you don't drive all the way over to Lake, and you don't get out of the car at Mammoth or Canyon or any of the smaller features or exhibits—you will almost certainly go to Old

Faithful to watch and feel an explosion of steam from a tiny hole in the ground.* You will probably find it a unique and enthralling phenomenon. You will probably conclude that it justifies the attention given to it. It's special. But the geyser's regularity and timelessness might make you wonder about people who stumbled across it long ago, with little advance warning that these experiences would be worthwhile.

Unfortunately a story like that isn't easy to find. Native American tribes regularly enjoyed Old Faithful and many other thermal features; their oral traditions may well have been as effective as our entrance-booth flyers at telling people what to expect. But we haven't been very good at preserving or analyzing those oral traditions, which makes it hard for us to understand the contexts from which those cultures perceived their worlds. In fact we haven't done much better with regard to the first Anglos to experience Yellowstone, because they didn't write stuff down either.[1] John Colter, after leaving the Lewis and Clark expedition, probably passed through Yellowstone in 1807–08. But the fact that he made the trip alone, on foot, in winter, made his trip sound almost more like legend than fact.[2] Over the next four decades, fur trappers wandered through Yellowstone, but they were stereotyped as fringe elements, like homeless people today. Stories told by the trapper Jim Bridger were doubted so often that he became famous less for his formidable exploits than for his tall tales. He told of a river warmer on the bottom than the top, as if heated by the friction of the rocks—a good description of the Firehole. But then, talking about a petrified tree northwest of Roosevelt Lodge, he repurposed an old tall tale about the tree being home to petrified birds singing petrified

---

* Major Yellowstone features that have grown into neighborhoods named like towns are (counterclockwise on the figure-eight road from the North Entrance): Mammoth (Hot Springs), Norris, Madison (Junction), Old Faithful, Grant (or West Thumb), Lake, Canyon, and Tower/Roosevelt.

songs. Eventually an older Jim Bridger story, about a mountain of glass that served not only as a mirror but also as a magnifying glass, such that it made an elk seem within shooting range when it was really twenty-five miles behind you, was repurposed by others who set it at Obsidian Cliff between Norris and Mammoth. Finally, completely fabricated stories, such as Bridger's alleged use of an echo as an alarm clock, proved marvelously entertaining but damaged his credibility.[3]

Trappers were followed by prospectors, who had incentives to either hide or lie about their destinations. They probably approached this little-visited land having heard some sort of story about its uniqueness, but for sixty-odd years after Colter, there are few accounts that we can look back on in detail. Only in 1870 and 1871 did teams of upper-class explorers set out to create a written chronicle of the region. Because they were the first to try to document Yellowstone's wonders, they're sometimes credited with "discovering" the place. They did so only if you define *discover* as "be the first to make known"—they certainly weren't the first to find it.[4] But the great thing about their stories is that we can see how they viewed Yellowstone, how they saw it as different from other places, and how their interpretation came to center on the notion of *special*.[5]

At the Grand Canyon of the Yellowstone, the painter Thomas Moran lingered over the view. It was midsummer—July 1871— and the canyon presented an epic panorama, full of color. Its golden-yellow cliffs were streaked with rusty reds, pearl grays, and deep blacks. The scene was dotted with vivid green mosses and paler green grasses. The base of the Lower Falls created a cacophony of white spray, which then collected itself to flow into a blue ribbon of river. The surroundings featured evergreen trees—blankets of lodgepole—plus clear blue skies, and, off in the distance, the tantalizing white snowcaps of the Tetons.

Moran, a rail-thin 34-year-old with a beard grown unkempt from a summer in the wilderness, often appeared to be at leisure, just looking around. In fact he was committing scenes to his prodigious visual memory. And so he lingered here, seeing the colors and the composition, soaking in the beauty and majesty, feeling the emotions they evoked. For four days, he walked up and down the canyon. Sometimes he made sketches, fished in the river, visited with geologists, or helped his friend William Henry Jackson set up photographic equipment. But much of the time he just sat, observing, memorizing, feeling. From which vantage did the elements come together most beautifully? Which views best captured the power and wonder of the natural scene? How did this scene provoke an emotional reaction in him, and how could he recapture that on canvas?

What's most fascinating about Moran's visit isn't so much that he was one of the first Anglo artists to see the canyon. Nor is it even that he was one of the *best* such artists, as demonstrated by one legendary masterpiece and several more artworks nearly as acclaimed. What's most fascinating is Moran's ambition. He was not a *plein air* painter, reproducing what he saw in front of him. Rather, he would take these scenes home to construct images that *interpreted* Yellowstone for others. He intended to transform the nature he witnessed into art, into a piece of culture for others to consume.

In varying ways, transforming raw nature into culture was what every member of his 1871 expedition sought to do. The trip was organized by Ferdinand Hayden, a scientist-bureaucrat in charge of annual federal geological surveys. Each summer Hayden assembled crews to go off and look at some place that few of his contemporaries had ever seen. But unlike previous explorers, he wasn't after gold, slaves, or furs. He pursued knowledge. Twelve years after the publication of Darwin's theory of evolution, Hayden sought fossils to understand the past, taxonomies to document the present, and maps to plan the future. He was not merely seeing nature in place, nor merely extracting from it the obvious riches of minerals or furs. He was articulating how an unfamiliar landscape could be folded into the era's dominant culture.

To do so, Hayden brought along a crew of about thirty: topographers and geologists and botanists, an entomologist, a meteorologist, and a zoologist; plus packers, cooks, hunters, and guides. He solicited interns from the families of congressmen because—unlike previous explorers—his trips were paid for by congressional appropriations, rather than private or military funds. Thus every member of the expedition served a cultural purpose: some explaining the place in terms of the existing scientific culture, and others setting the foundations to incorporate it into America's democratic and economic structures. In a similar trip the previous year, Hayden explored the Uintas, an inhospitable but rather ordinary mountain range on the Wyoming-Utah border, and the expedition's report rhapsodized over picturesque beauty and agricultural potential. Hayden compared a rugged Uinta plateau to "an elegantly prepared lawn" and peaks to "Egyptian pyramids on a grand scale"; he referred to the game trails between them as excellent roads. In other words, Hayden was trying to show the government and the railroad how places like the Uintas could turn into places just like the Midwest, the East Coast, or northern Europe.[6] In Yellowstone he would find a challenge even greater than the Uintas, because this equally cold and empty place was also far more strange.

The Hayden crew members who ended up having the biggest cultural impact—the painter Moran and the photographer

Jackson—also used the summer to become close friends. The two met in late June at a camp on a high-altitude, treeless meadow along what is today Interstate 15 about five miles north of the Montana-Idaho border. Sagebrush-sprinkled flats still glowed verdant with spring runoff, and probably sported wildflowers. The setting was scenic, with a wide, grand beauty befitting the notion of the nearby Continental Divide—but with a certain monotony to the beauty, a view that barely changed for twenty miles at a time. And the expedition, which had left the nearest railhead about three weeks earlier, chugged along at less than fifteen miles per day. Moran, who'd gotten a late start from the Union Pacific station at Ogden, Utah, leapfrogged the first two hundred and fifty miles in a four-day stagecoach ride. This was the well-traveled route to Montana's territorial capital at Virginia City; from there the expedition would curve northeast to pick up a military escort near Bozeman, and then southeast to the unknown territory along the Yellowstone River.[7]

Some of Moran's now-legendary early blunders made him appear ill-suited to rugged western travel. For example, on the stagecoach trip, he wondered aloud why the vehicle was so heavily armed. "Road agents," somebody replied, and he didn't recognize that phrase as a synonym for outlaws; he wondered why the driver would need a gun to interact with his own company's station agent. Other problems: He'd never ridden a horse. He carried a small carpetbag with clothing insufficient for the cool mountain nights. Worst, his stomach had a lifelong aversion to oils and fatty foods. On such a journey, of course bacon was a staple and the frypan a standard tool. Indeed Hayden's head cook, John Raymond, was nicknamed "Potato John" because of his habit of under-boiling potatoes. By the time Moran arrived, Potato John had already decided to give up on boiling and conquer all of his potatoes by frying them.

But the legends exaggerate: Moran was actually quite comfortable with enduring hardships for the sake of art. He was an experienced traveler, having spent several weeks camped out on Lake Superior, painting, and several months in England, studying the Romantic seascapes of J. M. W. Turner. He was a passionate fisherman, and showed his colleagues a new way to cook fish, wrapped in wet paper and baked under a campfire's hot coals. (Impressed, they didn't seem to realize what he must have seen as the chief benefit: food that hadn't been fried.) In Moran's day job at *Scribner's Monthly* magazine, he'd recently illustrated black-and-white woodcuts to accompany Nathaniel Langford's article on the 1870 Yellowstone expedition. Langford's stories made Moran decide to pursue these Yellowstone scenes in person. At that point in the history of landscape painting, Hudson River School painters had thoroughly canvassed the pastoral scenes in the East; to be new and different, Moran would happily endure rugged wilderness travel.

One of Moran's first opportunities to sketch a scene that no contemporary artist had previously visited came at a feature called the Devil's Slide. This stark cliff face receives little attention today, in part because it stands five miles north of Gardiner, Montana, the park's northern boundary. But if you did stop along the highway there, you could imagine how sediments were deposited like a layer cake—one layer full of oxidized iron to make it red—and then later heaved up on end to turn the layers into vertical stripes. A geology teacher would get very excited, and talk about how the sedimentary rocks are of different types, and note that they are eroding at different rates, making the red layer stand out like a playground slide.

In 1870, however, members of the Washburn-Langford expedition experienced very different reactions. Although they acknowledged this unusual geology as majestic and sculptural, a "marvelous freak of the elements," Langford wrote, they insisted on naming it after the devil.[8] Langford later regretted that decision because it felt unimaginative in the face of all the additional opportunities they subsequently encountered for hell-based names. They kept encountering hot, dry, mountainous, rocky landscapes—so unlike the gentle, well-watered, long-manicured English countryside that shaped their cultural expectations. So they assigned devilish names. Because how could you tame such a place? How could you turn this aggressive terrain into a recognizable landscape? This was an era when Americans compared Atlantic coastal towns to the English seaside, Colorado to the Swiss Alps, southern California to the Mediterranean. The Hudson River Valley paintings—and even Albert Bierstadt's more outlandish extensions of that school set in exotic Western locales—showed landscapes that could have been located in Europe, except for the fact that they were not yet developed. In other words, as a culture America was not yet mature enough to see its landscapes through anything but a European filter. A red-streaked cliff—massive, dry, and empty—couldn't easily be compared to anything in Europe. Langford found it amazing, but he wasn't self-confident enough to think of it as special. It was different, alien, "other"—so he ascribed it to Satan.

One remarkable achievement of Hayden's 1871 expedition was to invoke calmer reactions to such scenes, in part because the expeditioners applied more knowledge and wisdom than their 1870 predecessors had. Hayden the geologist could write matter-of-factly about the slide's composition. Jackson the photographer could show it in black-and-white, with the red de-emphasized and the protrusions foreshortened. Moran the artist could sketch it as a jumble of rocks and trees that weren't particularly red or even slide-like. Although they didn't change the name, their practical approach did make the place seem a little less terrifyingly foreign. In one of their earliest opportunities to interpret nature as culture, they found anchor points more welcoming than hell.

On July 21, after six weeks on the road, the expedition finally crossed into what is today the national park. They camped at Mammoth Hot Springs, where hot water pools in white travertine terraces resemble a wedding cake on steroids, and then at Tower, where a 132-foot waterfall spills from a jumble of minaret-like spires. In one of Moran's Tower watercolors, the towers lean together as if gossiping under dark clouds. A beam of sunlight catches the top of the ribbon of water and then broadens across a cliff face. In the foreground, trees and rocks pile together in heaps, pushing your view upward, from ground to waterfall to towers to clouds. In another painting, filled with light and color, two tiny figures are perched on a rock in the foreground, overwhelmed by a jumble of toothy spires. To some extent Moran was drawing from a body of preconceived types: waterfall, spire, tree, mountain. And his use of color relied on what he'd learned from Turner. But at the same time his colors, less hysterical than Turner's, felt more genuine.[9] And Moran's greatest strength was to capture in astonishing yet realistic visuals the emotional weight that caused Hayden to write of the towers as "gloomy sentinels," and a geologist who climbed one tower at sunset to feel precarious in "the approaching gloom of evening."[10] The place was a little bit scary.

Moran interpreted that fear by benignly incorporating it into the culture of the day—a culture fascinated by a theological notion captured in the word *sublime*. A mixture of awe and pleasurable terror, the *sublime* resulted from the way Christians of the time appreciated God's overwhelming power: they mixed exaltation (*God is good*) with righteous fear (*God is omnipotent*).[11] They couldn't separate the joy of a rainbow, that symbol of God's grace, from the helplessness they felt facing the destruction of the associated storm.

The classic example of pre–Civil War sublimity was Niagara Falls: to stand by the falls, to see them and their uncontrollable power, was to experience nature as sublime. It was scary—but scary-fun to search out and observe at a distance, the way we enjoy horror movies today. Ideally, if you stood there long enough, your reaction folded in on itself: you realized that if nature contained these boundless reserves, maybe humans did too. As you looked out, you looked in; as you felt a somewhat-intimidating rapture with God in nature, so with God in yourself. Like many acclaimed landscape paintings of the day, Moran's depiction of the waterfall at Tower spoke to his culture's love of the sublime.

Then Moran arrived at the canyon, and sublimity was not enough. The expedition camped at a spot between two waterfalls. In the Upper Falls, the Yellowstone River, having idled through scenic meadows for a dozen miles, suddenly throws itself off a cliff. A quarter mile downstream it dives again, perhaps more spectacularly, into the deep canyon. Hayden instinctively made a comparison to the nation's best-known natural feature: with a smaller volume, these were "not so grand or impressive" as Niagara, but "far more beautiful."[12] More than the power of the waterfall, what really made the scene was the diversity and strength of the colors surrounding it. As Rudyard Kipling later wrote, the canyon was "one wild welter of color—crimson, emerald, cobalt, ochre, amber, honey splashed with port wine, snow white, vermilion, lemon, and silver gray in wide washes."[13]

At the canyon the scientists didn't have much to document or explain, so they soon moved on to Mud Volcano and Yellowstone Lake. But they understood why Moran stuck around for an extra four days. This site achieved the first half of Moran's goal: to find a scene worthy of being depicted in a masterpiece. Now only the second half remained: to create that masterpiece. Hayden wrote, "Thomas Moran, who is justly celebrated for his exquisite taste as a colorist, exclaimed with a sort of regretful enthusiasm, that these beautiful tints were beyond the reach of human art."[14] But he could certainly try.

After four days at the canyon, Moran spent just another week with the expedition, hitching a ride back to civilization in early August while the others slogged on through the fall. He now had a quest. As he wrote to Hayden the following spring, "By all Artists, it has heretofore been deemed next to impossible to make good pictures of Strange and Wonderful Scenes in nature; and that the most that could be done with such material was to give topographical or geologic characteristics. But I have always held that the Grandest, Most Beautiful, or Wonderful in Nature, would, in capable hands, make the grandest, most beautiful, or wonderful pictures, & that the business of a great painter should be the representation of great scenes in Nature."[15] Others stood curious as to whether his talents would be able to pull it off. But the work of a landscape painter is not merely in mimicking colors—it's in choosing themes to represent.

On the evening of Thursday, May 2, 1872, crowds thronged through the first-floor entranceway and up the broad double staircase of a New York institution called Clinton Hall. A Parthenon-like building originally constructed as an opera house, Clinton Hall presided over one of Manhattan's richest cultural districts, at Astor Place. The building housed the nation's fourth-largest lending library, plus the city's largest fine arts auction business. It was an excellent place to view major new works of art, and the evening's exhibition featured a single item. Attendees filed, one at a time, in front of Moran's twelve-by-seven-foot canvas, *The Grand Cañon of the Yellowstone*. The attendees were a varied crowd: railroad financiers, literary types (*Scribner's* was underwriting the event), and artists. Dazzled, Moran felt like "all New York" was there.[16]

It had been a busy winter. In the nation's capital, a notion spread that the Yellowstone area should receive some sort of special designation. The idea's backers included Ferdinand Hayden, pursuing scientific fame, and the Northern Pacific Railroad, pursuing tourist dollars. Supportive politicians in Montana, which provided the best-developed routes into the proposed attraction, pointed to the precedent of Yosemite: in 1864, Congress withheld an extraordinary landscape from homesteading and granted it to the state of California as parkland. At Yellowstone, however, Montana and Wyoming were still territories, not yet states, so the park would have to be held at the federal level.[17] In Congress, a bill to create "the Yellowstone national park" proved fairly easy to support because it required no monetary outlay—total federal appropriations over the first five years of Yellowstone's operations totaled zero dollars. In March 1872, the bill became law.

That lawmaking process was aided by an exhibition of small Moran watercolors, accompanied by Jackson's photographs to show this place as not only stunning but also real. But Moran spent much of the winter working on the oversized canvas he was now unveiling. At first glance, the painting's central misty falls competed for the eye's attention with sun-dappled cliffs. Golds and greens dominated, split by the river's ribbon of blue. In the foreground, the eye could rest in shaded purples and browns, and might struggle in the gaslight to catch tiny details: explorers on a rock, their horses, a Native American, and a bear. On a distant plateau, geysers erupted; off in the far distance stood the snowcapped peaks of the Tetons. "One can readily imagine the tallest cliff to be a vast cathedral, with its outer walls painted in the fadeless colors of Pompeii," wrote one critic later that year, also comparing the falls' rising mist to a prayer. In describing the view, calling it "too grand and wonderful for words to describe," this critic seemed to confuse the work of art with the real-life scene it depicted—which was further evidence of Moran's triumph.[18]

Expensive, oversized paintings were in vogue at the time—but this one outshone them all. A *Scribner's* editor wrote, "I knew the artist was going to paint a big picture, but I didn't know how big it would be . . . When I think of his carrying that immense canvas across his brain so long, I wonder that he didn't go through the door sidewise, and call people to look out when they came near."[19] It included massive scale yet impressive detail; exquisite composition and vivid color. Furthermore, it felt less stagy and exaggerated than other oversized works, such as Bierstadt's. Looking at Bierstadt's 1860s paintings of Yosemite, one might ask, How much of this is real and how much is the artist's longing? By comparison, viewers instinctively felt that *The Grand Cañon of the Yellowstone* was realism. They felt Moran's fidelity to the specifics of what he'd seen. Although he wasn't afraid to rearrange the topography, he rendered many details faithfully. He said, "My aim was to bring before the public the character of that region. The rocks in the foreground are so carefully drawn that a geologist could determine their precise nature."[20]

However, what made the painting most effective as art, as a piece of American culture, was Moran's interpretation of the region's character. *The Grand Cañon of the Yellowstone* captured the way America in the 1870s was changing its notions of the sublime to take a more generous view of nature. With advances in science and natural history, people became less intimidated by vast natural features, more capable of appreciating them as benign creations of God. Now you could react to, for example, an impenetrable forest or a red-streaked cliff not by fearing or despising it but by contemplating the reason God put it there. Fear could become wonder. Nature's boundless power revealed God's omnipotence, complete with all of its mercy. A landscape of vastness and grandeur, one that made people feel insignificant before it, was evidence of a greater God, not a greater devil. Moran, far more successfully than his predecessors, could see Western landscapes—with their unsurpassed vastness and grandeur largely unspoiled by Anglo development—as profound and divine.[21]

Specifically, as lobbyists for the national park displayed Moran's watercolors (and later convinced Congress to buy his masterpiece), "popular descriptions of Yellowstone changed dramatically," wrote art historian Joni Kinsey. "Within just a few months the region was transformed in the public's imagination from a kind of hell on earth to a spectacular 'wonderland.' Tones of reverence and awe replaced the earlier satanic references . . . what had been perceived as distant, sinister, and hellish places before 1870 became, through his portrayals, places of magnificence and wonder that could stand as important symbols of America's uniqueness."[22]

Moran brought Yellowstone into an American culture that was bumping up against the limits of the Niagara Falls interpretations. Niagara suggested that America, with a uniquely rich natural environment, was uniquely blessed by God. But Niagara was geographically contained. You could see great lakes above and below the falls, and you could envision exploiting nature's resources to fulfill God's purpose. Before Moran, when painters tried to apply this template to the ridiculous scale of the West, with unfamiliar plains or deserts or mountains extending as far as the eye could see, the vision faltered. Nature felt too strong, its power more a curse than a blessing. But Moran brought a peaceful wonder to *The Grand Cañon of the Yellowstone*, as well as his watercolors depicting terraces, absurdly colorful pools, high distant mountains, and magnificent rock formations. At first the images might stun a viewer like the West stunned those who weren't prepared for it: so unusual, so different from Europe, so *weird*. But after spending forty days in the wilderness, Moran didn't come back with revulsion at an uninhabitable hell, or with the European envy of Bierstadt's Swiss-tinted mountains. He mixed awe not with fear but with wonder at uniquely epic and serene features of the American landscape. Moran's work tied together the unique, the natural, and the vast in a way that people could interpret as implying God's grace even in the West. Yellowstone, in his vision, was super-sublime.

When the West was strange, terrifying, and hellish, it represented all the ways America felt inferior to Europe, dirty and unrefined. Europe had grand old cathedrals, a history of art and civilization, a cultural legacy—a society that was *better* the same way that a rich French croissant was better than a tired camp-tender's biscuits. It was widely accepted that America had more nature than Europe, and perhaps even more natural grandeur ("my scenery can beat up your scenery"). But after the Civil War, ready for a new perspective that celebrated the newly unified country, America was ready to hope that nature also provided it with a *historical* culture that was just as valid as Europe's. This argument began with awareness of the cathedral-like valley of Yosemite and its ancient sequoias. Moran's paintings brought it fully into the mainstream. Yellowstone boasted ancient rocks and geysers and a cathedral-like canyon and lake. Its landscapes were beautiful and serene, and didn't have to conjure the devil. They could speak for God. And God, Americans of the time believed, had a plan for this nation. It was a Manifest Destiny for the special people of this special country to occupy these special landscapes from sea to sea.

Today, we look back on Manifest Destiny as arrogant, racist, and environmentally destructive. But it was the reigning philosophy of the day—and people of the day saw it expressed in Yellowstone. Yellowstone stood for what America thought was best about itself. This was the message that Americans had secretly hoped to see in images of the West, images that Moran finally gave them: *We are special. America is special, because of its wondrous landscapes.* America's landscapes were many, and varied, and frequently extreme. Yellowstone captured them in microcosm, with unique geysers just a few miles from a gorgeous canyon; with vast, dark forests coming right down to a huge, pristine lake; with abundant fisheries and extraordinary rock formations; with endless mountain vistas atop majestic canyons. Yellowstone had almost everything an American of the 1870s might want in a landscape.

And that meant, to those people, that their country did too.

With the excitement of all the wonders that Moran and the Hayden party experienced, we sometimes gloss over what they *didn't* experience. An abundance of wild animals, for example. The party's hunters continually returned to camp empty-handed; one member's diary includes repeated entries such as "squirrel and partridge for dinner as José got no game."[23] Jackson later reported that nobody on the expedition even *saw* a bear the entire summer, which was an exaggeration, but not much of one.[24]

Ecologists today are wary of using these anecdotes to say much about actual wildlife populations at the time: maybe this party was simply too large, noisy, unskilled, or unlucky to encounter many animals. But whether animals were absent or just hiding, the notion of abundant wildlife did not register with our heroes. The reasons for thinking of Yellowstone as special all centered on geology. But less than thirty years later, that situation would change. When the once-ubiquitous bison suddenly loomed on the edge of extinction, the nation again looked to Yellowstone—with a very different set of priorities.

2
HALF TAME

The newborn bison calf, a surprisingly light tan color, was less than two feet tall, not much bigger than a Labrador retriever. Alone on the side of the road in Yellowstone's Lamar Valley in May 2016, it appeared to be abandoned, shivering in the cold. So father-and-son Canadian tourists took pity on it and put it in their Toyota Sequoia to drive it to a ranger station. The well-meaning action resulted in a well-deserved $735 fine, because it broke perhaps the park's most-publicized rule: do not approach wildlife. The tourists should have walked and then driven away from the calf, should have left it by the side of the road. They were fortunate that their ignorance did not have more serious consequences: by approaching an unpredictable wild animal, they could have been injured; by handling it, they could have injured it if not themselves;

and by interfering with nature, they could have helped create unnatural conditions, harming the very wonders that they had come here to enjoy. Commentators on social media condemned them vigorously, especially after the Park Service announced that the calf was not able to be reunited with its herd and had to be euthanized.[1]

Park officials made it clear: it's not bison—or bears or other wild animals—that are the problem. It's people. They just can't seem to help getting too close. For decades everyone has received a warning poster at the entrance gate, MANY VISITORS HAVE BEEN GORED BY BUFFALO, with a comical drawing of a man and his cowboy hat flying apart from each other after a bullfighting-cartoon head-butt—but people nevertheless continually try to take selfies with bison. Some even approach within a few feet of a bison that has just attacked another human being.

Thus the public shaming: *How can these tourists be so stupid? Do they think Yellowstone is some sort of petting zoo? Do they think somebody can control these wild animals? Do they think that because a national park is a special place, nothing could ever go wrong?* There's a temptation to consider "the tourist" a less-evolved, less-intelligent form of life than, say, the bison.

That's the wrong reaction. Yes, wild animals are dangerous, and no, you should not approach them. But the bison calf was already motherless when it approached the tourists. And because it was motherless in the wilderness, it was doomed to soon be killed and eaten by a coyote, wolf, or bear, its role in the natural system reduced to *food*. When the tourists looked at a creature so beautiful and precious, of course they wanted to save its life. In this particular case, the Canadians were familiar with wildlife preserves in Tanzania, where abandoned animals could receive care. Only inside the boundaries of Yellowstone, with its rule to leave natural processes alone, would they be condemned for that mercy.[2]

The tourists were acting from an innately human need, one that has been shaping our view of Yellowstone since almost its earliest days. These "stupid tourists" were following a philosophy that has been held by many individuals considered to be highly intelligent—a philosophy that historically was good for both humans and wildlife in Yellowstone. Because the philosophy doesn't fit with what we now know of ecological science, nobody today should mimic their actions. But before dismissing these "stupid tourists," it's worth embracing the history of that clash between mercy and logic. After all, the clash gets at the heart of what it means to be a human being who lives in a world with other creatures.

Every time a tourist approaches too close to a bison or other wild animal—as misguided as that action may be—the tourist is in a sense recapitulating the entire history of people and wildlife in Yellowstone. First comes fascination, then empathy or pity, then the temptation to do something to help. There's a later stage, resulting from education about ecosystem science and the value of a hands-off policy, in which you gain the strength to resist that temptation and let nature take its course. The Canadians didn't seek that education. Yet even if they had received it, the irony would be that taking a hands-off approach to bison is possible only because previous generations of people chose the opposite tactic of merciful intervention. The bison avoided extinction only because people long ago drove around carrying the animals in the 1900s equivalent of Toyota Sequoias.[3]

To explain, this chapter tells the story of one of the earliest people to write about putting himself in harm's way in the face of the park's wildlife. It was 1897, and he was one of the world's most-loved naturalists, on a life-changing journey to Yellowstone.

On June 9, 1897, a couple exited their luxurious accommodations in a Northern Pacific railcar at Livingston, Montana. They crossed the street to eat breakfast at the Albemarle Hotel.[4] The 25-year-old former Grace Gallatin was a small, trim, attractive heiress, and the daughter of a financier. A dead shot with a rifle, Grace craved adventure and travel. She'd met her husband, who was now thirty-six, aboard a ship to Paris three years earlier, where she was headed to write newspaper columns and he was headed to study art. He was a tall man with a spare frame and a distinctive handlebar mustache. His passions and intelligence won him many friends, although a tendency toward arrogance sometimes later lost them. He was known as "The Wolfman," because he was obsessed with painting wolves, a passion that Parisian artists didn't quite understand.

At the time his name was Ernest Seton Thompson, although the couple's name soon became hyphenated (Seton-Thompson), and in 1901 reversed (Thompson Seton). Ernest, born in 1860 with the name Ernest Evan Thompson, was enraptured by a family legend claiming that his father, Joseph Thompson, was the rightful earl of Winton, Scottish nobility deserving of the name Seton. The complicated claim involved a tenuous link to a possibly illegitimate status, and Joseph—for reasons he didn't articulate—never pursued it. But Ernest, who called his father "the most selfish person I ever heard of or read of in history or in fiction," may have sought in lineage the love and value he didn't feel from his father in person.[5]

Breakfasting at the Albemarle, Ernest and Grace took an opportunity to write in their journals. Both of them were talented and ambitious, and planned to write and publish about their respective journeys. But Ernest—older, male, and well ensconced in a popular niche—already had an actual assignment in hand. *Recreation* was a conservation magazine published by an elite outdoorsmen's group called the Camp Fire Club, which Ernest had recently helped establish. Naming him a special correspondent, the magazine asked for a summer's worth of reports on Yellowstone's wildlife.

"At Livingston we entered the mountains," he wrote in the magazine. "Now, between ourselves, I have never had much love for mountains. They always seem to me aggressive, overpowering, inaccessible and brutal; and they always seem posing for admiration. They give one a shut-in feeling, and make things seem close and stuffy. I am a prairie bird, you see, and whenever I see a large mountain, I always think what a grand prairie it would make if it were taken away, altogether."[6] Seton's idea of an idyll was prairie Manitoba of the early 1880s, where he had gone to help a brother establish a homestead.

Ernest's parents had left Scotland when he was not quite six, to homestead a remote, woodsy patch of Ontario. For the next four years he wandered the woods, collecting bird nests and adopting small mammals as pets. He and some of his nine brothers made their own wooden toys and constructed model wilderness scenes by arranging twigs, grass, and lichen in candy boxes. He gravitated toward local old-timers who could show him stuffed bird collections or regale him with stories of hunting wolves or bears. He connected with the wild creatures and the people who loved them in ways he could not connect with his parents.

The family's Ontario farm did not succeed. (Ernest thought his father was lazy, although a more generous view would suggest that the former shipping executive wisely traded the grueling toil of attempting to tame marginal land for the city life of an accountant.) In 1870 they moved to Toronto, where Ernest continued to study birds, dogs, and cats. He wanted to be a naturalist, a career that his father believed would be unprofitable. So instead he trained as an artist. But in classes and competitions, where other artists painted pastoral or urban landscapes, Ernest painted wild lands. Where they painted still lifes, he painted more wild lands. And where they learned how to see and paint musculature from the study of nude models, he studied dog cadavers. After just one year he fled a prestigious London art institute for a farm on the Manitoba frontier.

Ernest proved no better at farming than his father. (Neighbors thought he was lazy.) His crop-tending was hindered by his fascination with the wild game in the woods and sandhills and the birds migrating over the broad plains. He went on long hunting trips. He tracked foxes through the snow. He collected skins and traded them with other naturalists. One night, by candlelight, he counted every feather on the wing of a grackle. The homestead's failure didn't concern him, because he gained the opportunity to acquire the material needed to write and illustrate the exhaustive guidebook *Birds of Manitoba*.

As an illustrator, he was universally acclaimed. But scientists complained that as a naturalist, he failed to objectively chronicle birds' habits. Instead he told stories about bird-heroes. Ernest wasn't trained in science; he just watched wild animals and let his imagination run. He thus connected with non-scientists, as a storyteller, far more effectively than he reached the establishment. He faced similar rejection from serious art critics, who preferred innovative techniques such as impressionism to realistic if sentimental scenes of wilderness. Each rejection by authority figures sent Ernest scurrying back to the frontier, to places like Manitoba or New Mexico, where he could bask in the untamed land and hear the stories of old-time frontiersmen. Eventually he came to see himself as a sort of middleman, a person who could best help society by bringing it more of the benefits of that wilderness.

He was, perhaps subconsciously, playing out a well-defined heroic role, best captured in the James Fenimore Cooper novels Ernest had read as a child. Cooper's Natty Bumppo, a white man raised by Delaware Indians, wasn't quite *of* the wilderness, but he wasn't able to live a conventional civilized life either. At his best, he could use wilderness skills to help the expanding Anglo culture live in better harmony with nature. He could thus lessen his loneliness and displacement (*Who am I? To what culture do I belong?*) with a level of social status that birth couldn't have accomplished.[7] Ernest decided that his way to help people appreciate the glory of the natural world—and for him to find his place in the limbo between the two—would be to write and illustrate stories about animal heroes for popular audiences.

That niche proved successful and lucrative. The 1890s featured a new wave of animal stories that incorporated accurate portrayals of the lives of wild creatures. For example, Rudyard Kipling considered his 1895 *The Jungle Book* to be realism, describing actual conditions of wilderness in India, despite its fantastical tale of a boy raised by wolves. (With typical egotism, Ernest would one day claim that Kipling copied him.) Ernest became one of the best of these naturalist-illustrator-storytellers, who might embellish science—giving his creatures names and implying emotions similar to human ones—but who didn't *fudge* science. Later, lesser talents preferred sentimentality to facts, and when Ernest was sometimes lumped in with them, he resented the additional slight from the establishment.

Later in life, Ernest used his fame to found a youth organization called the Woodcraft Indians, centered on outdoor knowledge and skills. His writing about Woodcraft influenced Lord Robert Baden-Powell, founder of the Boy Scouts, and in 1910 the two organizations merged in the United States. Although they had philosophical differences, and Seton engaged in lengthy political battles with Baden-Powell and other Boy Scout leaders, the Woodcraft/Boy Scout movement reflected the wider culture's revived interest in nature—and Ernest's own boyish approach to it.[8]

But first he achieved that fame by writing animal stories. To give them the authenticity both he and his readers craved, Ernest needed to have lots of experiences with animals. He grumbled that on the train from Chicago to Livingston, the only creature he'd seen was a grouse.

Back in 1871, the West had been so massive that Ferdinand Hayden considered himself an explorer, helping society by simply documenting the unseen wonders. But the ensuing twenty-six years generated a lot of change: Transcontinental railroad routes traversed both north and south; violent marauders along the way were reduced; eight new states were born, finally big enough to admit to the Union. As the national population nearly doubled, people poured into the Plains and intermountain regions. The mounting growth had devastating effects on wildlife populations.

The most famous endangered creature was the bison. Once, as many as thirty million of these shaggy beasts roamed the West.[9] Their massive, free-ranging herds defined prairie ecosystems like the one in Manitoba that Ernest so loved. But as railroads and fences sliced up habitat and hunters carried off hides, bison populations declined in freefall—which only increased the value of the few remaining animals to those who might want to shoot them. A similar fate afflicted many other species. Elk and grizzly bears, for example, were once prairie creatures. At the beginning of the century, Lewis and Clark were stunned by the wealth and diversity of wildlife they encountered in the Dakotas and eastern Montana. But these seemingly inexhaustible populations became exhausted more quickly than anyone could have imagined.

That's what fueled establishment of the Camp Fire Club and its more cliquish rival, the Boone and Crockett Club. Wealthy hunters and wilderness adventurers were concerned about the loss of habitat and game. Although it seemed impossible to stem the tide of civilization, they reasoned that perhaps wildlife could be better protected in remote regions administered by government authorities. Some of them started holding up Yellowstone as a great example.

However, as Yellowstone and areas around it grew, so did animal slaughter within the park. Thus the earliest politics of Yellowstone involved increasing attempts to protect wildlife from hunters. In 1883 regulations prohibited hunting in the national park; in 1886 corrupt civilian management was replaced by a more efficient and better-funded military; and in 1894 authorities gained enhanced enforcement power. These ever-toughening standards owed a great deal to George Bird Grinnell, cofounder of Boone and Crockett and editor of *Forest and Stream* magazine. The patrician Grinnell was the bedrock of the *conservation* movement—the first person to use conservation in its modern, environmental sense—with an interest in and genius for politics. Ernest Thompson Seton was a very different animal: he preferred making speeches full of stories and birdcalls to those that exhorted political action. But the two men were allies, and both saw Yellowstone as a sanctuary. Seton hoped that the political efforts led by Grinnell would allow him to see animals in Yellowstone, far more than he had on the train so far.

From Livingston, Ernest and Grace continued on the park branch railroad to its terminus at Cinnabar, named for the red of the adjacent Devil's Slide.[10] There they boarded a Tallyho stagecoach for Mammoth Hot Springs. This was the way tourists of the late 1800s saw Yellowstone: train to stagecoach. Many of them then took a set tour of the premier attractions: one day at Mammoth, the second at Norris and the Lower Geyser Basin, the third at Old Faithful, a fourth at Lake and Canyon, and a fifth back to

Mammoth. Concessionaires set up hotels and lunch counters at appropriate spots, and the $40 package tour covered everything, the stagecoach afloat in the wilderness like a cruise ship of today. Thus the experience depended a great deal on how much you liked your companions. When the British imperialist Kipling visited in 1889 and famously wrote, "I am in the Yellowstone Park, and I wish I were dead," he was referring to the dusty monotony of 150 miles of stagecoach rides and the inescapable obnoxiousness of his fellow passengers. ("It is not the ghastly vulgarity, the oozing, rampant, Bessemer-steel self-sufficiency and ignorance of the men that revolts me, so much as the display of these same qualities in the women-folk," he wrote. He could not believe that such boorish commoners had sufficient wealth and prominence to afford such a trip.)[11]

As an esteemed conservation correspondent, Ernest was able to sidestep the standard tour. At Mammoth he and Grace met with superintendent George Anderson, who provided them with a wagon and guide to take them to crude lodgings in the northeast part of the park, near Tower Fall. Their first-day tour guide was Colonel Samuel Baldwin Marks Young, who was about to replace the retiring Anderson as superintendent.

Arriving at the Pleasant Valley Hotel, they were greeted by "Uncle John" Yancey, an old Kentuckian who'd been kicking around the West since 1851. The log cabin had five guest rooms with numbers marked on their doors in chalk. Each had a single bedstead, a broken window, and a cracked wall pasted with strips of newspaper. The beds, a guest wrote, "showed that they were changed at least twice, once in the spring and once in the fall of the year." The food, unless you caught some fish in the river, was bacon and eggs for every meal, enlivened by breakfast slices of raw Bermuda onion, which Uncle John said was "good for the narvs." An adjacent log cabin served as a saloon, with a pair of upended barrels supporting boards that formed the bar. Drinks were ten cents apiece, but Uncle John never seemed to have any change. If you gave him a quarter, you'd better want two more drinks.[12]

The superintendent discouraged upper-class tourists from staying at the hotel, which filled mostly with miners on their way to Cooke City northeast of the park. But serious outdoor-lovers were also drawn by the setting and the fishing. Ernest and Grace actually occupied (and cleaned and improved) an adjacent tumbledown shanty. They stayed six weeks, going on guided trips to see elk, bison, antelope, and other wildlife. Ernest was particularly moved by the majestic elk, and titled his articles "Elkland."

Ernest's fascination with natural settings was boundless. He wrote of beaver dams and the associated marshland rich in habitat for muskrats, rock-chucks, coyotes, mule deer, and antelope. He wrote of the swarms of birds he saw. In each case he studied the animals' behavior, and rendered it in vivid if unscientific prose: "Frequently when 2 beaver would meet in the pond, i.e., the street, they would kiss each other on both cheeks and make a chattering noise just like Frenchmen."[13] He compiled a list, with notes from experts, of forty-three mammals believed to inhabit the park, which ranged from otter and mink to moose, elk, and wolf.

He was gloomy about bison. "The herd that numbered 300 or 400 some years ago has now dwindled to 20 or 30. It seems almost certain that they are less than 30 now and that they are doomed to extinction."[14] But the other news, he reported, was generally good. Elk numbered at least 30,000 and growing. Antelope, moose, and deer populations were also healthy. Predators such as the mountain lion, wildcat, and wolf were rare—which Ernest believed was a good thing. Like most naturalists of the day, he figured that fewer predators meant more game. Still, the Wolfman was disappointed not to see a wolf. He was even more disappointed by another missing animal—also a predator, but more beautiful, more endowed with humanlike qualities that gave it majesty and magic. Ernest had come to Yellowstone in large part because of its bears, and in his first eight weeks he didn't see a single one.

The Setons left Pleasant Valley in early August and traveled south to Yellowstone Lake, where they met with new superintendent Young. Ernest complained about the lack of bears. One of his reasons for coming to Yellowstone, he told Young, was the promise of as many bears as he liked. But all he'd seen was a single set of tracks.

"You are not in the right place," Young responded. "Go over to the Fountain Hotel and there you will see as many bears as you wish."[15]

The Fountain Hotel was located in the Lower Geyser Basin, an area of fascinating hot pools and paintpots eight miles north of Old Faithful. Unlike Uncle John's Pleasant Valley Hotel, this three-story structure was, for the times, modern and comfortable. Opened in 1891 to accommodate 350 guests, the hotel featured steam heat, electric lights, and hot-spring water in its baths. It even had a ballroom where a lady might wear a silk dress. There was not yet an inn at Old Faithful, so many tourists spent two nights at Fountain, seeing the famous geyser on a daylong side trip.

But to Ernest, the best feature of the Fountain Hotel was a quarter mile off in the woods: its garbage dump. "Early the next morning I went to this Bears' Banqueting Hall in the pines, and hid in the nearest bushes," he wrote. He was nervous: he carried no weapon, as they were illegal in the park. But he wasn't as nervous as the large black bear that soon came out of the woods to the pile: "sitting up and looking about at each slight sound, or running away a few yards when startled by some trifle. At length he cocked his ears and galloped off into the pines, as another Blackbear appeared. He also behaved in the same timid manner, and at last ran away when I shook the bushes in trying to get a better view."[16]

With increasing confidence that he would not be mauled, Ernest decided to get closer than this spot seventy-five yards away. But there were no bushes any closer. So he crawled into the pile of garbage itself, dug a hole, and hid in it, "with cabbage-stalks, old potato-peelings, tomato-cans, and carrion piled up in odorous heaps around me. Notwithstanding the opinions of countless flies, it was not an attractive place."[17]

But he was enthralled. Bears came and went. They arrived silently, without rustling leaves or sticks. They pawed through garbage and ate, each exhibiting its own personality. Ernest started naming them in his head. Fatty sprawled at full length, darting out a long tongue to reach some morsel, rather than moving his body. Slim Jim was long-legged and thin; it was amusing to watch him puzzle over a canned lobster. "Grumpy was the biggest and fiercest of the Blackbears, and Johnny, apparently her only son, was a peculiarly tiresome little cub, for he seemed never to cease either grumbling or whining," Ernest wrote.[18] Although he recorded evidence of illness—little Johnny had a gimp leg, mangy coat, and scrawny frame—Ernest the moralist couldn't help but see him as spoiled.

Grumpy chased four bears off the garbage pile, and Ernest made numerous sketches of Johnny sifting through the discarded food, at one point cutely getting his head stuck in a can. Later a grizzly bear approached. Grumpy sent Johnny up a tree while she scuffled with the grizzly. Losing the battle, she climbed the tree herself, and later slunk off. Ernest decided to make some bold sketches of the grizzly.

Meanwhile his wife, Grace, had been doing what most people did—touring the geysers. She spent the whole day admiring thermal features, but when she returned to the hotel at sunset, she couldn't find Ernest. She headed out to the garbage pit.

She soon saw the grizzly feeding quietly on the hillside. "It was very lonely and gruesome . . . the bear looked a shocking size, as big as a whale," she wrote. She started wondering if the bear had swallowed Ernest, "Jonah style. Just then I heard a sepulchral whisper," she wrote.[19]

"Keep quiet, don't move, it's the Big Grizzly."

Ernest was in his nest not far away. She edged closer, and he continued, "See, over there in the woods are two black bears. You scared them away. Isn't he a monster?" indicating the grizzly.

She paused to admire it for a while, then finally said, "How long have you been here?"

"All day—and such a day—thirteen bears at one time. It is worth all your geysers rolled into one."

Like Thomas Moran with his colors, in Yellowstone Ernest Thompson Seton had found his animals. And as with Moran, Seton's experience created an imperative to depict them in art. But Ernest hungered for more, so he and Grace returned to the area the following summer. This time they took horses on a backcountry trip starting in Gray's Lake, Idaho, southwest of Yellowstone. They crossed into Jackson Hole, where they spent a couple of weeks fishing and elk hunting under the Tetons, and then headed east through the mountainous country south and east of Yellowstone. Some of this area had been set aside in 1891 as a Forest Reserve, a precursor to the National Forest System, and they were accompanied by one of the reserve's chief proponents, who also happened to be a close friend.

Like Ernest, Abraham Archibald "Triple-A" Anderson got rich the old-fashioned way: by marrying an heiress. And like Ernest, Triple-A was an artist and outdoorsman. His art ran more toward portraiture, for which he received some accolades, although not the worship given the impressionists. But Triple-A's greatest talent may have been his social network. His friends included many prominent people, such as Thomas Edison, Theodore Roosevelt, and Mark Twain. In Paris, his mansion on the Boulevard du Montparnasse housed the American Art Association, a beneficial mutual-aid society that became a social center for expatriates.[20]

In addition to painting, Triple-A's other primary passion since childhood was hunting. So in the late 1880s he bought a ranch on the Greybull River in Wyoming. When he arrived, his spread—the Palette Ranch—was ridiculously remote. The nearest railroad station was in the coal-mining town of Red Lodge, Montana, a two- or three-day trek to the north. Of course remoteness was the point: Triple-A needed to get away from railroads and fences in order to get into the big elk herds. Thus his choice of the easternmost foothills of the mountains southeast of Yellowstone, on an elk migration route from summer range in the national park to winter range in the windswept lowlands. With elk came predators, including grizzly bears. Like Ernest, Triple-A was fascinated by bears, although he never outgrew his desire to kill the animal he considered his arch-nemesis. He later claimed to have dispatched thirty-nine in his lifetime, including four on a single day.[21]

Triple-A met the Setons in Jackson Hole, with sixteen horses and two hired men to conduct them over the mountains to his ranch. Along the way, Ernest tracked elk, Grace shot a pronghorn antelope, and the party sat out a storm in a cave warmed by a fire at its mouth.[22] In early October, on the Upper Wiggins Fork north of Dubois, Triple-A and Grace were riding their horses a couple of miles from camp when he suddenly stopped and pointed to the ground. Grace saw the track of a huge bear.

They were not in danger: the bear was headed in the same direction they were, and Triple-A believed the prints to be days or weeks old. But he was awed by their size. He got off his horse and measured: one hind track was fourteen inches long. "The hole looked big enough for a baby's bath tub," Grace wrote.[23] Triple-A said he knew of only one bear that could make tracks that big, even though this area was not in its usual range. It was the bear called Wahb.

Had a gigantic bear that Triple-A knew from his ranch really also made a track more than thirty miles southwest? At the time, wildlife science was not yet advanced enough to provide proof.[24] But long before science, grizzlies were inspiring legends as big as their size. Indeed Grace—and to a lesser extent Ernest and Triple-A—seemed to be under the impression that the giant grizzly Ernest had viewed at the Fountain Hotel had also been Wahb, as if Wahb (Shoshone for "white bear") had been a supermetaphor capable of leaping tall mountain ranges in a single bound. Indeed, Grace wrote, "I had heard so many tales of this monster that when I gazed upon his track I felt as though I were looking at the autograph of a hero."[25]

Tales about Wahb, and sightings of the gigantic tracks, continued as the party reached the Palette Ranch, a massive structure reminiscent of a European hunting lodge.[26] Its huge living room featured a stone fireplace, tapestries, fur rugs, and hunting trophies. The guest room boasted silk sheets and a crystal mantelpiece from Japan. The wine cellar was stocked from France. Yet just outdoors was a jumble of wilderness: colorful rock cliffs, grasses, sagebrush, and spruce-fir forests. The steep valleys boasted willows in their narrow bottoms, and the cliffs rose to snowpack above ten thousand feet. The palette included reds and russets of the riverside cliffs, spring greens of grasses or autumn yellows of cottonwoods, the whites of the snowcapped peaks, and the blue of the never-ending sky. Triple-A had a painting studio on the grounds, and another far out in the mountains. At the remote studio he would sometimes paint from nude models, and today the river there is still known as Warhouse Creek, presumably a more printable approximation of what some area cowboys believed was really going on.[27]

Triple-A raised cattle, as well as horses and hunting dogs. His war on grizzlies resulted in part from their tendency to eat his cows. Yet despite all the hunting parties that pursued grizzlies, and all the traps that Triple-A and his neighbors set for them, Wahb had never been caught.

Ernest was captivated by this story. He loved how, both inside and outside the national park, wildlife dominated the legends and folkways of the old-timers. The artist/hunter/storyteller Anderson was an oversized character, and so were some of his present and former neighbors, including the misanthropic nephew of a Confederate general, a German count who had come to Wyoming to redeem the insult of being too short to get into the kaiser's army, and a young horse thief not yet known by the name Butch Cassidy. But the biggest character in the valley was Wahb.

Ernest turned Wahb into one of his best-known books, *The Biography of a Grizzly* (1900).[28] Despite the factual-sounding title, he invented Wahb's life: a mother killed while raiding cattle, clashes with Indians and hunters, numerous escapes from government trappers, and a peaceful, accidental old-age death from inhaling natural poisonous gases at an obscure area of eastern Yellowstone called Death Gulch, now known as Wahb Springs. (The ending was unquestionably fiction: Triple-A later boasted of finally killing Wahb himself.)[29] The illustrated book was sentimental and anthropomorphized—the orphaned cub was shown whimpering, "Mother! Mother! Oh, Mother, where are you?"—but it had more scientific accuracy than many previous animal stories, and it gave Wahb a dignity that appealed to both children and adults.

Ernest portrayed his Wahb as eating at the Bears' Banquet at the Fountain Hotel, which he indeed suggested was an overt government policy toward wildlife. He was fictionalizing, but we can see how Yellowstone's actual policies inspired him. In Yellowstone, there was no hunting or logging, no pollution from mills or mines. In that era, those facts alone were amazing. So it seemed an obvious extension to show food being laid out for the animals every day. "The wild creatures crowd into the Park from the surrounding country in numbers not elsewhere to be seen," Ernest wrote, as if the bears, like the tourists, were making a pilgrimage to a special place. In Yellowstone, he said, wild animals "no longer shun the face of man, they neither fear nor attack him, and they are even more tolerant of one another in this land of refuge. . . . All seem to realize that in the Park no violence is allowed, and the most ferocious of them have here put on a new behavior. Although scores of Bears roam about this choice resort, and sometimes quarrel among themselves, not one of them has ever yet harmed a man."[30]

This passage is remarkable for several reasons. First is the claim that bears had never attacked people in Yellowstone. Seton probably believed it to be true, in part because the park did not systematically keep injury records until the 1930s.[31] Second is the discussion of bears' motivations as if they were capable of human rationality and emotion. Although this spiritual view of nature frustrated practitioners of emerging wildlife science, who wanted descriptions of animals to include only facts, Seton was especially notable for granting this moral wisdom *to a predator*, a class of animals that others often demonized.[32] Third is the notion that feeding bears garbage was good for them. Today what many nature-lovers value in bears is a sense of wildness and independence, an other-ness. But for many people of Seton's time—and perhaps for quite a few today—the spirituality that connected all human beings also extended to all other creatures, both domesticated and wild. If so, then the question was how to activate those connections.

It was the defining question of Ernest's life. On a youthful wolf hunt in New Mexico, he had felt a spiritual connection to "Old Lobo" as the life drained out of the legendary wolf's eyes.[33] Now Ernest wanted to help other people find such special kinships through love instead of slaughter.

What did that love look like? Clearly it required intimacy. And so, with similar motivations, guides in Yellowstone often left the remains of dinner strewn about the campfire, to draw bears close to their guests. A Yellowstone concessionaire ran a zoo on an island in the middle of Yellowstone Lake. And Superintendent Anderson kept a pet bear chained to the side of his house.[34]

Compared to these other attempts at intimacy, Ernest's vision was far more sophisticated and generous, even modern. In a zoo, for example, humans displayed wild animals in cages, showing not only the animal but also how humans controlled it. These ferocious animals had to submit. But in Ernest's vision of Yellowstone, humans could create conditions where animals didn't need to be ferocious, and thus didn't *need* to submit. They could be tamed by love rather than force.

Ernest didn't focus solely on Wahb. He told many Yellowstone bear stories in multiple articles and best-selling books, as well as on the lecture circuit. Little Johnny, the spoiled bear he'd observed from the Fountain Hotel garbage dump, became a celebrity. Indeed, according to Ernest, Little Johnny had a profound impact on popular culture: after Ernest lectured at Bryn Mawr in 1901, a student asked a New York toy manufacturer to make a couple dozen cute stuffed Little Johnnys. Then the following year, the media got hold of a story about a Mississippi bear hunt where President Theodore Roosevelt refused, on sportsmanship grounds, to shoot an old, lame bear that his assistants had tied to a tree. So the toy manufacturer, with plans already in hand, made a whole bunch more Little Johnnys, Ernest claimed, and christened them Teddy Bears.[35]

Little Johnny became an ongoing celebrity at the Fountain Hotel—as a name for successive generations of cute little lame bears. "Indeed, when I went back to the Fountain Hotel fifteen years afterward," Ernest wrote, "a little Bear came and whined under my window about dawn, and the hotel folk assured me it was Little Johnny calling on his creator."[36]

Little Johnny's exploits, in Ernest's increasingly fanciful versions of the tale, extended beyond cavorting with his mother in the garbage dump. By the end of that first summer he was supposedly caught and chained by Fountain Hotel employees. A newly hired Irish girl mothered him—not only fed him but spanked him as well. After a month of not being spoiled, he became well behaved. He docilely followed her around on her chores. Sadly his illnesses proved untreatable, and just before winter he succumbed. He died in the girl's lap, redeemed, in Ernest's tale, by her love.[37]

At the close of a century where America's growth and greed brought so many species to the brink of extinction, this was a powerful message. Humans, Ernest implied, could help animals by loving them. One form of love was to set aside a vast refuge where they would not be hunted, where they indeed would be fed. And the animals would feel gratitude for this action. They would feel the specialness of the refuge, and flock there, and behave there differently than they did elsewhere.

Was it a myth? Sure, in many ways. The 20th century generally doubted that animals had "souls" or "emotions," and although today that science is evolving, ascribing them *gratitude* still seems a stretch.[38] But if you take away Seton's reliance on emotional explanations, he does have a point: Yellowstone did nurture many animal species formerly far more common on the Plains, such as grizzlies, elk, and bison. It effectively served as a refuge that proved essential to these species' ongoing health—for example, the bison miraculously held on in Yellowstone, and a century later brimmed across its borders.[39] The park's elk thrived to the extent that by the 1920s "surplus" elk were transplanted from Yellowstone to reestablish herds throughout the West.[40] And Ernest's claims about animal behaviors do often seem to ring true: even today, in more-developed areas outside the park, many large mammals instinctively fear people, keeping far away because those people might be hunters with guns. Inside Yellowstone, by contrast, some animals will allow people to come perilously close, perhaps because they instinctively know they will not be hunted. They are unpredictable and unfathomable, but sometimes arguably arrive at behaviors that resemble what gratitude might produce.

"Whenever travellers penetrate into remote regions where human hunters are unknown," Ernest wrote, "they find the wild things half tame, little afraid of man, and inclined to stare curiously from a distance of a few paces." In his lifetime those remote regions had nearly vanished. But America had chosen to set aside Yellowstone, a place big enough to support elk, bison, and bears; remote enough to let them live most of their lives the way they always had; organized enough to prevent poachers from spoiling that paradise. "In this Reservation," he wrote, "and nowhere else at present in the northwest, the wild things are not only abundant, but they have resumed their traditional Garden-of-Eden attitude toward man."[41] Ernest was bored by Yellowstone's geology, but he was stunned at the wonder of its animals. Yellowstone fulfilled a need, on the part of Ernest and millions of others—including many today—to provide a preserve for creatures they saw as half tame.

Ernest's passion for the bear-dominated stories of old-time hunters, and the bear-dominated garbage dumps of Yellowstone, resonated with a subset of American values. Yet they clashed with another subset, one that was particularly evident when American men went on vacation wearing neckties. With the upper classes still carrying a lot of Europe envy, tourists often embraced formality: formal dress, formal balls, formal gardens. How could you appreciate the Yellowstone passions of people like Seton and Thomas Moran when your tastes precluded you from visiting the likes of the Pleasant Valley Hotel or the Fountain garbage dump? In the coming years Yellowstone would show America bridging that gap as well.

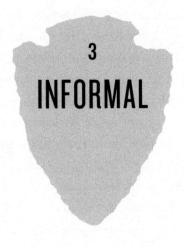

3
INFORMAL

When planning a first visit, a person today might fail to appreciate just how vast Yellowstone is. You might look at the figure-eight road on the map and wrongly think that you can do the whole thing in an hour. When you discover how far apart the main attractions are—especially with roads clogged by traffic- and bison-jams—you'll start crossing items off your agenda. You may even realize that you have time only for Old Faithful. Then, when you arrive forty-five minutes before the next eruption, you wander toward a nearby building, and so you also end up visiting the Old Faithful Inn.

You might feel a bit ashamed: you've come to one of the great wonders of the natural world, and you spend half your time in a man-made building. It'd be like spending most of a visit to Mount

Everest studying the architecture of a base camp. Surely the wonders of Yellowstone are the natural features themselves rather than the buildings that accommodate people experiencing them.[1]

And yet you have made a wise choice. When you know how to appreciate it, the Old Faithful Inn is one of the most fascinating destinations in Yellowstone. This remarkable building influenced many subsequent prominent structures in national and state parks. And it helped change people's expectations of park experiences—how we want buildings to relate to the natural environment, and how we want other tourists to relate to us. The inn complements the adjacent wonders in the same way that a visit to it rounds out your session of geyser-gazing. And one of the amazing things about the inn is how it came to be: constructed by an unassuming trio of heroes who almost certainly didn't realize the lasting significance of what they were trying to do.[2]

At the Hotel del Coronado near San Diego, when Harry and Adelaide Child arrived for a vacation on January 17, 1903, both the guests and the resort represented the cream of 19th-century society.[3] As the wealthy owners of businesses including concessions in Yellowstone, Harry and Addie must have approached the hotel from a private railcar. That's what many wealthy patrons did, on the dedicated rail line along the Silver Strand, the peninsula that encloses San Diego Bay. (Less moneyed guests took a ferry from downtown.) The rails ended directly outside the hotel's front entrance, giving the Childs a panoramic view of the world's largest wooden structure, dominated by white paint and red roof. The fifteen-year-old building was a Queen Anne crazy-quilt of turrets and dormers and windows and verandas. Behind them was an electric plant to power lights in every room—a first in hotels, installed by Thomas Edison himself. Many rooms featured views of the Pacific and the long sandy beaches extending to the south, but photographs of the day tended to focus on the visionary structure rather than its natural surroundings. Indeed the founders tore up the surrounding native sagebrush to construct a garden of subtropical plants entirely imported from abroad. Likewise, the building itself resembled an elegant Victorian seaside resort, as if plucked from Brighton, England, to be transported to the Pacific coast just a few miles north of Mexico. The interiors were all about elegance and shine; for example, in the hotel's dining hall, a team of four men needed ten days just to polish the wainscoting.[4]

As Harry Child entered the lavish lobby—alone, because etiquette required his wife to use the separate women's entrance—he probably felt at home among the well-appointed furnishings. They spoke of money, which was his language. The 46-year-old lived in Helena, Montana, a gold mining town of fewer than fifteen thousand people that boasted dozens of millionaires, what may have been the nation's highest per-capita wealth at that time.[5] Harry had made some of his own money managing gold mines. At one mine, when the employees didn't get paid, they kidnapped him; he ended up taking their side in demanding back pay from the mine's New York owners, and then outwitted thieves hoping to strip him of the mega-payroll before he could distribute it. Harry later invested in farms and ranches, eventually owning some of the largest spreads in the state. He stood only five feet five inches tall—with dark eyebrows, a bushy mustache, and center-parted hair—but made up for height with energy.[6] Some said he was ruthless or difficult to get along with, a perfectionist. But others described him as smart, articulate, and fair. One contemporary called him "a homemade efficiency expert" who liked to time various operations with a stopwatch, adding, "People liked him, however."[7] Another nicknamed him

41

"Harry Hardup" because "he owned only a young empire of land and 30,000 head of stock."[8]

In the women's lobby—where the opportunity to freshen up after a journey was said to be a luxury, helping women avoid unsightly main-lobby scenes such as fishermen displaying their catches—Addie was a force in her own right. After graduating from universities in Wisconsin and Massachusetts, she had gone to Helena to visit her sister, who was married to a mogul named Silas Huntley. Arriving, she discovered all of the town's eligible bachelors gathered at the incoming train depot. Somehow she selected Harry, and married him just a few months later in 1883. Now forty-one, she had raised two children and partnered with Harry in business. In 1891, the Childs and Huntleys acquired the Yellowstone transportation concession, owning and managing stagecoaches and horses to take tourists on their five-day tours. Ten years later they added the hotel concession, and then Silas died suddenly. Now Harry and Addie were among Yellowstone's most important curators of the visitor experience.

That authority brought pressures to improve the four hotels they'd inherited from the previous concessionaire. A four-story barnlike structure at Mammoth was functional but, despite garish green and red paint, not particularly interesting. An 1891 building at Canyon was referred to by a park superintendent as "a most unsightly edifice" and by a journalist as the "ugliest building in the world."[9] The Fountain Hotel, with Ernest Thompson Seton's garbage pit, was a decent if unremarkable example of the stick building style, a plain box. And at Lake, a dull clapboard building was rather Spartan-looking, and its fifty-one rooms were less than half what tours needed.[10]

Although the Childs had a quasi-monopoly on high-end hotels in the park, visitors had options beyond the Childs' control. If you brought or rented your own horses and equipment, you could camp wherever you wanted, or stay in crude lodgings, as the Setons did in Pleasant Valley. If you wanted more sophistication than that but were willing to sleep in a tent, you could travel the "Wylie Way." William Wylie established a series of semipermanent tent camps at the park's major attractions and sold his own stagecoach tours, 30 percent cheaper than Harry's. Wylie liked to hire school-teachers and college students rather than hospitality professionals, which made his tours more informal and education-oriented. Their homemade entertainment, such as campfire sing-alongs, appealed to middle-class visitors as well as anyone frustrated with the formality of upper-class tourism.

The Wylie Way and its emerging imitators presented a real challenge to the Childs. If their hotels were undistinguished or their service less than stellar, tourists wouldn't have much reason to spend the extra money and miss out on Wylie's relaxed camara-derie. Wylie even had a tent camp at Old Faithful so that his guests could spend more time admiring geysers and less commuting in stagecoaches. Thus Harry's priorities were to upgrade Lake and the other existing hotels, and most importantly to build something at Old Faithful.

Harry was pressured by the Northern Pacific Railway, whose passengers spoke of their desire for a nice place to stay at the park's premier attraction. In many ways, the railroad ran the park in those early years, though it learned to avoid the appearance of control. Instead it loaned the Childs huge amounts of money. Harry liked the security of the partnership, knowing that the enormous invest-ment forced Northern Pacific into a benevolent partnership—his tongue-in-cheek motto was never to be in debt to a railroad for less than a million dollars. Northern Pacific liked telling Harry what to do. When railroad executives said they wanted a hotel in the Upper Geyser Basin near Old Faithful—and relatively quickly, before a competing concessionaire tied to the Union Pacific could build one—they knew they could trust Harry to simply ask for a loan to get it done.

So even as Harry and Addie took in the southern California sun in January of 1903, they had crews working to cut logs and bring them to a site near Old Faithful. Although they didn't yet have a firm plan for what the new building or buildings would look like, it was easier to cut and skid logs across winter snows. The design, however it turned out, would undoubtedly require a great deal of wood.

In San Diego, the Hotel del Coronado's luxury experience was designed at great cost to meet the tastes of wealthy eastern and European rail travelers. Everyone who could afford it wanted that level of comfort and luxury: electric lights, indoor toilets, formal dress for dinner. Although Harry loved to camp in the great outdoors, when he was traveling with his sophisticated wife, they stayed in hotels that offered the very opposite of the outdoor experience.

Indeed, when they arrived, the Hotel del Coronado had just recently reopened after six months of renovations to improve its luxury status. Back in 1888, it had been built in a hurry, with architects completing drawings sometimes just a day or two ahead of construction. Now, as a resort city grew up around it, owners invested in transforming the rambling structure into a neighborhood centerpiece, while also creating a nearby dance hall, bathhouse, and dormitory. For these projects it employed a staff architect, Robert Reamer. Just twenty-nine years old, and with only a sixth-grade education, Reamer had already been working as a San Diego architect for six years. His fresh-faced, puffy-cheeked appearance made him look even younger than his years—Harry soon started calling him "the kid"—and his habit of quietly looking down at the ground made him seem even more humble than he was.

Early in his visit, Harry was struck by a recently remodeled clubhouse on the golf course. He asked the hotel's general manager, Elisha Babcock, about its architect. "[I] spoke in very high terms of you," Babcock later wrote to Reamer about that conversation. With the hotel renovations completed, Babcock was probably running out of work for a staff architect. Babcock continued, "This made him [Child] feel inclined to see if he could engage your services. I have known Mr. Child for years. He is intimately connected with the president of the Northern Pacific Railway . . . They want to build hotels, as much as possible, in the rustic and your taste in that line would redound to your credit."[11]

The rustic. Harry left no records of how he or Addie came up with that angle, or what exactly he meant by the word. Perhaps it simply referred to Yellowstone's remote location. But based on what happened next, it seems likely that the Childs were inspired by the tradition of the log cabin. These simple structures had become the standard of the American frontier due to convenience. Out in the middle of nowhere, you didn't have access to lumber or the equipment to mill it. You had raw trees (or worse, on a treeless prairie, raw sod). You also had endless demands on your time, so you wanted to turn the raw materials into a shelter as quickly as possible. Your log cabin might leave the logs' ends rough-hewn, the bark still on. If you bothered with a foundation, you might just collect some nearby rocks. The resulting living space was often small, dark, and dank, so as soon as you had enough time or money, you built and moved into a stick-frame house. But then decades later, you or your descendants might feel some nostalgia for the old frontier days, for the log cabin as a symbol of independence and informality. The log cabin was rustic, and rusticity was (you wanted to believe) what made America great.

Rustic building styles started going retro in the 1870s. In parks and gardens, landscape architects used weathered local stone and unpeeled logs to create natural-looking structures. Then as New York tycoons built Adirondack vacation homes, they enjoyed using natural materials to join their buildings to the environment, log cabin–style. They used oversized timbers to support heavy snow loads, overhanging roofs to keep icicles away from walls, and oversized stone fireplaces to retain heat. Although the elements were huge, the structures were small: a cozy lodge, clad in rough shingles, tucked into a mountainside, attuned to the natural surroundings.

As private vacation residences, these buildings were not open to the public, but the Childs, in their wealth, must have been familiar with the style. Thus, they must have realized that *log cabin* need not be the opposite of *luxury*. Some past proposals for lodgings at the Upper Geyser Basin around Old Faithful had involved collections of small huts (although others were for large, stick-style hotels), and the Childs might have been wondering if a good architect could help them make huts in a log-cabin style that would be nostalgic yet comfortable for upper-class tourists.

The Childs quickly decided that Reamer was their man. They brought him to Yellowstone by early February. As titular head of the company, Harry often gets credit, but Addie and Robert became fast friends and collaborators. Sadly, little is known today about how the three worked together; none wrote any sort of memoir. But over the years, as Reamer endured difficulties, including the death of his wife from kidney disease at age thirty, Harry and Addie became like a family to him. During his sojourns in Yellowstone, he often resided in their Mammoth home. In 1909 they even took him on a vacation to Europe.

One of the difficulties that Reamer endured was alcoholism. Later a rumor arose that Harry had discovered Robert on a California street corner with delirium tremens, and the first architectural sketches he drew on the train to Montana reflected his feverish state. The rumor seems false: the initial sketch was rather sober, and author Ruth Quinn has demonstrated Reamer's relative sobriety when they met at the Hotel del Coronado. The rumor might have arisen because Robert was one of those exceedingly rare birds: an architect with little ego. "My father was a quiet, modest man, quite reticent about discussing his work, particularly in evaluating it," his daughter later recalled. "He would pour everything into plans for a certain building, then once completed, seemed to turn away, seeking a new challenge."[12] For the hotel at the Upper Geyser Basin, Reamer got hold of a new challenge. In March, Harry left Yellowstone for Washington, D.C., to get federal approval for a single structure—no longer a collection of huts—that they were then calling the Old Faithful Tavern.

As an architect, Robert Reamer was gifted in many different styles. For example, he designed a San Diego carriage-and-livery building in an unexpected Spanish Mission style. Later in his career he designed extravagant movie theaters across the Northwest: art moderne, Moorish, and Chinese. Some of the residences he designed, as well as the now-demolished, much-mourned Canyon Hotel in Yellowstone, used Prairie-style horizontals so well that critics assume (there's no proof) that he knew Frank Lloyd Wright during his teenage years as a Chicago draftsman.

Reamer also had a huge capacity—even a need—for hard work. In part, it kept him off the sauce. In March, his old boss Elisha Babcock wrote to Harry, "Am afraid, if he is drinking, you are not giving him enough work."[13] So Harry loaded Robert with assignments, especially during that first busy year of 1903. The Northern Pacific finally completed its tracks for the final five miles from Cinnabar to Gardiner at the park's northern boundary. It needed a new passenger station, and at Harry's recommendation, Reamer designed it. He went for a rustic look: walls built of rough rock, overhanging eaves, a big stone fireplace, and a log roof. The station's porte cocheres—one long roof covering the area where passengers got off the train, and another shorter one where the Tally-Ho wagons picked them up to begin their Yellowstone tour—were supported by huge logs with the bark still on them, as if they were solid trees and the roof a leafy canopy.

Meanwhile, Yellowstone's road superintendent decided to build a stone archway just beyond the depot to formalize the entrance to the park. Reamer probably collaborated on the structure, though no records remain. One can make an argument for the arch as an interesting architectural statement, with its rustic basalt construction and its implication that a visitor's first impression of Yellowstone should involve a man-made structure seeking to make a cultural interpretation of what nature provided. But instead the arch became famous for its celebrity connections. In April President Theodore Roosevelt laid its cornerstone and made a much-quoted speech, as further discussed in chapter 4. By then Reamer was working on other projects: a nearby retail store, a colorful, barnlike building in Mammoth, and a simple lunch station at the West Thumb of Yellowstone Lake. And, of course, there were the hotels.

At Lake, the old hotel fronted the lakeshore on a small bluff a mile west of the outlet at Fishing Bridge. The outstanding setting included views across the sometimes-glassy, sometimes-choppy expanse of the lake to the distant Absaroka peaks. But the clapboard building itself had little ornamentation to make it feel special. Reamer's design more than tripled the number of rooms and expanded the size of the lobby. But more importantly, he gave the building character by adding architectural details: dormers, false balconies, and elaborate window designs. He imported Ionic columns to support exaggerated gables that made for a long front veranda facing the lake. The result was a distinctive building that soon became known, for its architectural style, as the Lake Colonial Hotel.

At Old Faithful, the hotel site was a quarter mile west of the namesake geyser, on the southwestern edge of the Upper Geyser Basin. These thermal features, collected along the Firehole River upstream from other geyser basins, represented an entire neighborhood of curiosities. When early explorers such as the Langford and Hayden parties encountered the basin, its geysers were much more active than today, with Grand Geyser erupting daily, and Splendid and Giantess erupting multiple times on the occasional days they chose to erupt. The effect was to create a valleyful of geysers, a district of meadows interspersed with "sinter"—the rock-like effluvia of thermal features—all of it bisected by the warm river and rimmed by forests of lodgepole. For twenty years geyser performances had been slowing; some turned into colorful pools and others into massive craters. Nevertheless the inn's site provided views of multiple attractions.

Through the summer of 1903 and the following winter, the architect shuttled between Lake and Old Faithful. A hands-on designer, he liked to supervise construction efforts himself—especially ones this massive. Harry employed ninety workmen between the two sites; he took out loans eventually totaling $220,000 from the Northern Pacific; he awarded a contract for the cutting of five thousand logs; and he shipped eight hundred thousand pounds of nails. He wanted both hotels open for the summer of 1904, which meant a particular challenge for Old

Faithful, since it had to be enclosed before the snow started falling in October. One legend—perhaps as exaggerated as the one about the DTs—claimed that Robert was so busy that he "forgot to shave, forgot to undress at night, or breakfast in the morning, he was so engrossed in his work."[14]

Such legends arise in part because nobody chronicled either of the building efforts as they were happening. Nobody kept a diary; no journalists came to visit. So we know very little about any complications Reamer encountered, or about how his or Addie's ideas took their physical form. We lack concrete details to bring alive their challenges: the isolation, monotony, and diet; the physical danger of building seventy-six feet in the air; winter's bitter cold; the pressure of being squeezed on one side by the deadline of next summer's tourists and on the other side by youthful inexperience. Nobody on site was experienced building at this scale, much less under these conditions.

The legends also arise because whatever those challenges, our heroes somehow overcame them. They beat their deadline and built the useful accommodation that the railroad demanded. Furthermore, they did so with profound creativity, in a departure from any previous building ever built. The main innovation was the overall vision: to blow up a log cabin to absurd proportions. Today the inn is widely believed to be the largest log structure in the world, nearly seven hundred feet in length. Its lobby is seven stories high, and standing in the middle of it, you see logs everywhere. A rustic stone stand-alone fireplace, sixteen feet square, boasts a full-sized hearth on each side, plus four mini-hearths in the corners. Its chimney, made from five hundred tons of rock, soars to the ceiling like an erupting geyser, commanding attention from throughout the room.[15]

Reamer took a vernacular building style, one used by everyday folks for everyday cabins, and turned it into high-class public art.

Unlike frontier shanties, the Old Faithful Inn was not small or dank. Unlike Adirondack resorts, it was not cozy or private. It was a grand hotel open to the public, with a lobby open even to nonpaying guests. And it was a brand-new use of the log-cabin architectural style, yet a use that perfectly fit the building's function and surroundings.

To accommodate the scale, the building is, structurally, not really a log cabin. The foundation is of stone and concrete, with much of the visible rustic stonework merely a veneer. The first floor has load-bearing unhewn logs, but the upper stories use conventional stick framing, and the entire building has plumbing, electricity, and heat, all from imported materials. Robert and Addie used logs, shingles, and rough wood paneling as *decorative* elements, to provide character. In other words, the use of on-site materials was to some degree practical but to a larger degree self-conscious. The logs and stones are there to remind you that you're in a place of logs and stones.

Meanwhile, the monumental scale reminds you that you're in the American West, where the vastness of the landscape would overwhelm a simple Swiss chalet or a quaint Adirondack camp. The inn refuses to defer to the landscape. Rather it establishes its own strong presence to strike a balance with the scenery. For example, it doesn't face the geyser it's named for; it faces what was originally the main entrance road from Fountain. Visitors could experience the architecture the way Harry and Addie experienced the Hotel del Coronado from their private railcar. Later, they could embark on a separate experience of watching the erupting geyser.

These experiences are separate but linked. Unlike the Hotel del Coronado, plopped incongruously on a southern California beach, the Old Faithful Inn feels like it has grown naturally from its site. It even has a bit of organic unbalance to it, with dormers scattered seemingly haphazardly. From the exterior, that dormer-strewn roof (originally painted red), the huge stones, and the piers of stacked timbers make for a stunning first impression.

Upon entering, the lobby does too. Although multistory lobbies are quite common today, this was a huge innovation in 1903: a space so tall and airy that it seemed to be both indoors and outdoors at the same time. This mixture—imagine celebrating the outdoors while being inside!—was a relatively unexplored idea at the time, and perfectly suited to the notion of a national park. The indoor environment provides many accessories to match the monumentality outside: doors two inches thick, a clerk's counter made from a single thick slab of wood, and a gigantic iron clock on the chimney's main face. The main stairway is constructed of twelve-inch-thick logs, seven feet long, cut in half to provide flat steps.

Yet one of the inn's greatest innovations is surely due to Addie Child, who was responsible for furnishings and decoration. For beyond the first impression of masculine strength in the face of wilderness, the lobby eventually shows a more delicate, feminine side. Close up, the balcony and stairway railings include arched, gnarled, and twisted branches. Rather than discarding such mutant pieces, workmen were instructed to save them for these ornamental purposes. The slender, curved, and kinky timbers create a lacy network across that high-ceilinged space. As sunlight dapples down from the off-kilter dormers and through the lacy branches, you feel like you're at the bottom of a leafy forest.[16]

Beyond its initial soaring impression, the lobby is full of tiny pleasurable spatial experiences. Its balconies have plenty of room for sitting and gazing. Dozens of scattered writing desks attracted the female journal-keepers of the day. The area around the massive fireplace was originally sunken behind a log fence, creating an intimate hearthside. Loose-cushioned settees, rockers, and armchairs invited people to sit and visit. "The sheer enormity" of the lobby, wrote architectural historian Laura Soullière Harrison, "is counteracted by the warmth and tactile qualities of the materials: the rough shingles, the gnarled wood, the multi-light windows."[17] And although Addie selected Mission-style furniture, solid enough to stand up to the oversized chimney, she refused to make the interior into a hunting lodge. There are no animal heads on the walls, no bearskins on the floor. Instead the rustic elements are more unusual and intriguing: a stone drinking fountain, a log-cabin mailbox, a rustic pine shoeshine stand. She created a space where both men and women can feel relaxed and fascinated, where they can mingle or cloister, perceive themselves both indoors and out.

Reamer and the Childs were creating a space of luxury, where the wealthy could feel comfortable. But because they created that comfort through rusticity and informality, odd contrasts ensued. Guests often commented on the log-walled dining room with its open fireplaces, although many still dressed for dinner. They loved the lobby's full tree trunks, which retained bark until the 1940s, although they also appreciated its grand piano. They marveled at the precariousness of the "crow's nest," like a child's treehouse perched high in the rafters, but they also enjoyed when crow's-nest musicians played classical music for dancing on the lobby's gleaming maple floor. Light fixtures captured the contradiction perfectly: custom-designed white candlesticks that were actually electric lights. What is rustic and what is luxury? What is nature and what is man-made? The Old Faithful Inn poses such questions with an insistence and creativity that rivals many modern museum exhibits. It's a work of man-made art that deserves comparison to the works of natural art that surround it.

The inn was a hit from the moment it opened. Architects loved it: *Western Architect* magazine did a photo spread noting, "The ax, saw, and hammer built the entire structure. There isn't a yard of plaster in the entire building . . . The hotel is simply the rough product of the forest." The administration loved it: park super-intendent John Pitcher wrote in his annual report that it was "a remarkably beautiful and comfortable establishment." And most importantly, tourists loved it. It became so well known that the 1915 World's Fair in San Francisco featured a larger-than-life-size replica of the inn. Around the same time, historian Charles Francis Adams, Jr., wrote, "All I can say is that the greatest travelers in the world say, 'There is nothing in the world like it or to compare with the Old Faithful Inn.'"[18]

The building's influence started extending to other national parks. The 1905 El Tovar Hotel at Arizona's Grand Canyon, though not as studiedly rustic as Old Faithful, likewise incorporated regional themes—in this case Hopi—in its interior design. The 1910 Glacier Park Lodge used massive bark-on tree trunks as central pillars in its expansive lobby, which also featured an open firepit. At Mount Rainier, the 1911 Hiker's Center and 1917 Paradise Inn aimed for similar rusticity; so did the 1924 lodges at Bryce and Zion and the 1927 Ahwahnee Hotel at Yosemite. Indeed, by the late 1920s, when this style of primitive monumentality branched out to buildings other than hotels, it came to be known as National Park Service Rustic. More recently it's gained the whimsical name *parkitecture*.

The building's influence may have even extended beyond national parks. For the following twenty years, American architecture and design included movements that highlighted rusticity, such as the Arts and Crafts style. By incorporating American folk traditions, these forms became less derivative of European influences—finally American artists were allowing themselves to be shaped by the natural forces that shaped the American character. In fact a similar trend surfaced in literature: the critic H. L. Mencken celebrated the vivid, earthy language of writers such as Mark Twain, whom he saw as far more authentically American than the formal stylings of someone like Henry James.[19] In other words, a vernacular-powered discovery of a uniquely American character was happening across a variety of arts—which means we shouldn't anoint the Old Faithful Inn as the sole wellspring of nationwide rusticity. But we can say that the building caught the zeitgeist, and expressed it in rare form. The country responded to that form, because what people saw as great and special and American, they particularly appreciated in Yellowstone.

Parkitecture preserves that form, to constant acclaim today. One reason tourists love it is nostalgia: The Old Faithful Inn obviously required thousands of hours of manual labor with old-fashioned tools; it presents a fascinating contrast with the industrial symmetry that has come to dominate both urban landscapes and tourist lodgings. Another reason is its harmony with its natural surroundings, the way it complements the scenery rather than pushing it aside. As Merrill Ann Wilson wrote of the inn, "Perhaps for the first time in American architecture, a building became an accessory to nature."[20]

But the most important reason that tourists respond to the Old Faithful Inn—and the reason it was such a profound and influential creation—may be its informality. The inn challenged the formal tradition of grand hotels in three important ways. First, by using nearby materials in construction, thereby mixing the outdoor and indoor, it eliminated the boundaries that set off formal spaces. The lobby, open to everyone, felt like a place where you could wear your hiking or fishing clothes, where you could be the same person you were in nature. Second, its intimate places encouraged impromptu encounters with strangers, who gave off few status signals because they were wearing outdoor clothes. In these encounters you might voice thoughts on the experiences you'd just shared—the geysers, colorful pools, vigorous hikes, or uncomfortable stage-coach rides—rather than being inhibited by the backgrounds that might separate you. The inn, like nature itself, was a space that neutralized class distinctions. Third, it was open to both genders, indeed to the entire public, thus encouraging the American ideal of classlessness. Was this person next to you a mogul or a cowboy, a peer or an employee? In the West, with its frontier danger, what mattered wasn't money or status symbols so much as skill. And now, extending those natural conditions indoors, the inn imposed a sort of frontier egalitarianism on its well-heeled patrons—and they discovered they liked it. When this upper-class space was invaded by people who couldn't afford to stay there, the guests didn't feel that their experience was cheapened. Previously, New York resorts such as Saratoga and Niagara Falls fell on hard times when rail connections and new construction made them easy and inexpensive for the masses to get to. These places lost their elegance—or at least their exclusivity—and the upper classes subsequently shunned them as vulgar. But the Old Faithful Inn's atmosphere couldn't be so easily vulgarized because its cachet wasn't created by its guests. It was created by the combination of nature and art.

Robert, Harry, and Addie's demonstration that luxury and comfort could coexist with rustic design helped Americans embrace informality. The Old Faithful Inn showed the folly of past American accommodations: as previously with scenery, America had foolishly believed that it needed to replicate Europe. Resorts in Newport, Saratoga, and Niagara—and even the new Western railroad hotels in Manitou Springs, Colorado, and Pasadena and Santa Monica, California—were built in imitation of those in Europe. The only thing that made these places American was the fact that from such a hotel you could take a day trip to some impressive natural scenery. Furthermore, these places inevitably failed to live up to the formal elegance of their European counterparts, which made them feel like cheap imitations. By contrast, the Old Faithful Inn was something new: a hotel that didn't look like anything that had been built before, a hotel located directly at the powerful natural wonder that people had come to see, and a hotel that brought American informality into its very design—a hotel as wondrous as the park that housed it.

If the informality of the inn presented Yellowstone's visitors with hints of how nature and culture might merge, it didn't fully embody the appeal of the nature side of that equation. Its feminine touches were a brilliant way to make Yellowstone appeal to the entire family, but they were tempering a very masculine appeal of the western frontier in general. Rusticity echoed the frontier, and over the next twenty years, the frontier would become increasingly romantic. What's more, perhaps surprisingly, it would become increasingly associated with Yellowstone.

4
RUGGED

For years I wanted to vote for Theodore Roosevelt as Yellowstone's Most Overrated Celebrity. The former president is remembered in the so-called Roosevelt Arch in Gardiner, in a 1920 rustic-styled lodge and cabins near Tower Fall, and indeed in many people's ideas of the park's history. Several times, when I told someone that I was writing a book about Yellowstone history, the response was, "How fun! You get to write about Teddy Roosevelt!"

At first I would say, "Well, no. Roosevelt did visit the park, and loved it, but he didn't really influence it." Roosevelt (who hated the nickname "Teddy") didn't create Yellowstone—that was Ulysses S. Grant, when T.R. (a nickname he preferred) was just thirteen years old. Roosevelt didn't expand it, didn't make lasting alterations to its management, didn't create the National Park Service. At age twenty-nine Roosevelt did co-found the Boone and Crockett Club, the hunters' organization that went on to successfully lobby for Yellowstone wildlife protections, but his policy influence was indirect. He wasn't even the first sitting president to visit—that was Chester Arthur, whose Yellowstone legacy is hard to find unless you climb a minor peak in the park's southeastern corner five miles from the nearest trail.

Eventually, however, I decided to listen to the people who were talking to me, rather than turning on the fact machine. Why *did* they associate Roosevelt with Yellowstone? Many cited his conservation policies. He established the first eighteen national monuments and the first fifty-one federal wildlife refuges; he doubled the number of national parks; and he quadrupled the acreage in forest reserves, also organizing them into the U.S. Forest Service. As president, he surrounded himself with conservation activists, including both the preservationist John Muir and the multiple-use advocate Gifford Pinchot. He was the first conservationist president, at a time when the nation, and the national parks, embraced conservation. He was also very good at linking conservation to democracy. For example, in his much-admired speech at the Gardiner Arch, he spoke of "the preservation of the scenery, of the forests, of the wilderness life and the wilderness game *for the people as a whole*, instead of leaving the enjoyment thereof to be confined to the very rich." He noted that "wild creatures have been so carefully protected as to show a literally astounding tameness." And he highlighted the phrase *for the benefit and enjoyment of the people* so forcefully that it sometimes ends up being attributed to him rather than the 1872 law establishing Yellowstone.[1]

More deeply, however, Roosevelt established a cultural narrative. In the story America tells about itself, Roosevelt was a sort of superhero who came out of the rugged West—along with a posse of writers, showmen, and artists—to rescue high society from the effete Victorian era. T.R. in a drawing room was like a bull in a china shop: causing all the men who'd been standing around in their formalwear to wake up and proclaim, "What the hell are we doing in a china shop? Bullfights are way more fun!"

America raced off to its bullfights—including a war against Spaniards, a crusade against monopolists, and a new appreciation of masculine physicality—while celebrating the West. The West was a region and philosophy and set of crazy characters that the once-sickly young Roosevelt credited with his transformation into an unstoppable force. As he spread that credit, thick and wide, a great deal of it pooled into the national park.

Like any superhero, Theodore Roosevelt had a story of redemptive rebirth. In the wake of an 1884 tragedy—the deaths, hours apart, of his mother and wife—the 26-year-old Roosevelt retreated to a ranch near Medora, North Dakota. For the next two years he toughened himself: hunting and horseback riding, serving as sheriff, and writing history books. As we polish the story into myth, we often picture him basically alone. But in fact his neighbors came from a similar upper-class background.

Howard Eaton, raised in a wealthy Pittsburgh family, had arrived in 1879 to start his own ranch. Soon his two brothers, Willis and Alden, joined him. In fact, a letter from Howard to a friend in New York was what prompted Roosevelt to visit North Dakota in the first place. Indeed the Eatons found themselves regularly entertaining friends from back east. Some friends started offering money to cover their expenses, starting in 1883 when several accompanied Howard on a pack trip to Yellowstone. As the cattle economy faltered, especially after the brutal winter of 1886–87, the Eatons started making better income from visitors.[2]

A husky man, tanned and blue-eyed, Howard Eaton had a powerful handshake and a surprisingly high-pitched voice. He typically dressed in canvas pants and jacket, a blue flannel shirt, and a white felt hat. His boundless reserves of hospitality made him the public face of the family operation. He loved outdoor living—riding horses for fun, not merely to get somewhere—and he also loved sharing that lifestyle with others. Among his early guests were a great number of restless teenage boys, whose parents sent them to the West to keep them out of trouble. Staff at the ranch—who were nicknamed "savages," as staffers at Yellowstone were as well—noticed how enthralled the visitors were with Howard's wide-brimmed white felt hat, leather chaps, oversized spurs, six-shooter revolver, and other accoutrements of ranch life. The boys dressed far more "cowboy" than any cattle tender did. In the wider culture, *dude* at the time referred to an overdressed fop, but when genial Uncle Howard called someone a *dude* or, for that matter, a *savage*, the terms were scrubbed of derision.[3]

When Howard and his brothers first arrived, before the railroad, North Dakota still boasted bison. Over the next twenty years, Plains wildlife populations went into free fall, and farmers fenced off the open range. So the Eatons decided to move. In 1903 they sold the North Dakota ranch and established a new one on the east slopes of Wyoming's Bighorn Mountains, eighteen miles from the rail line in Sheridan. It had a mountain setting for horseback riding, trout fishing, and big game hunting. It was also twice as close to Yellowstone for the trip Howard led there every summer.

Throughout the following decade, establishments that called themselves dude ranches started emerging elsewhere too. In many cases, the ranch was simply the home base of a hunting guide. Dudes—primarily upper-class young males playing out newly trendy masculine fantasies—would bunk there before and after the camping trip into elk country. Such was the case with a second hero of our story, Irving H. "Larry" Larom.[4]

Born in 1889, Larry was raised on New York City's Park Avenue by parents on the *Social Register*. But he was fascinated with the West: he hung a Bierstadt print in his childhood bedroom. When he was a junior at Princeton in the spring of 1910, his father took him to see Buffalo Bill's Wild West in Madison Square Garden, and then backstage to meet the showman himself. There, Larry was drawn to an oversized painting of Buffalo Bill's TE Ranch, an eight-thousand-acre spread in thinly populated northwest Wyoming.

Larry had an angular nose, thick eyebrows, dark hair pulled back from his forehead, and a mustache with a slight twirl. He had a slightly proper, reserved air that could make you wonder how tough he was.[5] That summer of 1910, Larry went west to find that out for himself. He was joined by Alexander James, son of the philosopher William James and nephew of the novelist Henry James. Larry and Alexander were the type of rich kids defined more by privilege than obvious brilliance: Alexander disappointed his father by failing the Harvard entrance exam five consecutive times, and Larry never got around to finishing his Princeton coursework. But out west nobody asked for a diploma.

Larry and Alexander took a train to Cody, Wyoming. In 1910, Cody was a struggling town that had not yet acquired its road into Yellowstone or its outsized cowboy character. All it had was Buffalo Bill's name—an attempt to capitalize on his celebrity—and a railroad stop. There the boys mounted horses to ride up the South Fork of the Shoshone River, where they gradually entered a world of high golden cliffs, massive peaks, and breccia spires. At first they traversed a dry flat with views of a newly created reservoir. Soon they passed Castle Rock, a lone fortress in the middle of the empty valley floor. Its presence had been noted in 1807 by John Colter, the first Anglo to see this country, but little appreciated since. The South Fork country was high in elevation, with cold winters and thin soil, and not on the way to anywhere at all. Railroad surveyors had come through here, searching for a direct route over the Continental Divide, but were stymied by the endless massifs on both sides, closing in like a funnel pointed upstream at a distant, impenetrable canyon.

They passed the TE Ranch, thirty-three miles upstream from town, and then came upon a large, flat-topped mesa called Ishawooa. On flat bottomland below the mesa, the South Fork ran in wide braids through gray cobble strewn with massive peeled tree trunks left behind by past floods. It was huge country, at a scale difficult for an easterner to comprehend. On benchlands covered in grass and sage, the views extended dozens of miles, far longer than the vistas obtained from some of the highest eastern peaks. Cows and cottonwoods dotted the valley floor, but from the benchlands they—and by extension any horse and rider—seemed infinitesimal. In this lonely expanse, you could start to understand what it took for someone like Colter to survive out here: the physical strength, the forbearance of cold, the comfort with being alone, the wisdom to choose good trails, and the courage to ford rivers or scale precipices when you chose wrong—and sometimes even when you chose right.

Here was the "dude ranch" where Larry and Alexander spent their first night. In its kitchen, the proprietor had nailed the windows shut to keep out the cold, and the resulting accumulation of grease and other odors caused Larry to gag and run outside. Then at bedtime, he and Alexander climbed an outdoor ladder to an attic. Bedsheets hung from the ceiling to break it into compartments. Each so-called bedroom had an army cot and a coal-oil lamp. Larry found that he was indeed tough enough to accept these conditions. But he would remember the night for the rest of his life, because it led to the insight that eventually defined that life: in general people of his class would really rather not live like this.

A few years and several visits later, in 1915, Larry and another friend—Winthrop Brooks, a Yale graduate whose family owned the Brooks Brothers clothing store—bought that ranch where Larry first stayed: 175 acres, 56 horses, and 38 cows. They envisioned turning the Valley Ranch into the sort of upscale resort that wealthy women would enjoy. Instead of a boardinghouse-style attic, guests stayed in private cabins. Instead of a smelly kitchen, they ate in a dining room. Instead of being hosted by a syphilitic hunter-trapper-guide, they had a refined man of breeding.[6] And instead of focusing solely on hunting, their vacation of fishing, riding, and swimming would be capped by a trip to nearby Yellowstone. Because of these innovations, Codyites sometimes credit Larry (Win soon returned to New York as a silent partner) with inventing the first real dude ranch.

Meanwhile something very similar was happening a few mountain ranges to the southwest. In 1908 a 25-year-old Princeton grad named Struthers Burt arrived in Jackson Hole, the gorgeous valley of the Snake River below the Tetons. (*Hole* was an old trappers' word for a valley surrounded by mountains; the town of Jackson lies at the southern end of the Hole.) Burt was visiting the newly established JY Ranch, with a breathtaking view across Phelps Lake to Death Canyon amid craggy, high peaks. The lake was chilly for swimming but often calm enough to serve as a mirror of the surrounding pines and mountains. The views were among the most scenic imaginable, but Struthers was equally fascinated by the ranch itself: he was determined to learn how to rope and ride.[7]

Burt had wide, observant eyes that seemed to pop out of a pinched face. He was an aspiring writer drawn to the romance of the place. Jackson Hole was a favorite haunt of the famous novelist Owen Wister, a Harvard classmate of Roosevelt's who crystallized the cowboy-as-mythic-hero in his 1902 best seller, *The Virginian.*

In 1911 Wister would build his own cabin near the JY; he and Burt were part of a pipeline between Jackson Hole and the upper-class neighborhood of the Philadelphia Main Line.

Upon his arrival, Burt was also impressed with the JY's proprietor and namesake, Louis Joy. After twenty-five years in the West, Joy knew the country but lacked social graces. Burt's connections to the elite seemed a good complement, and by the end of the summer he acquired a partnership in the operation. However, the two later quarreled, and in 1911 Burt struck out on his own. With a partner from Philadelphia, he established the Bar BC along the Snake River a few miles north. In the center of Jackson Hole, near Jenny Lake, it looked directly up at the three grandest Tetons. The setting could not have been prettier, although at more than one hundred miles to the nearest railroad, it was incredibly remote.

The Bar BC soon became the most successful and notable dude ranch in the Hole. People in Jackson Hole sometimes credit it with establishing not only a regional economic sector but also an architectural style. In "dude ranch vernacular," small guest cabins cluster around a main lodge—all of them made of rustic logs.[8] Like the idea of dude ranching itself, the style appears to have arisen independently for Burt, Larom, the Eatons, and dozens of others. And, of course, it mirrors the Old Faithful Inn's informal architecture, marrying a rustic homestead and a luxury retreat. Nevertheless, Jackson Hole took pride in Burt and embraced the dude ranching economy more quickly than Cody or Sheridan did. Indeed, as published authors, Struthers and his wife, Katherine Newlin Burt, became the industry's best publicists. And their emphasis on culture, with theatrical performances and literary discussions under the spectacular vista of the Tetons, polished the idea of the dude ranch to an unprecedented gleam.

Our three heroes—Eaton, Larom, and Burt—had common goals. It's not enough to simply say that they wanted to make a living as dude ranchers. Nor is it enough to say they were entrepreneurs hoping to dominate a new economic sector. What they wanted was to fulfill themselves, and their customers, through vigorous application of Rooseveltian masculinity.[9] Each was seeking to establish a utopia centered on outdoor recreation. Their ranches were a combination of resort and Outward Bound–style adventure where young people could use the natural surroundings to discover their true character. It was a heavily nostalgic experience that called on the traditions of the Old West. Surviving frontier conditions required physical strength—and, some liked to believe, moral strength. Now that frontiers were tamed, how could you build and demonstrate that strength? Dude ranching was an effort to stimulate rugged character by simulating the frontier.

Given their wealth and connections, any of our three heroes could have found another way to make a living. Larry had sold real estate in New York; Struthers could write from anywhere. They could have established vacation cabins in the West, like Wister and Buffalo Bill did. Then they would have spent their summers fishing and riding rather than teaching others how to. But their vision of the West—with its grand vistas, unspoiled country, and physical demands—suggested a new vision of society. They were like Boy Scouts who pursue merit badges not only in archery and forestry but also in lifesaving and citizenship. In Rooseveltian America, our heroes wanted their clients to be able to follow Roosevelt's transformational path. The dude ranch turned the experience into a sort of assembly line, as the romance of outdoor living was enriched by discussions of literature, encounters with earthy cowboys, and visits to an extraordinary national park.

Creating that experience involved hardships. In 1923, near what might be considered the height of dude ranching, Larry wrote despondently to Win Brooks, who was now rising the corporate ladder at the family business in New York. After nine years, Larry said, he was still making less money than his cooks. "Every day requires more work, more planning, more direction, more desk work. . . .The glamour of the West and all that rot has long since faded away. My only pleasure is in making this company a success, not in my surroundings, nor in the gossiping trash we call neighbors, nor in the long winters, spring floods and summer cloudbursts. This is the toughest damn country to make a living in there is, and despite our temporary difficulties we are the only ones who are getting anywhere."[10]

Larry might have been referring to surrounding cattle ranches amid an agricultural downturn, because in fact several dude ranches were getting somewhere. The industry benefitted from lucky timing. When the world war engulfed Europe in 1914, many of the young people who might have toured the Continent chose to instead see America first. A dude ranch could substitute for Paris or Rome, with mountain scenery replacing ancient cathedrals in exactly the way Thomas Moran had painted. Especially for young women, a trip to the West was now *safe* in a way it hadn't been during the genuine frontier days. Native Americans had been fully dispossessed of their lands and shunted off to reservations. Wolves and grizzlies were nearly exterminated, and outlaws were equally rare. Railroads continued to expand. And in contrast to the unknown, unmapped wilderness that faced John Colter, dude ranches featured a regulated environment with knowledgeable guides.

Indeed the experience was a little like a summer camp. Many of the guests were college students or recent graduates. They were finding themselves, delightedly discovering their talents. Romances were common. In the first years of the Valley Ranch, Win Brooks married one of his female dudes (they were often called *dudines*), and Larry almost married another. Other guests married each other or married locals. Some of them bought their own spreads and became locals themselves.

It was a very exclusive summer camp, highly discriminatory. Guests arrived by invitation only, after providing references. Dude ranch proprietors, many of them Ivy Leaguers, announced their own references—Larom's letterhead included not only his and Brooks's names but also their alma maters. Exclusivity was deemed important because the guests would be spending an entire summer in very close proximity at a remote location. They needed to be compatible with each other and their hosts, and so the admissions process resembled that of an Ivy League school—all the way down to excluding Jews, African Americans, and other minorities.

A place that eliminates class and ethnic tensions by eliminating classes and ethnicities is really more of a hideout than a utopia. The dude ranch wasn't an authentic representation of American society. Nor was it authentic to the frontier it honored, because many of the risks that defined that frontier had been sanitized. Indeed it wasn't even an authentic ranch, because it didn't depend on cattle sales—although dude ranchers often claimed to be running legitimate cattle ranches, this was at best an unsustainable hope and at worst a mere part of the sales pitch. In some ways, our heroes were running summer-long costume parties.

Burt almost admitted so. He wrote in a memoir that cowboy/cowgirl attire was "the one national costume we have." The dude rancher, he said, "knows that when Eastern damsels put on overalls and wear egregious scarfs they don't look in the least like cowgirls, but he encourages them to do these things because it is good for their souls."[11] With an understanding of the artifice inherent in his industry, Burt made a compelling argument that it was justified. But it's not clear whether other dude ranchers, much less the dudes themselves, possessed Burt's self-consciousness.

Whether or not dudes knew they were pretending, other westerners knew. Many cattle ranchers scorned dude operations. On the lonely frontier, the ranching tradition had long embraced extreme hospitality—you always welcomed all guests free of charge. Dude ranchers consciously violated that tradition in order to nurture a meaningless product: even if the goal was to toughen effete easterners, catering to their whims seemed a demeaning occupation. It was not, to the western mind, authentically masculine. And so the dude rancher ended up occupying a strange and lonely middle ground: to his guests, he was a rugged Roosevelt full of native skills, but to his neighbors he was an effeminate, toadying fake.[12]

The dude ranchers also faced conflict with their neighbors over land. In their wide-open vision, they could ride all day without encountering civilization. Burt called this frontier reenactment a "museum on the hoof." But they didn't own all that land, and people whose livelihoods depended on sheep and cattle had different ideas about what to do with it. For that matter, Jackson Hole in particular started proving attractive to a variety of businesses catering to a new class of automobile tourists. The side road to Burt's Bar BC eventually gained a baseball diamond, rodeo grounds, and a billboard advertising the HOME OF THE HOLLYWOOD COWBOY. In the late 1910s, Burt opposed the notion of preserving the Tetons in a national park, an idea then envisioned as an extension of Yellowstone. He wanted a utopia run by himself, not the government. Historians have told a fascinating tale of how development and progress forced Burt to reverse positions and ally with the government to save Jackson Hole from commercialism.[13] But equally interesting is that utopian experience itself.

On a dude ranch you could spend your days riding, fishing, or just sitting around admiring the scenery. Mountain climbing and river rafting were not yet widespread pastimes, but if they were your passion, you probably would have been indulged. You were surrounded by people like you: young, healthy, and well-bred. Your vigorous exercise in the clean mountain air promoted a strong appetite and sound sleep, so much so that you might not even care that the vegetables were canned and mattresses lumpy. Every morning you woke up to the smell of sagebrush and the burble of a river. City life became a distant memory. You gained the time and inspiration to turn inward, focus on the self, clear away the clutter to appreciate what was important about life.

As a percentage of total western tourist traffic, dude ranches were never significant. But because they delighted the elites, their influence exceeded their numbers. For example, acclaimed author Mary Roberts Rinehart published a 1916 travelogue, *Through Glacier Park: Seeing America First with Howard Eaton.* Novelist Caroline Lockhart, a friend of Larom's, published a best-selling 1921 comic novel, *The Dude Wrangler*, with a hero resembling Larry. Then came Burt's 1924 memoir, *Diary of a Dude-wrangler.* All highlighted the informal atmosphere of the dude ranch and its salutary effect on character. Compared to stuffy and socially restricted eastern resorts, out west you could relax and be yourself.

Although few dudes experienced the scope or fame of transformation that Roosevelt had, many were clearly enriched. Some decided to buy their own western ranches, to be run as a cattle operation, as a summer retreat, or as their own dude ranch. Thus the utopian impulse started extending beyond the boundaries of any one ranch, to entire communities. In Cody, Larom co-founded the Cody Stampede rodeo, a massive Fourth of July celebration where dudes and townspeople mingled, happily and drunkenly. The town of Cody increasingly filled with former dudes and dude-sympathizers; in the 1920s its diverse residents included an art-loving Italian count, the family of a bookbinding mogul who'd commanded an all-African-American regiment during World War I, and a gay Harvard-educated literary scholar.[14] In such a neighborhood, Larry could market his dude ranch as a *civilized* wilderness. He could host western-themed shindigs for the neighborhood—featuring chuckwagon dinners, Crow Indian guests, and displays of rodeo talent—knowing that his dudes would nevertheless encounter neighbors of their own class. Like Triple-A Anderson in the next major valley to the south, several of those neighbors were men married to heiresses. It might be going too far to say that their passion for hyper-masculine pastimes such as hunting, horse-racing, rodeos, and military history arose from inadequacy at not being the family provider—but one can at least point out how easily they could afford those passions.

In Sheridan, Eaton likewise helped found the Sheridan Wyo Rodeo, and dudes extended the informality of the ranch into town. Haydie Yates, a former Larom dudine who moved to Sheridan to edit the newspaper, described the Sheridan Inn when she lived there in the winter of 1930 as "the gathering place of ranchers, state politicians, pensioners of one sort or another, rich ne'er-do-wells, spinster schoolmarms, dudes in expensive buckskins and dudines in fringe and fashionable permanents, sourdoughs, old-timers, and jolly rumrunners . . . The narrow dark halls were perpetually whirling with drifting eddies of people going in and out of each other's rooms."[15] For women of Yates's sensibilities, riding a political tide that had recently given them the vote, Sheridan was an ideal society: safe, economically rewarding, sexually liberated, and classless.

Jackson Hole perhaps most of all represented a playground on which dude culture could imprint its values. With a high elevation ill-suited to farming, Jackson Hole had no meaningful economic base before the arrival of dudes and then automobiles. To this day, the Jackson area feels like an anomaly in Wyoming—because its founding character was shaped by upper-class vacationers.

Indeed the dude ranch utopia also extended beyond those communities to the lands within the formal boundaries of Yellowstone National Park itself. (Those boundaries, drawn by an uninformed Congress in 1872, were an arbitrary political designation, which is one reason it's worth examining the culture of dude ranches not far outside those boundaries.) As an unspoiled natural preserve, Yellowstone's backcountry preserved the frontier character that the ranches strived for. It also anchored wildlife populations and the ranches' yearly routine. As curious as it is that our three heroes seemed to separately "invent" dude ranching, what's even more interesting is that these simultaneous inventions happened only in the Yellowstone area. Only later did this fully formed notion of dude ranching extend to other places in the Rockies.[16] The reason: the highlight of a dude's summer was a pack trip into Wonderland. Larom sometimes packed dudes over the steep passes south of his ranch into the scenic glory of Yellowstone's little-visited southeast corner, then around Yellowstone Lake to the more commonly viewed wonders. Meanwhile, Eaton took dudes every year on a trip through the park lasting fourteen to twenty-two days, at a time when the standard visit was just seven days.[17] The Eatons traditionally arrived at the North Entrance by rail, and camped the first night at Sheepeater Cliff, eight miles south of Mammoth. Although named for the Sheepeater Indians that once lived nearby, the site's chief attraction is a demonstration of weird geology: it looks like nature built a hill out of thousands of unused columns from Greek temples.[18] Yet Eaton probably highlighted it as one of his favorite spots because of its setting as a campsite. The Gardner River flows smoothly through a broad bottom, its ripples often the only sound for miles. Here the packers set up their canvas tents and built an evening campfire. The dudes gathered and listened to nostalgic stories of the West, of the olden days when every valley was this pristine, and this safe, and full of friendly storytellers like Howard.

Thus for dudes, the national park became entwined with the entire summer's experience. Yellowstone was a place, like Wyoming or the West in general, where you could ride horses through unspoiled country, sleep in the fresh air, and see extraordinary sights. A geyser was not merely a freak show but part of a package of natural wonders that contributed to a character-building experience. Indeed the Yellowstone visit became wrapped up in the personalities of the dude ranchers and your fellow dudes. To a dude, Yellowstone could be as much about a guide's folksy frontier stories as about geology or wildlife.

The park embraced that perspective. The early activities of the National Park Service, organized in 1916, centered on marketing national parks, convincing the public that these were special places worthy of government expenditures. In this marketing, Yellowstone wasn't just a geological oddity—it was a repository of national character. Thus, when Yellowstone superintendent Horace Albright visited Cody to dedicate an oversized statue of Buffalo Bill on the Fourth of July, 1924, he said, "We must be guardians of the spirit of discovery, pioneering, and progress. And this spirit can only be preserved by maintaining here forever at Cody and in Yellowstone Park . . . the picturesque customs and costumes of a day that is gone." By lumping together the town of Cody and the preserve of Yellowstone, the pioneering spirit and the bygone costumes, he was re-creating Yellowstone in the dude ranchers' image. When he spoke of "this conservation of the spirit of the Old West," he highlighted the park's chief attraction as not geysers or wildlife or scenery but the rugged frontier.[19]

One of the amazing features of Yellowstone was that it was big enough to accommodate these new visions. Starting in 1915, automobiles were allowed into the park. But Eaton, Larom, and many other dude ranchers continued the old-fashioned horseback pack trips. To keep their horses from being spooked by the loud new machines, the Eatons followed a trail parallel to the roads. After Howard's death in 1922—of appendicitis at age seventy-one—the park reverentially dedicated his path as the 157-mile Howard Eaton Trail. Today this road-paralleling trail is largely abandoned, because people would rather follow trails that take them to a destination that their cars can't reach. But at the time it was a demonstration of Yellowstone's immensity: the park had room for horse-packing to coexist with auto touring. Likewise Sheepeater Cliff could be preserved as a place for Howard's parties to camp in solitude, not competing with a hotel or restaurant, because Yellowstone was big enough to house those facilities eight miles away at Mammoth.[20] In short, Yellowstone's vast, unspoiled reaches meant that the park could simulate the frontier long after even Jackson Hole felt over-commercialized.

The decade of the 1920s represented the height of dude ranching. Our heroes succeeded: they made a living, established a new economic sector, and created an experience that transformed the lives of hundreds of their customers. However, after hard times during the Depression and war years, the industry fell out of the national consciousness. Dude ranches do still exist, in surprisingly large numbers, but they're generally tucked away far from beaten paths or social-media memes. Today, the most popular place to see and experience the dude ranchers' vision for Rooseveltian masculinity is in Yellowstone. It's the only American landscape that can show the general public the immensity that inspired and fueled the rugged dude utopia. Specifically, the best living example of our heroes' vision is at Yellowstone's Roosevelt Lodge.

The lodge sits alongside a meadow that was long a desirable campsite. In 1906 it became one of William Wylie's semipermanent tent camps for tour groups, and Wylie named it after the president, who had recently camped nearby. In 1919–20, the successor to Wylie's company, now offering independent lodging, built a permanent log structure on the site. The construction had the explicit goal of creating the atmosphere of a dude ranch. A central lodge of unpeeled logs was surrounded by dozens of tiny log cabins. Designed to especially support weeklong, or even monthlong, stays, in the early years it hosted scientific studies, field laboratories, lecture series, and a boys' summer camp.

Today Roosevelt Lodge has a different ambiance from other park accommodations. Tucked at the northeast corner of the park road's figure-eight, it's not directly adjacent to a natural wonder like Mammoth or Lake or Old Faithful. Although it often gets lumped together with the waterfall, campground, and store at Tower, the two attractions are actually three miles apart. Day-trippers are likely to stop at either one or the other—more likely the quickly digestible attraction of Tower Fall. Roosevelt Lodge, in contrast, relies on activities that call back to the rugged frontier living memorialized in dude ranches. For example, it's one of only two places in the park with corrals for horseback riding. Furthermore, in its popular Old West Dinner Cookout, guests ride in a covered wagon out to a picnic site where steaks are grilled and coffee brewed over an open campfire. After dinner, the concessionaire's website advertises, "you'll find your boots tappin' to old western songs sung by our singin' cowboy."[21]

A cynic might despair at how fake it is. The cookout is a watered-down simulation of a dude ranch, which was itself a watered-down simulation of the frontier. This is hardly authentic Rooseveltian ruggedness—it's more like a theme park. The covered wagon hints at Conestoga wagon trains that didn't come anywhere near here, and the dropped *g*'s of the advertisement's language suggest stoic cattle herders and salty prospectors whose activities were actually banned inside the national preserve. The event calls to the romance of a Hollywood vision of the Old West more than anything unique to Yellowstone itself.[22]

But families love it. Like the dudes of old, they love the idea of the frontier. They love to don the national costume—cowboy outfits—and revel in outdoor living. On the wagon ride they are often wowed by wildlife, including bison. They're surrounded by a newfound community rather than isolated in their cars or hotel rooms. Because it's for a single dinner, not an entire summer, the community need not be discriminatory—and thus even people of varying backgrounds discover their shared interests; all grow in their shared appreciation of deeper human relationships to the natural world. These relationships are often highlighted by the storytelling prowess of the wagons' drivers, who speak of the old days when this valley was pristine. The experience is, in other words, a very close approximation of the campouts that Howard Eaton used to conduct, in which Yellowstone served as a backdrop and symbol for the rugged frontier character that came to define the national identity.

I have long been fascinated by that speech in which Yellowstone's superintendent traveled to Cody and blessed a statue by endorsing the romance of Buffalo Bill, dude ranching, and Rooseveltian masculinity. It seems incongruent with the park's traditional focus on natural history—but it's not surprising. Horace Albright and his boss, Park Service director Stephen Mather, were products of that Rooseveltian moment themselves. They were educated, successful men who were motivated to become conservationists because they found fulfillment in outdoor enterprises. What might be surprising is that their ambitions for Yellowstone were far larger in scope than even that speech would suggest. They were building a brand-new organization, the National Park Service, on the foundation of a few famous natural places, including Yosemite, Mount

Rainier, and the recently established Glacier and Grand Canyon national parks. Albright believed that Yellowstone, the nation's first and biggest park, deserved top billing on that list. But how would he win that competition? Albright needed to do more than merely associate the Yellowstone area with Rooseveltian myth. He was on a quest to establish the mythic character of Yellowstone Park itself.

5

PATRIOTIC

I made the mistake of watching Ken Burns's TV series *The National Parks: America's Best Idea* only after I'd already done a fair bit of research for this book. So although I found the documentaries beautiful, accurate, and well told, I also found them a bit thin. "The idea!" I found myself saying back to the TV. "Why aren't you talking about who invented it?"

Burns's team deserves credit, first for seeing the national parks as a story of ideas, and second for making that story compelling. They justifiably pin the birth of this *best idea* to the creation of Yosemite in 1864; as Burns said, "It was the first time in human history [that] land was set aside for everyone."[1] That was a uniquely American notion, he says—the equality of it, the link between landscape and democracy. A wondrous natural place would not be reserved for royalty or monks, or commercialized by the highest bidder.

It's all true, and very inspiring. "But," I kept asking my television set, "when did it become an *idea*?" Burns shows lands being preserved at Yosemite in 1864 and Yellowstone in 1872, but my research was suggesting that those were more *impulses* than ideas. They were reactions to the overcommercialization of places like Niagara Falls: national leaders knew that they didn't want another Niagara, even if they couldn't quite articulate what they *did* want. Then, because of that lack of vision, the impulse foundered. In the 1880s, federal overseers signed giveaway contracts that almost did turn Yellowstone into another Niagara, until Congress stepped in to rescind them.[2] Even at that point, its vision was still negative ("No, we don't want that much private development"), not positive ("Here's what we want, and here's a budget to accomplish it"). So Yellowstone was finally turned over to the military, because the military was the only federal entity that had room for it and wouldn't trash it. The nation's park was like a boat stored in the army's backyard for an incredibly long winter, when nobody had yet seen or even imagined the lake without ice.

The *idea*—the National Park Idea, complete with capital letters—wasn't articulated as such until the founding of the National Park Service in 1916. The new agency promoted and even somewhat fabricated the Idea, applying it retroactively to the parks' history. That need not sound fake or evil: it was a grand, heroic action that helped establish the Park Service as perhaps the most-admired arm of the US government throughout the 20th century. And what's particularly fascinating is that the heroes who constructed the Idea decided to set its story in Yellowstone.[3]

Steve Mather came to the national parks in crisis—his midlife crisis. After making a fortune in borax, he discovered that what he really loved was camping in the wilderness. But on his horse-packing trips in the mountains near Yosemite and Mount Rainier, he got fed up with the poor trails and swarms of cattle.[4] In 1914 he complained to the Interior Department and soon found himself invited to improve the parks' management.[5] The fourteen national parks had each been created as one-offs, with idiosyncratic management plans. Some were controlled by the military, others by political hacks. (At Glacier, the story went, one of the politically connected rangers had to be assigned to patrol along the railroad track so he wouldn't get lost in the woods—and then had to be given a partner to shout at him when a train was coming.)[6] It was the height of the Progressive Era, with the founding of government bodies such as the Federal Reserve and Federal Trade Commission. So how about coordinated, professional management for the national parks?

Steve, then forty-seven years old, was well suited to the role of parks advocate. A tall, lithe man with piercing blue eyes, prematurely white hair, and a ruddy complexion, he was deeply driven and inwardly restless but outwardly amiable, gracious, and charming. His constant enthusiasm earned him the nickname "the Eternal Freshman." He liked people and believed in them, which made him very persuasive when dining with politicians at fancy Washington clubs. He was also willing to spend his private fortune on his public job, including paying for those dinners and even for the salaries of his staff. But Mather had a deep secret that nearly derailed his mission, and in fact the founding of the Park Service was equally indebted to his assistant, Horace Albright.[7]

Horace was a son of the California frontier who followed a professor to Washington. He figured he was on a temporary sojourn before using his law degree in a business career. Tall, brown-haired, and bespectacled, he was known as modest, patient, and tactful, full of integrity and idealism—but relentless. A *Scribner's* magazine profile later noted, "he never fails to get what he wants."[8] A meticulous, efficient administrator, Albright was the perfect complement to the big-picture salesman Mather. Then, just four months after the pair convinced Congress to create the National Park Service—and both agreed to stay on to run it—Mather got sick.

Today we would describe it as bipolar disorder. Then they called it "nerves." During a national park conference in January 1917, ebullient Mather suddenly flipped into despondent, suicidal Mather. He was hustled to a sanitarium, and Albright, then just twenty-eight years old, became acting director. He wrote reports, set policies, hired administrators, and toured existing and potential new parks. In a letter at that time, he wrote, "Organizing this new Service, with few precedents to go by and no one but myself to make decisions is a terrible burden . . . I have no blueprints and no architect."[9] But he did well enough. Indeed when Mather returned eighteen months later, Albright was ready to get out from the older man's shadow, though he wasn't yet ready to abandon his infant agency. He asked to be named superintendent of Yellowstone.

Horace saw the new job as an exciting administrative challenge, because Yellowstone was a microcosm of the Park Service as a whole. The agency's founding legislation, which Horace helped write, expressed lofty ideals: a mandate to help people enjoy nature while leaving it "unimpaired for the enjoyment of future generations." But the trick would be translating this poetry into management. Yellowstone was like a start-up company: it needed a civilian employee base, modernization for automobile travel, a system to organize and control concessionaires, and top-notch customer service. After all, the Park Service had been created because of the chaotic conditions and environmental degradation that Mather witnessed on his pack trips. If on-the-ground admin-istrative functions couldn't eliminate those problems, the agency would be a failure.

Unlike most start-up founders, Albright had to accomplish all this under public scrutiny. He was a public employee with a public mission—one that was not yet widely accepted. He and Mather were haunted by Hetch Hetchy, a scenic valley in Yosemite that was being dammed to provide drinking water for San Francisco. To defenders of national parks, it seemed self-evident that a park was more valuable than a reservoir—but there weren't enough such defenders. So the challenge for Albright and Mather was bigger than that of regulators at a place like the Federal Trade Commission: they needed the public to not only respect what they did but also love it.

In other words, they needed marketing. Happily, Mather was a marketing guy. He'd made his fortune not by mining borax better or cheaper than competitors but by transforming its public image. Among other tactics, he launched a "Hints from Heloise"–style campaign encouraging housewives to invent new uses for the easily dissolved white mineral. Soon many homes boasted a box of borax: combination water softener, eyewash, and skin cream. Over thirty years, borax use increased by 1,500 percent. Meanwhile, Steve distinguished his own company's brand of borax by establishing its *creation myth*. At its borax mine in Death Valley, California, in the 1880s, a twelve-ton wagon was required to transport the product 165 miles to the nearest railroad. The load was so heavy that it was pulled by eighteen mules and two horses. Steve arranged for a write-up of this legend and rebranded the product "20 Mule Team Borax." Steve probably knew that his story contained romantic exaggerations, but he was the type of enthusiastic guy who found even borax to be deserving of romanticism. And he intuitively grasped that a creation myth—whether it's for a tech company founded in a garage, the Pilgrims landing on a rock at Plymouth, or George Washington chopping down a cherry tree—needs to be a great story more than it needs to be factually perfect.

Steve's mission to transform the perception of national parks required frequent communication with the public: press releases, speeches, ceremonies, and lots of invitations to journalists to attend semi-invented events. In Steve's view, any activity should be an opportunity to tell the story of the parks, to reiterate how special they were. He engaged with a wide range of partners with different visions: railroads plus emerging automobile clubs, frontier-obsessed dude ranchers plus comfort-oriented vacationers, nature-gazers plus nature-recreationists. The clashes inherent in balancing the agendas of competing factions suggested another marketing angle: showing the parks as an emblem of the nation's democracy. At Yellowstone, Horace's job included seizing opportunities to push these messages wherever he could.

In 1922 came one of the biggest such opportunities yet: the fiftieth anniversary of the 1872 law setting aside Yellowstone as a national preserve. The literal anniversary, March 1, passed unnoticed because Yellowstone was basically closed in the winter. But in correspondence later that spring, Horace wrote, "We have talked about the semi-centennial so much that it looks like we will have to have some sort of a celebration."[10] What kind of event would make people admire Yellowstone? What would tell its story, emphasize the ways it was special? And whatever the event was, could they get President Warren Harding to attend? The obvious idea, Horace said, was a pageant.

The idea doesn't seem at all obvious today. But at the time, pageantry was booming. Before the era of mass entertainment media, pageants provided a creative outlet for the emerging industrial and middle classes, combining the ancient arts of oration and parade. Leaders of a movement to spread pageantry around the country wanted every small town to write and perform a play about community history. They'd chosen the word *pageant* (over *folk play*) to speak not of religious themes but an outdoor setting, exaggerated costuming, and a nonprofessional cast. As the head of the American Pageant Association put it in the *New York Times* in 1913, in a pageant "place is the hero and development of the community the plot."[11] That gave pageants a patriotic, even propagandistic, purpose: transmitting proper values and ideals through story (while also keeping the performers and audience out of saloons). This made them a perfect vehicle for national parks.

Albright and Mather toyed with a pageant illustrating the evolution of vehicular transportation in the West: Indian travois, prairie schooners, stagecoaches, the more comfortable Concord coaches, the even more magnificent coaches of the 1910s, automobiles, and buses. But such a theme failed to sufficiently celebrate Yellowstone, to make it the hero rather than just a setting. Organizing such a pageant would also take up way too much time. "It is certain that anything that is attempted will involve an enormous amount of work on the part of the men already overburdened with executive duties," Albright wrote.[12] And Mather responded, "Furthermore, if you were to have a pageant at Mammoth, the even distribution of visitors over the park would be unsettled, not only for one day but for several, and it would probably result in a congestion that might be disastrous and give us a black eye."[13]

But Steve also mentioned having a recent conversation with a botany professor who fondly recalled an 1872 scientific expedition to Yellowstone. For Horace, that apparently stimulated the idea of staging the celebration as a sort of Old Explorers' Reunion—and indeed he knew just the people to highlight it.

Near the park's West Entrance, in a broad, scenic meadow abutted by a high cliff, the Gibbon and Firehole Rivers flow together to form the Madison. Bison often graze nearby, especially in the spring when the grasses are green. The blue streams wander lazily through oxbows, pines blanket the distant hills, and if puffy white clouds dot the big blue sky, you feel like your mountain portrait is complete. Modern roads follow ancient trails along the watercourses, giving the place the name Madison Junction.

On July 14, 1922, Albright and a collection of dignitaries gathered in this meadow for the semicentennial ceremony. Witnesses included members of the National Editorial Association—newspaper editors on a junket. The guests of honor included Cornelius Hedges, Jr., and W. A. Hedges, the two sons of one of the most famous Yellowstone explorers; plus Charley Cook, a less-famous explorer who was delightfully alive and kicking at age eighty-three.

These men were then referred to as *discoverers* of Yellowstone. Today we find such a notion absurd, because clearly indigenous people had been present for centuries. But even then, the word *discoverers* had to be taken with a grain of salt. Because in addition to natives, lower-class Anglos—from John Colter to fur trappers to prospectors—had been wandering through Yellowstone for decades. The difference was, people like Charley Cook (maybe) and Cornelius Hedges (certainly) were vacationers of meaningful social status who visited Yellowstone for the purposes of education and aesthetic appreciation. They also wrote stuff down.

Cook was the borderline case: he and two friends were well educated but not socially prominent in 1869, when they left Helena to remarks such as "good-bye, boys, look out for your hair," "if you get back at all you will come on foot," and "it's the next best thing to suicide."[14] They had trouble publishing their written account because editors and publishers didn't believe them. The fact that they brought pickaxes to Yellowstone, as if they might do some prospecting, seemed to harm their credibility. But their stories inspired a bigger expedition the following year, complete with local big shots and a military escort.

One local leader was Cornelius Hedges, an attorney. With a bushy mustache and dark, prominent eyebrows, "Judge" Hedges wasn't exactly a rugged outdoorsman. But over the years the legend of his contributions to the expedition grew, primarily due to a story told by his co-expeditioner Nathaniel Langford.

Langford detailed their journey in *Scribner's* soon after they returned. But in the 1890s, when interviewed by a man compiling the first guidebook to Yellowstone, he added a scene that he hadn't mentioned before. (Nor, for that matter, had Hedges or Henry Washburn mentioned it in their published chronicles—indeed seventeen different accounts of the expedition had been published without mentioning it.) Later Langford expanded it in a 1905 memoir, written in the form of a diary, that he titled *The Discovery of Yellowstone Park, 1870*. Perhaps, looking back, he exaggerated. Perhaps ambition clouded his memories. Or if we take the generous view, perhaps with the passage of time he gained perspective to understand the scene's importance.

In the story, Langford recalled camping at Madison Junction on a September night near the end of their journey. They'd traveled eighteen miles that day. Around the campfire, and again in the morning, "the entire party had a rather unusual discussion," he wrote. Amazed by the geysers, canyon, and lake, they expected these places to become important tourism sites. So maybe they should each file a homestead claim near the prominent points of interest. Or maybe they should all file claims, and "the whole should be thrown in a common pool for the benefit of the entire party," he wrote.[15]

"Mr. Hedges then said that he did not approve of any of these plans—that there ought to be no private ownership of any portion of that region, but that the whole of it ought to be set apart as a great National Park, and that each one of us ought to make an effort to have this accomplished." Langford wrote that Hedges's brainstorm met with immediate approval.

Today, although historians are willing to accept that such a conversation took place, they don't see it as necessarily meaningful. Hedges was merely articulating a commonly held view, a previously expressed impulse, to somehow honor this magical land. As far back as 1832, in a trip up the Missouri River, painter George Catlin proposed that the government preserve a large expanse of land, a *"nation's park* containing man and beast, in all the wild and freshness of their nature's beauty!"[16] In 1865 Hedges was with acting territorial governor Thomas Meagher when they heard stories from a Jesuit priest who had toured Yellowstone, and Meagher "said that if things were as described the government ought to reserve the territory for a national park."[17] The impulse seemed to well up in anyone who visited: in his semicentennial speech, Charley Cook recalled saying, at this very site in 1869, that Yellowstone "ought to be kept for the public some way."[18] And Hedges had surely heard of Yosemite, which had by then already been set aside as a California state park. Indeed, he was soon advocating for a redrawing of territorial boundaries that would allow Montana to appropriate Yellowstone for public use—in other words, despite Langford's claim that Hedges invented this big, new idea of a national park, Hedges's actions suggested that he favored the smaller, more familiar idea of a state (or territorial) park.

But to Horace Albright, and indeed to many people in the 1920s, Langford's story was gospel. Around a campfire at Madison Junction, Hedges invented the National Park Idea.

That's why Horace set up this Old Explorers Reunion. That's why he located the semicentennial celebration at Madison Junction. This was yet another opportunity to polish the magic of national parks. Horace had been talking up the story since writing his first agency annual report. He was turning Cornelius Hedges's fireside comment into the national parks' creation myth.

Any creation myth is valuable, but this one in particular offered Albright all sorts of advantages. It portrayed Yellowstone's discoverers as selfless, setting a tone for all future national parks. If Hedges, Langford, and friends had foresworn the opportunity to get rich by filing their own claims, then parks should always be held separate from economic interests. *"I'm sorry, sir, but putting a dam in this place would go against the wishes of the people who discovered it."* The same spirit would frown on any railroad that wanted to build through the park, anyone who wanted to mine or graze or cut timber inside a park's boundaries, or even any concessionaire who seemed a bit greedy. Albright had already faced each of these political challenges, and found this story to be a powerful emotional argument against them.

The story's idealism was also a useful recruiting tool. Previously, Yellowstone's employees were ordered there by the army. Now, during the urban boom of the Roaring Twenties, Horace had to find people willing to live in a remote place and collect a small paycheck for often-demanding work. By citing the story, he could portray the job as a romantic calling for those inspired by the discoverers' noble dedication to nature and the nation.

Furthermore, the creation myth offered Albright an additional Yellowstone attraction. People enjoyed stopping at Madison Junction to see the birthplace of The Idea. It was a patriotic pilgrimage to a spot that embodied American ideals. In the same way that you visited the Statue of Liberty to become inspired about American ideals regarding immigration, or Philadelphia's Liberty Bell for independence, you could visit Madison Junction for equality. The parks were created for everyone—which meant everyone had to visit.

And again, Yellowstone was so immense that it could easily incorporate this new reason for visiting. Madison Junction was always a beautiful campsite, but providing a patriotic overlay didn't crowd out some other meaning. Nor did a stop at Madison need to replace any of the other attractions on a park tour, unless you were in a hurry. It merely added to the tapestry.

Indeed, by comparative standards Yellowstone had actually been lacking in this area. Over the fifty years of national park development, tourists expressed increasing interest in history. For example, Arizona's Grand Canyon showed off the traditions of the nearby Navajo and Hopi nations. Mesa Verde's sole purpose was to highlight the Ancestral Puebloan culture. The Glacier Park Lodge arranged for dances by Blackfeet warriors in ceremonial dress. But Yellowstone had a more complicated relationship with Native Americans, which put a damper on its ability to highlight history.

The problem was that Yellowstone was founded amid the Indian wars, four years before Custer's debacle on the Little Bighorn. The 1877 flight of the Nez Perce involved a dramatic hostage incident inside the park's boundaries. Afterwards, to assuage Anglo fears, Yellowstone leaders started asserting that natives never lived in the park, always avoided it because they were scared of the geysers. We now know that the assertion was false—many tribes treasured the area, and a Shoshone band called the Sheepeaters lived there full-time, probably into the 1870s. But in the 1920s the assertion still permeated Yellowstone's self-image, which made it difficult to celebrate ancient area history.

Now, with the origin of the National Park Idea, Yellowstone could boast its own lure for the history-oriented tourist. Indeed by offering a history of middle-class Anglos, it gained even broader appeal. As the first park to be dedicated at the federal level, Yellowstone wasn't just a set of natural wonders or the remnants of a past civilization. Yellowstone showed the dominant culture expressing itself.

You could argue that in building this symbolism, Albright was using patriotism toward selfish ends. He gave people a sense of collective ownership so that they would oppose the selling off, development, or other degradation of the national park system that employed him. He was manufacturing an emotion for political purposes. But that interpretation is too cynical. Albright did believe in the wonders of American democracy, including the egalitarian approach to natural wonders that Theodore Roosevelt captured in his speech at the Gardiner Arch. Albright's feat was to link this positive and useful emotion, patriotism, to a set of concrete symbols: Madison Junction, Yellowstone, and the national parks in general.

In his speech at the semicentennial, Albright described the scene at this site in 1870, and then quoted Hedges: "'We should preserve [these wonders] as a national park.' And right there," Albright hammered home, "the National Park Idea was born. These men were big enough, broad enough, and public spirited enough to lay aside all their personal ambitions and the wealth that was before them, and it was unanimously agreed then that a national park should be created."[19]

Albright then read a series of telegrams from high-ranking officials. Most of them summarized the event's significance, likely working off notes provided by Albright, and thus reemphasizing his themes. For example, President Harding's message included, "We now realize that with its establishment as the first National Park came also the recognition of the principle that scenery of supreme majesty is a national asset worthy of preservation for the use and enjoyment of future generations as well as those of our time." Wyoming senator Francis Warren joked, "I am sorry Jim Bridger is not alive today to see how many people now enjoy the park and can testify to its wonders, and the fact that Bridger was not suffering from hallucinations as believed in those early days." And Montana senator Thomas Walsh highlighted "the semi-centennial of the entrance of the Washburn Langford party, through which [Yellowstone's] wonders were made known to the world." In other words, the National Park Idea had become so dominant that Walsh believed that its campfire conception—rather than passage eighteen months later of a law setting aside the park—was the reason for the day's celebration.[20]

Only one telegram got the facts of the Hedges story correct. Arno Cammerer, a Park Service assistant director in Washington, wrote, "When Cornelius Hedges at the campfire in the Yellowstone, that cold September evening in 1870, said that there should be no private ownership in the great Yellowstone region but that the whole of it ought to be set apart as a great National Park, he voiced a thought which has been accepted and grown into a strong and unshakable national conservation policy for which future generations, perhaps more so than those of our time, will show deepest gratitude."[21] Cammerer's words were cautious enough to celebrate the moment and its role in the movement—without making romantic claims about an idea being born.

But romantic claims, of course, are the entire point of a creation myth. Debating their literal truth is an exercise in seeking to deny the power of mythology. Any origin story stretches the facts in order to capture a set of values that sets the entity apart. And the *values* have to be genuine, or else the story won't take hold. (Indeed, the success of a factual challenge to any creation myth generally depends on changes in underlying values that allow the challenge itself to take hold.)[22] With his vision and heroic action, Horace

Albright understood the values that a national park service needed, and he found a story format in which to express them compellingly.

In the end Horace got his pageant too. He reconnected with Garnet Holme, his old drama coach at the University of California in Berkeley, who had since stitched together a career directing pageants. Garnet had been born in England, attended Cambridge, gotten involved in theater, and discovered he was a better manager than actor. After directing hundreds of Shakespearean productions for English touring companies, he came to California in 1904. Now in his fifties and without children of his own, the gray-haired, large-nosed Holme nevertheless had a particular knack for working with kids and other amateurs, which aided his career as he bounced around the state. He became particularly famous for adapting and directing *Ramona*, which was performed for more than ninety years by a cast of three hundred in Hemet, California. After Horace connected him with Steve Mather, in 1924 Garnet was named "Pageant master of the National Park Service."[23]

Garnet was thrilled. He had no budget or official salary, but Mather paid him privately. Garnet also had a uniform, access to appreciative audiences, and great subject matter for patriotic, morally uplifting theater. Although he sometimes staged works by others—just three days after his appointment became official, he put on *Rip Van Winkle* at Sequoia National Park—he took particular pride in writing pageants that portrayed park histories. Holme believed in the mission of the Park Service, and he was increasingly interested in using folklore to shape mythic backstories of parks and other places. (Sadly, his scripts often garbled native folklore with aggressively Christian themes of the dominant culture; the fault may lie with Garnet's background as the son of a Christian clergyman.) His first original production was for Yosemite. And after meeting with Horace in the winter of 1926, he sketched an outline of what a similar historic pageant might look like in Yellowstone.

It was met, truth be told, with some skepticism. When Jack Haynes, the director of Yellowstone's small museum, received the script from his counterpart in Yosemite, he responded, "Regarding your letter of February 9 [1926] and the enclosures; who is Garnet Holme? Also by whom is the pageant planned to be given? Your communications are the first advice upon this subject which we recall having received." Haynes also seemed offended by the liberties Garnet was taking with facts, for example adding the trapper Jim Bridger to the tourist party that encountered the Nez Perce in 1877. You can almost hear Garnet's defensiveness in his cover letter: "This is a composite picture, but in order to hit the high points in the short time, the dramatist must have liberty to vary somewhat in place and time. A program can give the correct details and dates."[24]

Even Horace Albright objected to one historical inaccuracy, putting that Nez Perce encounter *before* the dramatic wilderness journey of Truman Everts, a member of the Langford-Hedges party who got separated from his companions for thirty-seven days. In fact the Nez Perce adventure happened six years later, and reversing the episodes would strip both of them of their meaning. Albright also noted, "I do not know where we would go to get real Indians. . . . Also, I do not know just how you could get wild animals for one of your scenes." Garnet was further proposing to bring as many as twelve professional actors who would need lodging at Old Faithful for a week; Horace tried to get the railroad and hotel interested in a donation, but Garnet's plan was logistically ambitious. And yet the biggest problem that strikes the modern reader comes in the second half of the proposed script, labeled Allegory as opposed to History. Garnet explained, "The second part (Allegorical): Uncle

Sam does not know what to do with the newly acquired territory. To him comes GREED, POLITICAL INFLUENCE, [capitalized to indicate that each would be personified by an actor] and Trappers, all pointing out the way to make the parks *pay*. He determines to commercialize the possibilities, when the figure of THE COMMON GOOD appears and begs him to pause."[25]

As a moralizer, Garnet had learned well his history and politics. He instructed other actors to portray wealth, selfishness, monopoly, "GOLD, SILVER, and other MINERALS, WATERPOWER, SKINS OF DEAD ANIMALS, LUMBER, and similar commercial propositions." Even if actors in the historical part of the pageant conquered hostile savages and endured the terrors of nature, to establish a sanctuary would require constant vigilance. Garnet dramatized how new threats kept popping up to imperil the meaning of a national park. His script instructed the personified threats to "do a curious dance, ending up with the symbolical murder of a little child called IDEALISM." Then, in the allegory's conclusion, geyser-dancers would tend to the child and bring it back to life.

At the time, when allegorical dances were common features of pageants, it presumably would have played much better than it reads now. (Although Garnet's biographer, Phil Brigandi, notes that he rarely employed allegories, and wonders if this one was driven by Albright.)[26] Nevertheless, Horace expressed only guarded support. He expected the pageant to at least pay its own expenses, and with a 25-cent admission he couldn't figure out how to make the budget work. "We are all very enthusiastic and want to go ahead but are afraid that financially the play will be disastrous," he wrote Garnet in July of 1926.[27] He suggested that instead, as a sort of pilot project, local talent put on a pageant with similar themes. Since it was already midsummer and Garnet couldn't drop his other gigs to travel on his own dime to Yellowstone, he was happy to agree. The pilot pageant, which apparently used little of Garnet's script and instead primarily dramatized the Langford-Hedges expedition, was deemed a success. Horace indicated that revenues might indeed pay for Garnet to put it on professionally in the future.

The following year Garnet pressured Horace to follow up, but got no response. Of course Horace, who was running a booming national park, had hundreds of responsibilities, and this one may have simply fallen through the cracks. But given Horace's legendary administrative skill, it seems more likely that at least subconsciously, he realized that he'd achieved his goals. The notion that the National Park Idea had been birthed in Yellowstone no longer required dramatization by a pageant. The story—and a new meaning for Yellowstone National Park—was firmly lodged in the public imagination.

By popularizing what has become known as the Campfire Myth, Horace Albright rededicated Yellowstone to a wider audience. You didn't have to be excited about geology or wildlife or frontier conditions to love Yellowstone. You could come because you wanted to be a better citizen, take a civics lesson, become inspired about your country's ideals. Yellowstone had been discovered and set aside by vacationing middle-class folk just like you, who had a spirit of patriotism just like yours. It was a museum of democratic equality. This message came along just in time. In the 1920s Yellowstone was being overwhelmed by waves of new types of visitors seeking new types of experiences. Among its other challenges, the Park Service needed to figure out what to do with the automobile-based masses.

6
TEACHABLE

I once developed a crude chart of the annual number of visits to Yellowstone compared to total US population. I was hoping it would help me identify events in Yellowstone that caused the park's popularity to accelerate or crumble. I imagined such potential turning points as the military taking over for corrupt civilian administration in 1886, the huge late-1950s infrastructure-building program known as Mission 66, or maybe the reintroduction of wolves in 1993.

But when I crunched the numbers, the chart didn't show any of this. It showed that before 1910, visitation was by today's standards minuscule. For example, in the entire 1910 season, just 19,575 people entered the park, or fewer than attended a single Jack Johnson prizefight in Reno, Nevada, that summer. Visitation rose noticeably in the late 1910s, and dramatically in the '20s. It took a small dip at the beginning of the Depression and a bigger one during the rationing of World War II. Then it grew staggeringly in the late 1940s and '50s, and has somewhat leveled off since the mid-sixties.

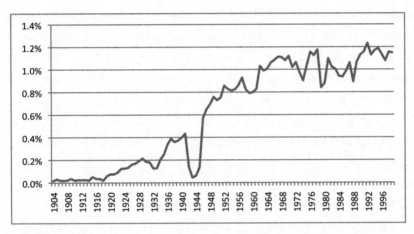

My Crude Chart of Yellowstone Visitation as a Percentage of U.S. Population[1]

My chart looked like one of automobile usage. Before 1915 few roads were good enough to take you very far, and by the 1960s most every family that wanted a car had one. I started wondering whether the biggest factor behind Yellowstone's visitation was the wider culture's embrace of automobiles.

We give credit to the National Park Service, and certainly after 1916 the new agency's skilled management and increased resources helped Yellowstone deal with the influx of automobile tourists *more effectively* than it otherwise would have. But the cars might have come anyway. The job of Yellowstone's leaders was to *react* to that cultural trend. They needed to reposition Yellowstone to continue to be relevant for the days when visitors arrived by car instead of rail, and for the middle classes instead of just the wealthy. How could Yellowstone remain an icon as American society changed?

At Angel Terrace, one of the springs at Mammoth where hot water bubbled across white terraced pools, Dr. Hermon Carey Bumpus started getting excited. He was watching rock being made! A thoroughly bald man with a bushy mustache and playful eyes, Bumpus would have been your favorite science teacher. He loved science, but even more than that he loved getting people excited about science. He loved getting people to wonder, and then grasp, what was special about the world around them. How lucky they all were to live in a world where the scientific revolution provided explanations! Though eminently trained in research, the effervescent Bumpus preferred the classroom—or even better, the outdoors—where he could help people discover the magic of science in the world around them.

Today he was learning, not teaching. It was September 2, 1925, and he was touring Yellowstone with chief ranger Sam Woodring and museum director Jack Haynes. Angel Terrace sat above the other hot springs, far from the hotel at Mammoth village. They had inspected other terraces and springs on their way up. The features at Mammoth change constantly, and Angel Terrace that summer might have been one of the more active or more accessible springs. Whatever the reason, it was the place where Hermon's attention was thoroughly captivated by a bubble rising through the pool. The water, hot and acidic, dissolved limestone on its way up to the earth's surface; now, as it cooled, some of those minerals could become gas and sediment. Hermon watched the formation of a globule of calcium carbonate. The globule increased steadily in weight until it sank to the bottom of the pool, a new layer of terrace. Meanwhile the bubble edged to the rim, where it eventually burst to leave the remaining precipitate to build up a wall. Hermon had seen such walls and shallow pools in the features on the way up, and now he was seeing how they formed. It was like a series of exhibits in a museum dedicated to explaining nature's processes of creating rocks.

Hermon knew such museums. He'd worked at one. In 1900, the American Museum of Natural History in New York plucked him from the faculty of Brown University to be its curator of invertebrate zoology. Born in Maine, Hermon Carey Bumpus had been named after, respectively, the biblical mountain, a missionary, and his ancestor Edouard Bon Passe, the first French Huguenot to arrive at the Plymouth colony in 1621. Growing up in Boston, Hermon became fascinated by snakes, frogs, rocks, and trees. As a student at Brown, he studied reptiles. For his PhD at Clark University, he studied lobsters. When he returned to Brown to teach, he became known as a catalyzer, someone who enjoyed starting a new organization or promoting a new idea, and who was happy to gradually step back as it came into its own. He had strong opinions, not always in the mainstream for the times. "To know the names of the flowers, plants, and birds one saw and to know something of the geology of the terrain where one lived seemed to him far more important than to know the French subjunctives or to be able to read Greek or Latin," his son later wrote.[2]

In 1900 the New York museum was looking for just such a self-starter, because it was in the throes of major change. Until that time museums were generally collections of artifacts, samples of the wonders that an explorer brought back from a faraway place. A museum was like a gallery to house the collection—easier for the explorer than keeping them in a room at his house. But was that really the way a museum should work? Shouldn't the museum's primary purpose be to educate the visitor? If so, shouldn't it be organized around the visitor experience?

Hermon helped lead this revolution. For too long, he wrote, museums had "assumed that the specimen was of more value than the visitor; that the institution existed for things rather than for human beings."[3] If you were going to teach people about science, you had to intrigue them, entertain them, show them the wonder of the world around them. You shouldn't just display some obscure animal's tissue preserved in a glass jar, labeled in Latin. You needed attractive exhibits and explanatory labels that would entice the visitor to learn more. Even taxidermied animals, rather than merely preserved, should be grouped realistically in an outdoor-like atmosphere.

After his first year in New York, Hermon became not just a curator but the museum's director. A colleague described him as "aggressive, astute, and very progressive, but always kind and sympathetic."[4] In 1906 a leading magazine said that his "work in the Museum of Natural History in New York is revolutionizing museum methods."[5] Writing about a flamingo exhibit, it said, "One man in a million may see the actual [flamingo] as [the explorer] saw it, but every man may go to Seventy-seventh Street, Central Park West, and see as accurate a representation of it as art and science combined may show . . . In spite of himself he [the visitor] has been forced to use his mind."[6]

In the age of Progressivism, leaders of societal institutions believed that democracy required them to help lift people out of poverty and ignorance, even if that meant tricking them into using their minds. To some Progressives, concentration of knowledge in the brains of museum staff was as bad as concentrations of wealth in the pockets of capitalists. The magazine profile continued, "Out with it, Sir Curator, we must have all your knowledge that we can digest."[7] Of course some curators resisted the change, as did some wealthy museum donors, who still expected a museum to memorialize their collections and egos. The revolution eventually succeeded, as demonstrated famously today by the dioramas of the American Museum of Natural History. But the process was not easy. In 1910 Hermon was forced out. He found a job in academic administration, later became president of Tufts University, and took early retirement in 1919. At the age of fifty-seven, his goal became broadening the visitor-focused museum revolution, bringing scientific education to everyday folk using formats they would find easy to consume. The crusade was led by an organization he'd helped found, the American Association of Museums.

The association, housed at the Smithsonian, modeled its campaign after Andrew Carnegie. From 1883 to his death in 1919, Carnegie gave money to more than twenty-five hundred small and midsized communities to build libraries. He wanted to provide opportunities for education and learning, like the opportunities he benefitted from in his childhood as a poor Scottish immigrant. So why not spread museums the way Carnegie had libraries? Local museums could highlight regional animal and plant life, inspiring young scientists the way youngsters like Hermon and Ernest Thompson Seton had been inspired. In pursuit of this goal, the American Association of Museums lined up philanthropists, including Rockefellers. And it also came across a new category of opportunities.

National park leaders such as Steve Mather and Horace Albright could see the trends: people were increasingly coming to national parks by automobile rather than train. They no longer had a stagecoach driver acting as guide to explain what they were looking at. So how could the Park Service ensure that visitors were fully equipped to appreciate the wonders they were seeing? In the early 1920s Yellowstone started a Museum and Information Service. It opened an official park museum at Mammoth, appointed its first official naturalist, and asked rangers to give their first public lectures. Parks were now in the business of *interpretation*, although of course budgets were constrained. As Horace Albright wrote, all Yellowstone had was "some interesting exhibits at the headquarters information office, which with some chagrin, we call a 'museum.'"[8] The museum's acting director, Jack Haynes, was unpaid; he worked another job as the park's official photographer and another job as the owner of photo and souvenir stores at the park's major attractions. But at least the museum was a start. Albright continually pursued opportunities to link the park to the science of natural history, through the museum or perhaps by starting some sort of school or institute. But visitation numbers were rising faster than budgets. Any expansion of the park's mission—into, say, education—would likely require external funds.

That's what brought Hermon Carey Bumpus to Yellowstone in 1925. He was the museum guy, with expertise and perhaps even access to Rockefeller money. Would he be able to reconceive Yellowstone as a national outdoor museum?

Hermon's first day in Yellowstone was a busy one. His train arrived in Gardiner at 11:15 A.M., where Jack Haynes and Horace Albright met him and took him to Mammoth. After lunch and a visit at the superintendent's office, Jack and ranger Sam Woodring took him all over the terraces and springs. Hermon was fascinated by the microorganisms that gave the springs their vibrant colors. He expressed an interest in seeing them under a microscope. Furthermore, he pointed out, such opportunities should be available to average park visitors. This focus on user-friendly science was the message Hermon would express repeatedly, in different forms, throughout his association with Yellowstone.[9]

At Angel Terrace and nearby Orange Spring Mound, Hermon marveled at the way standing trees were being swallowed by the developing travertine formations. Near Bath Lake, Jack placed a funnel over some venting gas, and used it to extinguish the flame of a match. At Liberty Cap, Hermon pondered the feature's unusual shape, pressed his hosts for the reasons, and was intrigued by the theory that its cause was chemical: compared to flat terraces, bulbous Liberty Cap contained higher proportions of magnesium carbonate.[10]

They also visited several sites that today are no longer part of most tourist itineraries. At the Stygian Caves, there were toxic gases capable of killing small birds. Hermon collected several carcasses and brought them to a naturalist for identification. He suggested stuffing and displaying these birds nearby. The number killed, he said, wasn't much greater than the toll of an average house cat. So the site should be developed as a tourist destination, "to show an interesting process of Nature with the story told both in popular and scientific terms."[11]

Mammoth at the time also had a zoo, which Hermon loved: a badger, three coyotes, two porcupines, a magpie, some bears, and a bison calf. He suggested larger quarters, and perhaps a visit to the acclaimed St. Louis Zoo for inspiration. But overall he liked the zoo very much, believing that tourists deserved close-up views of the animals. Likewise Hermon loved a nearby corral displaying a bison herd. In the nearly three decades since Ernest Thompson Seton had witnessed what he feared were the last of the bison, the creatures had made a remarkable recovery—but largely in captive settings. Park employees grew hay to feed to these bison, which were called the "show herd" because they were kept here at Mammoth where they'd be easy for tourists to see. Another "tame herd" was being fed in the more remote Lamar Valley, and a "wild herd" was surviving surprisingly well in the backcountry without human aid. A new museum near the show herd included photos and specimens related to Charles J. "Buffalo" Jones, the man then generally credited with saving the species during its 1902–1905 nadir.[12] Hermon thought that this museum could be developed into one of the leading attractions of the park.

The following day Hermon and Jack drove south from Mammoth toward Old Faithful, stopping at more than a dozen places along the way. One of them was Obsidian Cliff, a two-hundred-foot outcrop of unusual rock. Obsidian forms when silica-rich lava cools so quickly that it doesn't have time to make crystals. Instead it becomes a black glass that, compared to other rocks, is very easy to cut into sharp edges. Native Americans had long quarried this unusually pure and large deposit for arrowheads. (The quarries go back eleven thousand years, and the arrowheads show up as far away as Ohio and Texas.)[13] Hermon was again fascinated. He proposed building a shrine.

In his report on their trip, Jack Haynes regularly put *shrine* in quotes, as if this was a word that Hermon kept using that Jack didn't really like. One way to think of a *shrine* is as a location that embodies values that orient the culture.[14] But Hermon was probably thinking more practically: he had traveled in Europe, where he'd seen roadside religious shrines, often freestanding structures that sometimes resembled miniature chapels. Hermon found them architecturally interesting and, as an educator, potentially incredibly useful. At a spot like Obsidian Cliff, where the stagecoach might have stopped and the driver told the story of the rock and the arrowheads, maybe you could impart that information to the new tourists—now driving their own automobiles on their own schedules—with one of these little shrines, filled not with spiritual totems but instead with explanations of the surrounding natural science. Jack seemed receptive to the idea, if not to the religious phrases that Hermon insisted on using to describe it.

Just a few miles before Obsidian Cliff, Hermon and Jack had met up with Herbert Maier, a renowned architect serving as Hermon's executive assistant. During the remainder of their trip, Bumpus and Maier would identify dozens of potential sites for these "shrines," and also likely discussed at length what they might look like. The shrines did not receive budgetary priority, but finally by 1931 enough money and time were available to build the first one. The site chosen was Obsidian Cliff. By then park officials had won their battle against the word *shrine*, and the open-air mini-museums were known as kiosks or wayside exhibits. The kiosk that Herbert designed for Obsidian Cliff was the first wayside exhibit in any US national park.[15]

At Norris Geyser Basin, the party ate a picnic lunch and received a tour of the geysers from the resident ranger. Hermon was especially fascinated by the remote Cinder Pool, a twenty-foot-diameter spring that was half covered with pea-sized black sulfur beads. Hermon took some home to study, though neither he nor anyone since has quite been able to explain how or why the beads form. Hitting the road again in the afternoon, they stopped briefly at Madison Junction, which Jack identified as the place "where the National Park Idea was born," and Hermon suggested that another "shrine" be erected to tell the story.[16]

Later that afternoon they visited a cabin on Nez Perce Creek that Jack believed was built by General Oliver O. Howard's troops in 1877. That year a band of Nez Perce Indians, having been forced out of their ancestral home in northwest Oregon, spent the summer on an epic flight from the US Army. Their route took them through the heart of Yellowstone: up the Madison River and this creek, through the Hayden Valley, and out toward the northeast. Coming just one year after Custer's misfortune at the Little Bighorn, the conflict was embarrassing for the army, which pursued the tribe relentlessly. National attention increased with each skirmish, especially when the battles entered the five-year-old national park, and even more so after the Nez Perce took some tourists hostage. Today, it's hard to find an account of the flight that mentions the army constructing a cabin at this site. But in 1925, some sort of old cabin existed there, and Hermon was fascinated by it. He "made a minute study of its floors, doors and roof," Jack reported. "He suggested that at this point a historical story of intense interest could be told, and if possible the Ranger Station might be located near by, that wild flowers should be made to grow there, and relics of the Indian invasions of the park should be encased there with appropriate stories. 'This is the most valuable historical thing in the Park that I have thus far seen, and it certainly should be preserved,' are his words."[17]

Today, it's easy to chuckle at Hermon's views. Most entertainingly, isn't the very definition of a wildflower that it's wild and can't "be made to grow"? (Most troublingly, how could natives be "invading" a place they had used for centuries?) But to Hermon, and park leaders at the time, Yellowstone was full of wonders that should be manipulated or combined in even more impressive ways. Whether displaying bison at Mammoth or cultivating wildflowers at an old cabin, Hermon favored bringing the wonders of nature to the public—just like a city museum did. To Hermon, the advantage of Yellowstone was that it was a museum located adjacent to the source of the wonders being displayed. Today many of us puzzle over that intermediate step: when we go to Yellowstone we don't want a museum or zoo, we want to see the wonders in their original state. But in the 1920s, when museums and zoos were relatively new indicators of cultural sophistication, the nation wanted them in its parks too. Park museums, Steve Mather wrote, "are to be regarded as places to stimulate the interest of visitors in the things of the great outdoors by the presentation of exhibits telling in a clear, consecutive way, the story of the park from its geological beginning through all branches of history up to and including the coming of man and his works."[18]

Despite being a natural scientist, Hermon felt no conflict between human and natural history. Although he saw Yellowstone as a wildlife sanctuary and a spot dedicated to extraordinary geological features, he expected those elements to coexist with stories about people in the landscape. His Yellowstone was not a wilderness, not a preserve. It was a living resource to teach people—about nature and history both. Any enhancement or development that could better promote that learning was a good thing.

On the third day Bumpus, Maier, and Haynes toured a dozen or so features in the Upper Geyser Basin, an area increasingly referred to simply as Old Faithful after its most famous geyser. Then they met with rangers to talk about erecting a branch museum. Bumpus suggested constructing a model geyser so that rangers could make explanations to tourists before taking them on a tour. Much debate centered on the location and feel of this museum building: it needed to be set back in the trees so as not to visually compete with the geysers, yet not too far back, because it needed to be convenient for tourists and offer them a view of Old Faithful in eruption. It wasn't clear how much seating capacity would be required, or even whether Old Faithful inn guests deserved their own lectures and tours, separate from the lower-class campers. Later that day Bumpus, Maier, and Haynes drove down to the South Entrance, ate supper at what is now Flagg Ranch, and then returned to the Lake Hotel. They stopped continually to investigate lakes, waterfalls, and views of the Tetons. Bumpus alternated between suggestions for additional "shrines" and satisfying his own curiosity, as when he made a minute study of mosses, ferns, and lichens at the base of Moose Falls.

The fourth day they spent at Lake and Canyon, including an afternoon meeting with Horace Albright at the Canyon Hotel. Horace wanted to build a fish hatchery at Lake, a project that was complicated by the fact that tourists seemed as interested in the hatchery as they were in the lake itself. Should a hatchery be scientific administration that operated in the background, behind closed doors—or should this human manipulation of the natural environment be one of the park's attractions? Hermon argued for the latter: a hatchery, an aquarium, and a museum exhibiting birds from nearby would all enhance the Lake/Fishing Bridge area, giving visitors a reason to spend several additional hours there. Another enhancement he favored was salt licks along the road through the Hayden Valley. They should be placed, he said, so that tourists could see the animals from various points along their route. Today, the notion of luring wildlife with salt licks is seen as a dangerous and unnecessary interference in nature, unscientific and maybe even immoral. But Hermon and his colleagues were using the best science of the day. Indeed, also sitting in on the meeting at the Canyon Hotel was Dr. Henry Conard, a professor at Iowa's Grinnell College who spent summers as a Yellowstone naturalist-ranger. For men like Conard and Bumpus, science dictated saving the animals, providing them with an enriching life—and ensuring that the public could appreciate them. Given the animals' precarious standing—given what had happened to bison in the rest of the West—shortcuts such as salt licks and fish hatcheries were not merely acceptable but desirable.

They spent a final night at Camp Roosevelt, which was Hermon's favorite spot. The ersatz dude ranch honoring the conservationist president was where Horace Albright wanted to center the park's educational efforts; it was where Dr. Conard conducted lectures and collected botanical specimens. It served as a field laboratory that housed visiting students (away from the more crowded tourist sites at Old Faithful, Lake, Canyon, and Mammoth), who studied trout, beaver, buffalo, bear, moose, elk, deer, and antelope. "Dr. Bumpus was particularly pleased with the visit at Camp Roosevelt, and enjoyed every minute there," Jack wrote.[19] Dr. Conard took them to see a petrified tree and some beaver dams. They chatted around the fireplace. And they saw some bears.

In the morning Hermon hand-fed three bears a box of marsh-mallows. It was clearly a highlight of his visit, much like bear feedings were for thousands of tourists into the 1960s. To have a wild, dangerous animal eat out of your hand was an extraordinary thrill, evidence of a deep connection between humans and wildlife. Of course, even at that time feeding bears was officially illegal. It was dangerous, the bears impossible to control. Some people were injured (especially those who teased their bears, as if to emphasize the desired power dynamic). But few were arrested or even scolded. The superintendent himself loved feeding bears, and was often photographed doing so with celebrity visitors, such as President Warren Harding two years previously. And Dr. Hermon Carey Bumpus, beloved scientist and teacher, got a kick out of it too. Hand-feeding bears was an essential stepping stone toward later environmental philosophies. Only by seeing the animals close-up could people start to ponder their similarities and differences from ourselves. And only in pondering those differences could people come to admire the nobility of their life in the wild. In 1925 even Hermon, with his life spent studying the animal kingdom, needed to start with step one: the close personal connection made by feeding a bear some marshmallows.

After the final night at Roosevelt Lodge, Bumpus, Maier, and Haynes returned to Mammoth, where they met again with Albright. Hermon reported that he would enthusiastically recommend to the American Association of Museums that they fund museums in Yellowstone. Although Haynes and Albright had previously favored one huge museum at Mammoth, Bumpus argued for spreading museum exhibits throughout the park. In addition to the "shrines," he proposed midsized buildings at Old Faithful and

Lake, and smaller ones at places of Indian history. He coined the term "trailside museums" for these buildings.[20] They'd be intimate treatments of nearby subjects: the science of thermal activity at Old Faithful; additional geology at Norris; area bird and fish life at Lake; Indian history at Nez Perce Creek or at some tipi rings near Mammoth; fur trade history at Mammoth; bison at Mammoth or in the Lamar Valley. The exact placement and design of the structures would be the job of architect Herbert Maier.

It all took several years to come to fruition. Bumpus and Maier also toured other national parks, and Yosemite—which had the added advantages of proximity to San Francisco and being director Mather's favorite—became the first recipient of the association's philanthropic arrangements. The Yosemite Museum, designed by Herbert Maier, opened in 1926, and after it was favorably received, the Laura Spelman Rockefeller Foundation in 1928 funded the construction of Yellowstone's trailside museums: Old Faithful (the first to be built but replaced with new visitor centers in 1971 and 2010), Norris, Madison Junction, and Fishing Bridge.

In designing these museums, Herbert used a highly rustic style with plenty of battered rubble masonry, peeled logs stained a warm brown, and large decks built around existing trees. It's easy to draw parallels to the Old Faithful Inn—and in twenty-five years, rusticity had shaped a great deal of architecture nationwide. Indeed Herbert had started exploring this style at Yosemite, but in Yellowstone the design really came into its own. He consciously avoided rigid, straight lines so that the buildings would appear to have been constructed by pioneer craftsmen. The rocks were left so roughly natural, and the buildings so horizontally low, that they seemed to fade into the surrounding landscape, hinting at the smallness of man in relation to nature. Huge logs made the buildings feel strong, but delicate touches included, for example, elk skulls and antlers on simple wrought-iron chandeliers at Fishing Bridge.

FIGURE 1 (LEFT): Yellowstone National Park is located in the northwest corner of Wyoming, with portions overlapping into Montana and Idaho. Because of the rugged mountainous surroundings, early white explorers generally entered from the north, from Montana. *Map from Alethea Steingisser via Wikimedia Commons.* FIGURE 2 (BELOW): The figure-eight road in Yellowstone accesses the park's most famous attractions, counterclockwise from top left: Mammoth Hot Springs, Norris Geyser Basin, Madison Junction, Old Faithful/Upper Geyser Basin, Grant Village, Lake/Fishing Bridge, Canyon, and Tower/Roosevelt. Motorists can use five entrances, again counterclockwise: North (Gardiner, Montana), West (West Yellowstone, Montana), South (Grand Teton National Park and Jackson, Wyoming), East (Cody, Wyoming), and Northeast (Cooke City and Silver Gate, Montana). *Courtesy of the National Park Service.*

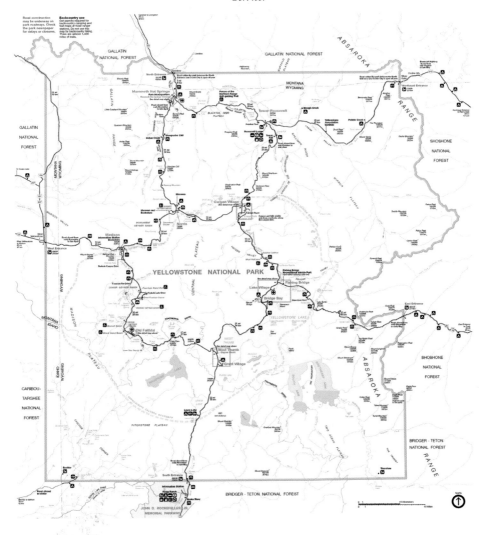

FIGURE 3 (ABOVE): Especially in the offseason, driving in Yellowstone offers opportunities to get ridiculously close to wild animals such as bison, as demonstrated by this photo taken from the driver's seat of the author's car in January 2016. *Photo by the author.* FIGURE 4 (BELOW): Five miles before crossing today's park boundary, the 1871 expedition led by Ferdinand Hayden encountered an unusual geological formation featuring a vertical red band of rock. Previous parties had called it the Devil's Slide, but Hayden and painter Thomas Moran would help America move beyond hellish metaphors for Western landscapes. *Tony Hisgett photo via Wikimedia Commons.*

FIGURE 5: Ferdinand Hayden, as photographed here by William Henry Jackson during Hayden's 1871 Yellowstone expedition, used his knowledge of geology to make these wonders seem special rather than frightening. *Courtesy of the National Park Service, Yellowstone history #02943.*

FIGURE 6: Painter Thomas Moran, pictured here in 1883, joined the 1871 Hayden expedition to Yellowstone in search of colors and views that would yield a masterwork. As an artist, he was doing more than rendering a natural scene—he was *interpreting* Yellowstone as culture. *Courtesy of the National Park Service, Yellowstone National Park, YELL 14297.*

FIGURE 7: Moran produced a series of chromolithographs based on the 1871 expedition, including this 1875 image of the Grand Canyon of the Yellowstone. *Buffalo Bill Center of the West, Cody, Wyoming, USA. Gift of Clara S. Peck. 18.71.8.*

FIGURE 8: In Moran's chromolithograph of Tower Fall, people (near the rock in the foreground) seem insignificant in the face of powerful nature—the sublime. *Courtesy of the National Park Service, Yellowstone National Park, YELL 21.*

FIGURE 9: Thomas Moran's 1872 masterpiece "The Grand Cañon of the Yellowstone" portrayed Yellowstone's—and thus America's—landscapes as not hellish but sublime, not terrifying but special. *U.S. Department of the Interior Museum, Washington, DC, INTR 03001.*

YELLOWSTONE NATIONAL PARK.

FIGURE 10 (ABOVE): This 1904 picture map from the Northern Pacific Railroad looks at Yellowstone from the north. In that era, many tourists arrived at Mammoth Hot Springs, in the lower right corner, and proceeded somewhat counterclockwise: Old Faithful in the upper right, Lake in the upper left, and Canyon in the middle left. Ernest and Grace Thompson Seton avoided the crowds by staying at Pleasant Valley in the rugged riverside country to the lower left. *Henry Wellge drawing via Wikimedia Commons.* FIGURE 11 (OPPOSITE TOP): Author–naturalist–illustrator Ernest Thompson Seton visited Yellowstone in 1897, when the nation was particularly concerned about vanishing bison and other creatures. In his vision of Yellowstone, it was a preserve for "half tame" wildlife. *Library of Congress LC-DIG-ggbain-02076.* FIGURE 12 (OPPOSITE BOTTOM): Grace Gallatin Seton, Ernest's heiress wife, was a writer herself. Her accounts of their trips in greater Yellowstone humanize her husband's single-minded passion for viewing animals. *Library of Congress LC-DIG-ggbain-06053.*

MRS. ERNEST THOMPSON SETON.

FIGURE 13: The Setons stayed at the Pleasant Valley Hotel, not far from today's Roosevelt Lodge. The hotel's proprietor, "Uncle John" Yancey, shown here probably about 1885 with a dog between his legs, provided few tourist comforts. *Courtesy of the National Park Service, Yellowstone National Park, YELL 32242.*

FIGURE 14: Artist/hunter A.A. (Abraham Archibald) Anderson, shown here on horseback later in life, established the Palette Ranch southeast of Yellowstone in the 1880s. His travels with the Setons, and his stories of a bear named Wahb, demonstrated Yellowstone's change from a geology-based park to one celebrating wildlife. *Buffalo Bill Center of the West, Cody, Wyoming, USA. MS 089 Jack Richard Photograph Collection. PN.89.106.21000.01.*

FIGURE 15 (OPPOSITE): As light filters through the expansive interior of the Old Faithful Inn, highlighting delicate, almost lacy features, it almost feels like being in a leafy forest. *Jim Peaco National Park Service photograph 17928d.* FIGURE 16 (ABOVE): Architect Robert Reamer, shown here at left with his foreman in front of the Canyon Hotel in 1910, is most famous for designing the Old Faithful Inn, a remarkable building that blends effectively with its surroundings. *A.L. George photograph courtesy of the National Park Service, Yellowstone National Park, YELL 89281-43.*

FIGURE 17 (OPPOSITE TOP): Although Theodore Roosevelt's *policy* role in Yellowstone is overstated, he did enjoy the park, as shown here at left camping with outdoor writer John Burroughs and guide Billy Hofer (seated at right) in 1903. Roosevelt epitomized a sort of rugged outdoor life and frontier nostalgia that the public came to love in Yellowstone. *Library of Congress LC-DIG-ppmsca-18937 via Theodore Roosevelt Birthplace National Historic Site.* FIGURE 18 (OPPOSITE BOTTOM): On April 24, 1903, President Theodore Roosevelt, front left, watches the laying of a cornerstone for an arch at the park's northern entrance in Gardiner, Montana. Roosevelt's speech that day, citing Yellowstone as an institution of democracy, tied the park to his rugged image. *Courtesy of the National Park Service, Yellowstone National Park, YELL 37105.* FIGURE 19 (ABOVE): Howard Eaton, a neighbor of Roosevelt's in North Dakota, is generally credited with inventing the dude ranching industry. He took dudes on an annual tour of Yellowstone, on horseback even after automobiles were allowed inside the park. He's shown here on horseback at the Upper Geyser Basin, near Old Faithful. *Courtesy of the National Park Service, Yellowstone National Park, YELL 15674.*

FIGURE 20: Dude rancher Larry Larom, shown here at the gate of his Valley Ranch on the South Fork of the Shoshone River in 1957, sought to simulate the frontier for his well-heeled guests. At the height of dude ranching's popularity, in the 1910s and '20s, he, like Howard Eaton, took guests on a tour of Yellowstone, making the park a foundation of their view of the West. *Buffalo Bill Center of the West, Cody, Wyoming, USA. MS 089 Jack Richard Photograph Collection. PN.89.18.3057.1.*

Adjacent amphitheaters at Old Faithful and Fishing Bridge were likewise constructed of peeled logs, even using the logs as bleachers.

Herbert's innovation was to apply rustic informality *to a museum.* Just as Robert Reamer dared to extend this uniquely American frontier style to the unlikely purpose of resort lodging, Herbert extended it to education. Because he believed that any building in a national park was a "necessary evil," he designed his buildings to feel like they had grown organically at the site.[21]

Furthermore, Herbert's client in these efforts was not an entrepreneur like Harry Child but the federal government itself. (The Rockefellers requested anonymity, so the funds appeared to come from, and were administered by, the Department of the Interior.) Thus rustic, informal architecture gained institutional approval, and soon was being used throughout the Park Service. In 1933 Herbert became a Park Service administrator, no longer designing buildings but influencing policy. His career change coincided with New Deal programs that provided money and labor for other government buildings designed by his protégés. In both national and state parks, these buildings served a variety of purposes, including administration buildings, maintenance facilities, and bathhouses.[22] Thus did "parkitecture" come out of Yellowstone to conquer the nation.

As he designed the museums, Herbert consulted continuously with Hermon Carey Bumpus, but in large part Bumpus was content to step back. He had set the process in motion, and for that became known in the museum trade as the "father of museums in national parks."[23] His interest, however, was broader than structures—it was in getting people excited about science. His trip with Jack Haynes generated dozens of specific recommendations for improving the communication of scientific principles. For example, he wrote,

"Lay emphasis in the written and verbal announcements of Nature Ranger Guide trips that it is FREE."[24] He recommended short nature trails, with plenty of places to rest, and signs or brochures to explain geology. For the yellow buses that had replaced stagecoaches as the way to lead tours through the park, he recommended "lecterns" be mounted on seat-backs so that you could read about the wonders you were seeing outside the window. He applauded the development of rangers' evening "campfire talks"—tourists gathered around a campfire not just to sing songs or be entertained but to increase their knowledge of the science behind the wonders they experienced during the day. He commended *Trailside Notes*, a naturalist-penned guidebook for automotive travelers, and made detailed suggestions for its authors. He arranged for Dr. Carl Russell, a naturalist from Yosemite, to oversee various types of educational work in Yellowstone. By 1931 he became chairman of an advisory board on educational programs throughout the Park Service, then of a broader Park Service advisory board.

Although often described as a "museum specialist," Hermon in Yellowstone transcended that role. As his son later wrote, "He believed that the surroundings of the museums—not the contents— were the exhibits, and that the museums should serve as sources of information about the works of nature that were left at their sites undisturbed."[25] And in so doing Hermon helped transform and democratize the Park Service's mission. Through his work, explanations of the science behind the wonders was available to all, not merely to those who could afford a tour guide. (And where guides and stagecoach drivers often told the most *entertaining* stories, Hermon's shrines and museum exhibits increased scientific accuracy.) The vacation-as-education, once reserved for the upper classes in Europe, was now available to middle classes in the parks. "Knowledge creates interest," Steve Mather wrote, "and interest adds to enjoyment."[26]

With this work, Hermon Carey Bumpus helped transform public education. Learning didn't have to be based in a building or a book. You could use science to augment people's fascination with natural wonders. The experience-based approach took advantage of the teachable moment. And thanks to Bumpus, the Park Service offered this education to everyone—of any age or class—in the belief that learning made you a better citizen. In a pilgrimage to Yellowstone, your experience with its natural wonders not only helped you better appreciate America's greatness but also expanded your intellectual capacity for such appreciation.

Bumpus's innovations transformed Yellowstone at an essential time: during the rise of the automobile. Auto-based tourism increased Yellowstone visitation exponentially, and the do-it-yourself nature of the "shrines" and roadside museums provided the park with an infrastructure that could accommodate those crowds. Furthermore, the automobile expanded Yellowstone's audience from the wealthy to the middle class, in an era when the middle class was interested in self-improvement. By stimulating the mind as well as the senses, Bumpus expanded commonly held ideas of a park's purpose. A city park might be a place of recreation: a lake, a forest, a trail. By contrast, a *national* park wasn't just about more impressive lakes and forests, it was about a broader mission, incorporating nature and knowledge into a deeper understanding of the nation and world.

Indeed, what may be most remarkable about Bumpus's quest was the scope of that mission, the number and diversity of teachable moments that Yellowstone could provide. You saw Old Faithful erupt, and you wanted to learn about the geology that created this wonder. You saw paintpots and fumaroles and colored terraces and mud volcanoes, and were primed to gain understanding of geology's magnificent complexity. Within a few miles you saw a grand canyon, an obsidian cliff, a petrified tree, and some impressive waterfalls—Yellowstone was one of the richest geological laboratories in the world. Laid on top of all that were the plants and animals, from bison and bears down to the mosses and lichens at Moose Falls. And laid on top of that was all the human history, Indians and explorers and the National Park Idea. These were all magical place-based experiences that could also become educational experiences. And so for millions of everyday Americans, the desire to visit Yellowstone, to *see* these wonders, was given the opportunity to mature into a desire to *understand* them.

Yellowstone was thus evolving far beyond its original conception as a location of some geological curiosities. It was taking on new meanings, layering on new and different values, becoming a richer, more complicated expression of evolving American ideals. Yellowstone had geology plus wildlife, it embodied informality and the frontier spirit, it tapped into desires for patriotism and intellectual self-improvement. This was all very practical, reflecting the age-old American character. Yet another bedrock American value was not yet well reflected in public views of the national park. Americans had always been profoundly religious, capable of seeing God's hand everywhere, and longing for overt spiritual meaning in everything they did. People brought their religion to these wonderful landscapes, as Nathaniel Langford did when his party named every third or fourth feature after the Devil. But was it possible for people to *find* their spiritual values in Yellowstone?

7
SPIRITUAL

To those with only a passing familiarity, it may seem a little annoying that twin pillars of the national park system both have long names beginning with *Y.* Yosemite, Yellowstone . . . which one's in California? Which has more bears? Don't they basically serve the same function and appeal to the same crowds? (I waited until halfway through the book to bring this up, just in case there are Yosemite fans out there still puzzling that I haven't yet discussed Half Dome or the Tioga Road. *It's too late now, people! You might as well finish this book about the other Y-park!*)

The confusion is understandable. Two mountain parks, renowned for scenery, founded at about the same time, with natural wonders that evoke the same types of emotions. What's more, there's the legacy of one of the greatest artists of the 20th century.

The photographer Ansel Adams was a Yosemite man through and through. He was profoundly influenced by childhood visits; he married a woman who'd grown up there and took over her parents' business there; he took some of his greatest photographs there—some of his earliest photographs, ones that led him to his inimitable style. Yet Ansel eventually became associated with *all* national parks. One of his books covered Yellowstone and the Tetons. People remember him as the national park guy with a particular love for the one that begins with the letter *Y* . . . and doubt creeps in . . . Wasn't it Yosemite?

So when I say that this chapter focuses on Ansel's experiences in Yellowstone, you may be surprised or even irritated. Shouldn't we keep Ansel in Yosemite rather than contribute to the confusion?

Sorry. Although it's true that Ansel didn't spend much time in Yellowstone, he did visit. And although his relationship with Yellowstone was complicated—nothing like his deep love for and thorough knowledge of Yosemite—those complications are instructive. Ansel had a profound impact on Americans' relationships to national parks in general. He changed the way the public perceived the system, including Yellowstone as that system's cornerstone. The story of Ansel in Yellowstone shows us how midcentury American history required the park to become something new.

At a train depot in Livingston, Montana, Ansel Adams slept fitfully on a wooden bench, 280 pounds of camera equipment piled next to him. It was June 11, 1942, and his train had arrived at 2:15 A.M. After dawn he would get on a bus to Gardiner, where Yellowstone officials would loan him a car to drive around the park and take photographs. He would have preferred to drive his own car from his home in California: he could carry more equipment and stop anywhere he wanted. Indeed he would soon devise a camera mount atop his station wagon to support his wooden tripod, unwieldy 8x10 view camera, glass plate, and any needed filters—because he liked to stand on the car's roof to get a better shot. But amid the gas rationing of World War II, on this trip he was forced to travel from park to park using public transportation.

At age forty, Ansel was tall and bearded, with a nervous energy and a talkative, high-spirited personality that made him seem even larger. For more than a decade he'd been noted for the technical brilliance of his photography—its composition, clarity, texture, and print quality. He'd received kudos from experts such as Alfred Stieglitz (who'd given him a one-man show), published several books, and taken the occasional teaching position. Among his technical accomplishments was development of what he called the Zone System, which codified exposure and development times to provide better control over light and shadow in the final image. With some of his most famous images already committed to their plates, he had begun to establish what would become one of the most remarkable careers in American photography. Early on, he flirted with avant-garde techniques such as soft-focus and etching, but then he settled on a modernist style with a sharp contrast between light and shadow, given incredible precision by his large-format film. Likewise, early on he flirted with various subjects and themes, including portraits, factories, and still lifes, before settling on his true passion: the outdoors.

Ansel's Yosemite photographs endeared him to federal officials. Just before the United States entered the war, the Department of the Interior gave him a contract to capture images of its lands—national parks, Indian reservations, and reclamation projects—to be used as photomurals in a new headquarters building. He earned $22.22 per day, the highest rate the government could pay an outside consultant, for every day that he billed. And on every day he didn't bill, when he used his own film, he retained ownership of the images he shot. It was a desirable contract for an artist struggling to make a living, and he hoped for annual renewals. But then the war slashed nonessential budgets. Higher-ups told him that the project was ending and that he should proceed to shoot Yellowstone, Glacier, Mount Rainier, and Crater Lake—all in the last twenty days of June.

From the train to Livingston, he wrote to his friend Nancy Newhall that she should share the story of his logistical difficulties with William Henry Jackson.[1] The previous year, Ansel and Nancy's husband, Beaumont, had looked up the 98-year-old frontier photographer in New York, where they'd found him lively and opinionated. Ansel admired old Will and oversaw the production of some new prints for an upcoming retrospective of Will's work. Of course Will's own 1871 Yellowstone trip had been full of logistical difficulties, with his huge plate camera and portable darkroom, but at least he had mules and assistants to pack them. Traveling alone, Ansel was ferrying all of his equipment across train stations and bus stops by foot.

Part of Ansel's admiration for Will lay in his appreciation of the legacy of Will's work. He knew how those photographs helped designate Yellowstone as a national park, just as Carleton Watkins's photos did for Ansel's beloved Yosemite. Indeed, a few years previously, Ansel himself had produced a limited-edition book, *Sierra Nevada: The John Muir Trail*, which helped secure similar protection for Kings Canyon. But where Will's interests beyond his art ran to business, Ansel's character was inherently more political. His Sierra Nevada book was not written as a job for hire; it was commissioned by the Sierra Club, where Ansel was a board member, for purposes of persuasion. Ansel did not want the preservation of scenic landscapes to be a side benefit of his art—that preservation was the very reason to create his art.

Indeed, his insistence that photography be defined as art likewise signaled Ansel's ambition. Jackson was merely a documentarian on the Hayden expedition, because at that point in photography's evolution, it was expected only to show what things looked like. Jackson used his technical skill at photography to make a living, and only in retirement fully expressed his artistic self by returning to his childhood love of painting. But Ansel wanted to use his technical skill to express all of his artistic creativity through the newer medium. In a letter to his friend and mentor Stieglitz that Ansel penned after Jackson's death later that summer, he wrote, "[Jackson] was a grand old man of a grand old period and leaves a grand old nostalgia. . . . I think he represented an astounding physical and 'expansional' period; he had a fine mechanical technique; he was spunky to the last. I don't think a single revelation of the spirit ever loomed on his horizon."[2]

Revelation of the spirit: that's what Ansel wanted from landscape photography. When Ansel made his first famous work, *Monolith, the Face of Half Dome*, in 1927, he had just one glass plate left for the shoot, and he used a process he later often talked about: visualizing what he wanted in the image before recording it. Then, looking at the final product, he saw that the process had worked. He later wrote, "I had been able to realize a desired image: not the way the subject appeared in reality but how it *felt* to me and how it must appear in the finished print."[3] Like the painter Tom Moran, he had come to Yellowstone to depict the emotions this place evoked, to capture those emotions as the art of the era.

Indeed, not only photography had changed; so had painting. Since the glory days of Tom Moran, impressionism, cubism, and modernism swept through the culture, and now a standard landscape painting seemed a bit dull. It had no cutting edge of technique, like a landscape rendered by Monet, of perspective, like a scene rendered by Picasso, or of political statement, like a Stieglitz photograph celebrating industrial strength. Moreover, modernism, arising with industrial society, celebrated human power to alter the environment. Thus Yellowstone, a place that amazed people by being relatively unaltered, had not attracted major artists for decades.

Critics of modernism, however, were unhappy with industrial society. Industrial jobs were boring and repetitive; industry's tenements were lifeless and soul-crushing. Where could the average person find spiritual fulfillment? In religion, perhaps, for believers. But many artists and philosophers of the day saw religion, like traditional forms of art and philosophy, as overmatched by the rapid changes of industrial society.

Ansel saw a clear path around this stalemate: spiritual fulfillment came from interaction with the natural world. He'd felt it as a child. He was an oddly artsy San Francisco boy, home-schooled and consumed by music, when at age fourteen he spent four weeks in Yosemite. Armed with a tent and a Brownie camera, he quickly developed a deep psychic connection to his surroundings. He saw in nature a source of individual spiritual insight. He eventually came to believe that nature's spiritual power could redeem society. This was hardly a new idea; people have been finding redemption in nature for millennia. But Ansel was able to articulate it with particular beauty, with new modernist-tinged techniques, at a time when America really needed it.

Leaders of the conservation movement had often spoken of the spiritual benefits of special places—and often clashed with those who found other benefits from these places. For example, in the mid- and late-1800s, John Muir and Frederick Law Olmsted both promoted the notion that people could deepen their sense of connection to the world by merely being present in a rich natural environment. You didn't even need jaw-dropping scenery to connect with forests, meadows, or wildlife.[4] Though he didn't talk about it in these spiritual terms, National Park Service founder Steve Mather clearly felt this connection to nature on his long pack trips through the Sierras—and his desire to bring that fulfillment to others was what led to his government service. Indeed Mather's best lobbying efforts involved taking congressmen and other leaders on these pack trips themselves. In Mather's vision, the grand scenery of national parks such as Yosemite and Yellowstone also encompassed room for spiritual growth in solitude.

But by the 1930s it was increasingly hard for a park to offer both, because of the increase in tourists and the autonomy granted by their automobiles. People drove themselves, camped themselves, fed themselves, and entertained themselves—which sparked demand for roads and roadside culture. Even if stores, restaurants, hotels, gas stations, and souvenir shops could be corralled away from the natural features, the associated crowds turned anything associated with these features into a group activity. As people descended on Yellowstone in unprecedented numbers, convinced that this grand scenic place had to be experienced, they no longer encountered nature in that "primitive," frontier-ish way. A new political movement arose, epitomized by the 1934 founding of The Wilderness Society. It saw tourism development as inherently opposed to wilderness and scenic appreciation. It thus saw national parks as such a popular success that they were a failure.[5]

Here was where Ansel's genius was so valuable. He grasped that the new masses of tourists were seeking to renew individual spirituality through solitary intimacy with an ancient landscape. He saw this quest as soiled by "resortism" that promoted outdoor recreation and amusement. Ansel believed that national parks needed to be reestablished as places of spirituality rather than outdoor exercise. And he believed this goal could be best accomplished with art. Art could speak directly to people's spiritual yearnings. In 1951 he would write to a Park Service official that the literature and photography of the conservation movement was unbearably boring, and that it needed to return to the spirit of Middle Ages art, soaked in religious values that inspired the viewer to a higher vision.[6] This 1942 trip was headed toward that vision.

"I quickly became enamored of the geysers of Yellowstone," Ansel wrote in his autobiography many years later. "It is difficult to conceive of any substance in nature more impressively brilliant than the spurting plumes of white waters in sunlight against a deep blue sky. I was delighted photographically with the geysers at dawn, as well as at sunset."[7] Indeed a large portion of the Yellowstone photos he submitted to the government were geysers, six of them labeled identically as Old Faithful "taken at dusk or dawn from various angles during eruption."[8] (Ansel was notoriously bad at recording the times and dates of his photographs, as if the sheer joy of artistic creation crowded out of his brain any capability of note-taking.) The images all center on billowing columns of white steam in sharp focus. The surrounding landscape is plain and featureless: an oversized pitcher's mound from which the steam explodes and a forested ridge in the distant background. Center stage belongs to this extraordinary natural wonder and the amazement felt by the viewer upon whom it bursts. Some images are shot into the sun, which is blocked by geyser-steam that rises to seemingly merge with the clouds. Cloudy skies almost always play a role in Ansel's famous images, because they present magnificently complicated textures. He must have been delighted at the possibilities of working with a form of clouds that emerge from the ground.

Ansel was not fortunate enough to capture one of the unpredictable eruptions of the beautiful Fountain Geyser, but he did make several striking images of its placid, steaming pool. As at Old Faithful, the rising steam and background clouds—here complemented by wind-driven ripples across the pool's surface—suggest a fleeting momentary beauty, while the heavy permanence of the surrounding rocks and trees suggests the possibility of infinite such moments.

Elsewhere, Ansel showed steam rising from vents on Roaring Mountain and along the Firehole River. He surveyed the terraces of Mammoth Hot Springs, depicted some conventional mountain scenes near the Northeast Entrance, and made close-ups of unusually textured rocks. But the other feature that particularly captured his interest was Yellowstone Lake. He took several shots across the watery expanse to snowcapped mountains pressed into distant insignificance by a vast sky. He clearly enjoyed the varying textures of lake, land, and clouds, occasionally contrasted with a foreground shoreline or geyser-cone. In his photographs, the sheer size of the lake gives a sense of the land's epic scale, with jumbles of mountains and rivers far beyond the reach of any automobile.

After just a few days in Yellowstone, Ansel ferried his equipment back to the train station. He had several more parks to visit before his July 1 deadline. And he made it: the trip proved a success. Although his patrons never executed the photomural project, Ansel did get paid. And several of his images entered the public domain, the pantheon of great art inspired by a great place.

None of the published photographs—twenty-seven in the national archives, plus at least nine to which he retained copyright, now at the Center for Creative Photography in Tucson—contain people. Ansel set up shots that put the viewer alone with a geyser, a steaming pool, or a huge mountain-rimmed lake. You feel, as Ansel did, redemption in solitary contemplation of the untouched beauty of the natural world. He could show, in clean, crisp, clear lines, what solitude with nature felt like. It was incredibly meaningful to anyone who yearned for a connection lost in their urbanizing, modernist, car-centered world.

The emotion Ansel sought was, in fact, something of a religious experience. Nature, in his view, had a healing power. Wilderness was a manifestation of God. But compared to the 19th-century fear of God's awesome power, by World War II many people's primary fears were of other humans. They could contrast Hitler's industrial might with nature as an embodiment of American virtue. It was tempting to see wilderness as pure divinity, contrasted with the fallen world of humanity. If the pain of being human resulted from our self-imposed exile from the rest of God's creation, then nature was a source of salvation from the sins of modern life.

In the letter Ansel wrote to Nancy Newhall about the train to Livingston, he said, "I get a strange mood when I am away from New York—a mood of living in a tremendous land—fresh, end-less, and friendly . . . All that intense, burning fencing with life and people doesn't seem to make sense seen from the Wyoming mesas. I often wonder about you two [Nancy and Beaumont]—you are both much bigger in spirit than the world you have chosen to live in."[9] The human spirit, Ansel said, was cramped by human society. That philosophy's appeal grew as the war's horrors later came to light: the Holocaust, the need to drop an atomic bomb, the devastating proof that World War I had not been a war to end all wars. Despite advances in technology, humans still suffered—often created suffering. Nature offered a safe haven.

That's what the national parks were to Ansel: sanctuaries. He extended Horace Albright's phrase beyond patriotism: "The *national park idea* is to me a very definite religious idea," he wrote to Park Service director Newton Drury in 1952. "To me, the only valid meaning is one not related to recreation . . . [in other words] the more obvious resort activities. . . . Every time I observe a tepid and flippant attitude towards the primeval park scene I have the same resentment that I would have were I to hear a Bing Crosby song in a great cathedral."[10] His metaphor ages poorly: to capture the vulgarity that the classically trained Ansel saw in the pop star Crosby, we might today need to substitute "Justin Bieber" or "Kid Rock." But the comparison is still fascinating: to Ansel, in a national park any attitude less than reverence was a vulgar affront to a primeval religious shrine.

In many ways the midcentury Park Service supported this view. It consistently rejected proposals to develop golf courses or commercial ski resorts within Yellowstone. It took an increasingly antagonistic attitude toward a swimming pool that had existed for many years at Old Faithful, finally closing the recreational facility in 1951. It has never allowed river rafting within park boundaries. No movie theaters were ever built; even today only two hotel rooms in the entire park have televisions.[11] The implication is that such lowbrow forms of entertainment are not worthy of the park's higher calling. (It's a fine line that draws controversy even today. Why is fishing an acceptable human use of Yellowstone rivers but not kayaking? Why horses but not mountain bikes? Recreationists plead their cases, and the best response is: Because we're protecting spiritual values and we have to draw the line somewhere.) But in other ways the Park Service didn't do enough for Ansel. Although he was complaining about Yosemite, not Yellowstone, when he wrote to Horace Albright in 1957 of "dancing, vaudeville, and popular music, urban cocktail lounges and food services, hideous curios, slick roads, and a general holiday spirit," Yellowstone certainly had some of those features as well.[12] Ansel wanted to bar all such activities. "The sanctity of a church, a gallery of art, or a great temple of Nature depends on appropriate use."[13]

Ansel was aware that such sentiments could make him sound like an elitist killjoy. He believed that the spiritual validity of wild, beautiful places arose in part from our simplicity of experience in them. That usually meant sacrificing comforts and undergoing difficulties—and saying so could seem a little smug. To avoid arguments about elitism, he tried to focus on the *purpose* of the parks and *activities* in the parks rather than the *people* who partook in those activities. All people were welcome in national parks, so long as they used those parks for the right purposes. As he wrote to Albright, "I have always considered that the prime objectives of the national parks were to provide inspiration, self-discovery of spirit in the wild places, and appropriate recreation. . . . This concept places the national parks at the highest level of an advanced civilization."[14] Of course, defining "appropriate" recreation was a difficult line to trod, one that tripped up many wilderness advocates. Indeed Ansel himself took many of his famous photographs while driving around in a station wagon—hardly the sort of ruggedly pure wilderness activity he seemed to insist on for others. During his long service on the board of the Sierra Club, he often struggled to effectively articulate such distinctions in words.

And again, here Ansel's advantage was that his primary contribution was images. His images showed those unpeopled scenes, suggested that glorious solitude, made you feel that spiritual fulfillment. He was still vulnerable to similar types of criticisms—that these masses of rock and vapor were cold and distant. With all of the technical perfection and elegant formality, you might wonder if people could ever play a role in his natural world. As one critic famously exclaimed of one of Ansel's landscape photographs at a 1938 museum show, "Doesn't anybody *go* there?"[15] Ansel turned out to be incredibly fortunate to make his first visit to Yellowstone during wartime gas rationing—he could get his shots of solitude because for the moment people indeed *weren't* going there.

Ansel's photographs offered society the advantage that now people didn't *have to* go there. He distilled the spiritual objectives of national parks into prints you could frame and hang on your cubicle wall. He thus deliciously escaped one of the drawbacks of Yellowstone's landscapes: the difficulty of achieving a sustained combination of beauty and graceful solitude. Although Yellowstone unfolds vast quantities of empty backcountry, much of it is monotonous lodgepole-pine forest. (Despite some breathtaking nuggets, for a steady stream of awe-inspiring solitude, many backcountry travelers prefer other parks such as Glacier.) But Ansel could provide that emotion in a single Yellowstone photograph. He didn't merely urge people to go to the wilderness to get inspired—he brought the inspiration to them.

One other factor contributed to the appeal of Ansel's art: the fact that you could try to mimic it yourself. Although artistically oriented people always enjoyed going out into nature to sketch or paint—to revel in the process of capturing and expressing beauty with their own hands—the pastime was generally limited to those who believed they had talent in the visual arts. In the discipline of photography, however, you had a machine to augment your talents. You could capture the scene without knowing how to draw. The average tourist certainly lacked Ansel's eye—not to mention his darkroom techniques, elaborate equipment, and unstinting dedication—but she did have access to the same Brownie-esque type of camera that started him on his life's journey. And, as Kevin DeLuca has written, "The camera, not God, created sublime, Edenic wilderness."[16] Framing your camera shot, you could edit out people and create pristine conditions. Cheap, simple cameras of that era usually captured only black and white, but Ansel's work served as an example of how much you could do without color. (Although he did use color when an assignment called for it, he preferred black and white for artistic reasons: the ability to focus on texture, shadow, and contrast. That choice had the happy side effect of allowing more of his fans to imagine themselves in his shoes.)

Indeed, even as the wilderness movement was criticized for elitism, Ansel's art depicting that wilderness was seen as populist.[17] He made art for the millions designed to encourage public participation in national identity. With a heroic, inspirational mood, his works were black-and-white Bierstadts, almost bombastic in their insistence on how stunning were the wonders they portrayed. Yet people found the bombast appropriate, the wonders—real! right there in a photograph!—truly stunning. They saw Yellowstone, and life, through his spiritual eyes.

He didn't like to talk about it publicly, because he wouldn't disparage any national park in public. But in truth, Ansel didn't much care for Yellowstone. It might have been an issue of scale: many of Yellowstone's features, such as geysers, wildlife, the Mammoth terraces, and the Canyon waterfalls, typically appear in the medium distance. Ansel excelled at longer distances. As he wrote in his autobiography, "No matter how sophisticated you may be, a large granite mountain cannot be denied—it speaks in silence to the very core of your being."[18] Yellowstone's many diverse wonders included few towering granite peaks.

By contrast, Ansel loved the Tetons, which presented a visitor with large, arresting mountains in the far distance. He took dozens of beautiful shots of the three craggy peaks with the Snake River twisting in the foreground. He could move up and down the Jackson Hole valley for different perspectives on his subject, and catch the sun hitting the Tetons from different angles. Where Yellowstone is a broad volcanic plateau, the Tetons, just twenty-five miles south, lie on a fault line. A sudden shift in the earth's plates caused the Tetons to rise sharply above the Snake River, with no foothills. Ansel understood this science but preferred to see the mountains in more spiritual terms. "The grand lilt of the Tetons is more than a mechanistic fold and faulting of the earth's crust," he wrote, "it becomes a primal gesture of the earth beneath a greater sky."[19] He loved the notion of *gestures*, as if the ground was speaking to the clouds or the horizon. His famous images, such as *Moonrise, Hernandez, New Mexico*, are full of them. But he couldn't find many such grand gestures in Yellowstone, which he described as a collection of curios: geysers, bubbling mud pools, oozing terraces, and herds of captive bison.[20]

He returned to Yellowstone in 1946 on his own, and in 1948 as a celebrity on a photography workshop tour. Participants on the latter trip had the opportunity to see the sights of the national park and also a nearby dude ranch. (The two activities did not fit together as well as they had during the dude ranching heyday twenty-five years earlier. Now, as Ansel wrote, "Them what likes scenery don't hanker after rodeos, and vice versa!"[21]) He needed to take engagements like this to generate income; not until the 1960s would his art alone provide enough to live on. And he might have been a bit grouchy on this trip, coming at the end of a long summer's travels to Alaska and the northwest parks. He wrote to Nancy Newhall, "Yellowstone is simply horrible. Millions of people, cars, bears, garbage."[22]

It's easy to see how "millions of people" would have gotten in the way of his attempts to create photographs of empty landscapes. It's also easy to see how he would complain about cars. Park officials often encourage visitors to get out of their cars so as to appreciate solitude and wilderness—but such moments are a small portion of your visitor experience. Before the car, they were the majority of your experience. When your spiritual wonder comes only in scraps, only in fleeting moments, it tends to be less powerful. And Ansel could remember a Yosemite of his childhood when all the solitude he could ever need was easily and abundantly available.

The final two elements of his complaint, bears and garbage, likely went together: he objected to Yellowstone's history of formalized bear-feeding shows, where garbage was set out for bears to scrounge—in front of bleachers for people to watch. These events, along with black bears begging on roadsides, must have felt to him like curios. But it's interesting to note that he didn't object on ethical grounds. Indeed, just as his photographs excluded people, they also excluded animals. Ansel's appreciation of nature generally came from earth gestures, from rocks and clouds—not from wildlife. He was not an Ernest Thompson Seton, spending an entire day watching beavers. He had nothing against wildlife, but the central focus of his spiritual quest was solitude with rocks and clouds. For Ansel, wilderness was all about the spirituality inside a person, not the habitat for wildlife.

Through the midcentury years, into the 1960s, Ansel's magnificent vision energized the conservation movement. Activists (including Ansel himself) wanted to preserve opportunities for solitude, and thus pushed for preservation of wilderness areas, especially through formal legal protection. Thus they tended to work not with the national parks but with the U.S. Forest Service, which had greater quantities of vast, roadless areas that could be protected. The Forest Service had a mandate for *multiple use* of its lands, and although setting aside a chunk as wilderness meant excluding from that chunk other uses such as logging, it was easy to argue that some small portion of Forest Service lands should be set aside in this way. The Park Service, on the other hand, had a mandate to manage its lands to provide for enjoyment—to conserve them unimpaired for the future, but always for enjoyment. It was harder, at that time, to argue that enjoyment should mean excluding roads and campgrounds and restaurants and hotels.

Indeed in the 1950s people flocked so heavily to the parks that a massive infrastructure upgrade was required. With Yellowstone as a centerpiece, the Park Service found a way to process large numbers of people by embracing modernist architecture and suburban development (what used to be museums would now be *visitor centers*, modeled on shopping centers). Although the Park Service argued that this development style helped preserve natural wonders and keep the backcountry pristine, Ansel and other activists were frustrated because it sought to accommodate the crowds rather than somehow limiting them. Among wilderness activists, national parks—especially the crowded ones such as Yellowstone—became examples of resortism that were the antithesis of wilderness.[23]

But for the general public the opposite was true. Yellowstone represented nature. In Yellowstone people found an intimacy with the natural world. Although it might have been only a scrap compared to what Ansel wanted them to find, it was still profound. The ability to access it easily—driving your car, sleeping in a real bed—made such experiences available to millions of people who would not otherwise have considered them. And they did *want* these experiences, in part because they had seen Ansel's artwork. Now millions of city and suburb dwellers could pursue a vacation in nature because of a spiritual glory that Ansel had highlighted, using an art form that they could try to imitate.

Ansel became an unofficial face of the national parks. As photography companies such as Kodak popularized his photos, they too benefitted from playing up his connection to the national parks, with the associated patriotic emotions. Furthermore, Ansel and his family continued to live in Yosemite, where his children grew up and eventually inherited the family photo studio. Indeed, being a

Y-park probably gained Yellowstone far more benefit from associations with Ansel than it deserved.

And yet that popularity would have quickly faded if Yellowstone had failed to provide the spiritual depth that people were looking for. In spite of crowds and cars, you *could* feel a close personal relationship with an overwhelming natural spirit in Yellowstone. Even today, walk a hundred yards from the Lake Hotel, and you are alone with the vast lake, the distant mountains, and your memories of photographs in which Ansel demonstrated the rich wonder of that solitude. Stop along the Firehole River, with steam rising from the far bank, and you see how Ansel didn't *compose* his photograph so much as he noticed the beauty with which nature had already composed it. Watch Old Faithful erupt, even with strangers standing all around you, and you become enraptured by the whooshing sounds and the billowing steam and the bizarre magnificence with which nature created these inexplicable marvels. Even when crowded, Yellowstone's landscapes are big and rich enough to provide you with the spiritual wonder that you had so yearned to find.

Still, for all of Ansel's genius at capturing the wonder of the experience, there were elements of the wonder he didn't address: the animals. Fascinated by bears and other creatures, people hungered for fuller understanding of these animals' lives. In the 1960s, evolving science and technology would start the world down this road—and lead to unforeseen controversies.

8
POLITICAL

One reason that I wanted to research and write this book was that as someone who's *interested* in Yellowstone, who consumes a lot of popular media about it, I felt like I wasn't getting a complete picture of its personality. For example, as I'm writing this chapter, the past month's headlines have included YELLOW-STONE BISON TO FACE SLAUGHTER; WAR ON YELLOWSTONE LAKE TROUT CONTINUES; and DELISTING THE GRIZZLY: A RECIPE FOR MORE BEAR DEATHS.

In short, typical media coverage suggests that Yellowstone is important primarily as a setting for arguments about environmental politics. The coverage suggests that this place has an inherently political vibe. It's like a coffee shop next to a state capitol building—a place you could go to get the real scoop on hotly debated issues before they make it into the newspaper. Is that Yellowstone's true character?

I suspected not—at least not entirely—because I also knew something about all these qualities that this book has described so far. But I did need to understand why Yellowstone was so political—why it generated more of those types of headlines than similar places like the Grand Canyon or Zion. Clearly the answer was tied to the presence of so many bison, grizzlies, wolves, and other extraordinary animals. But even less glamorous species—such as the fragile trout subspecies called the Yellowstone cutthroat, which is the potential beneficiary of the "war" on nonnative lake trout—garner particular political attention within the park's boundaries.

Yellowstone's debates about wildlife science and policy date back to its earliest days. In the 1880s the issue was poaching. In the 1930s scientists disagreed with campaigns to eradicate coyotes and other predators. But those efforts struck me as comparatively noncontroversial: the easy-to-understand antipoaching movement was widely popular beyond Yellowstone's outskirts, and the predator debate didn't leach out into national consciousness. By contrast, today a saga like reintroducing wolves, eradicating lake trout, or taking grizzlies off the endangered species list involves dozens of studies and meetings and position papers and court cases and congressional speeches, generating a cottage industry of political churn that can command public attention for decades. So when did Yellowstone wildlife science become so political?

I knew that many environmental debates had become more heated in recent decades, from water pollution to genetically modified foods to climate change. I wasn't surprised to realize that environmental stories matter more in a national park that epitomizes our relationship with nature. I was a little bit surprised to be able to pinpoint the Yellowstone shift to a single story. But then I realized that story's great elements: it featured a stunning advance in ecological science, and it took place during the cultural turbulence of the 1960s and early '70s.

♦

When the grizzly bear raised its head slightly, the three scientists knew the end was near. For almost an hour they had ignored the snow flurries blowing around them and the cold penetrating their fingers. They'd ignored the sounds of howling coyotes and honking Canada geese, the distinctive calls of sandhill cranes and that extraordinary experience of autumn in Yellowstone, the bugle of the bull elk. They'd focused little on their Hayden Valley surroundings, the patchwork of meadow and forest so teeming with wildlife that some people consider it the beating animal heart of Yellowstone.

The scientists blocked out all of this beauty to focus on the drugged grizzly in front of them. It was September 22, 1961. Twin brothers Frank and John Craighead, forty-five years old, had a youthful, clean-cut appearance, with brown hair swept back from open, often-smiling faces. As boys in Washington, D.C., they'd become interested in falconry, which they pursued with such passion and talent that they published their first *National Geographic* article at age twenty-one. Later they conducted survival training programs for the military, pursued PhDs, and built identical log cabins in Jackson Hole. Today they were assisted by Maurice Hornocker, a graduate student of John's at the University of Montana. And today, they had a chance to make history. To do so, they had mapped out a set of procedures to perform while the bear was out of commission, and they'd followed those procedures closely. Now, with the work basically complete, instruments showed the grizzly's respiration rate had more than doubled, meaning that the anesthesia was about to wear off. But something was wrong.

An associate, Mike Stephens, who was several hundred yards up the valley, called in by walkie-talkie. According to Frank's memoir, he said, "It's colder than hell out here . . . What's holding things up?"[1]

Their goal was to place a specially designed radio on the grizzly: a two-ounce transmitter, a fourteen-ounce battery, and a tiny loop antenna, all in a collar fitted around the bear's neck. They'd tested empty collars on previous grizzlies, and they believed the bear would tolerate wearing it for months.

Up the valley, Mike was carrying a radio receiver. Earlier, he had reported that the collar's signal was weak. Now, Frank asked if it was any stronger. "No good," Mike said.

That was bad news: something must have failed. But what could it be? They had already double-checked the tuning of the transmitter, the acrylic seal, and the connection to the antenna. They'd stayed up late the previous night dipping the battery pack in rubber to waterproof it, coating and wrapping the other components, and sanding and wrapping the assembly as a whole. They'd made the unit as shockproof and bearproof as they could. They'd been working for two years to this moment, spending copious amounts of grant money and endless hours of time. Why couldn't Mike hear the signal?

The bear raised its head again, this time a little higher.

"We'll have to give it up," John Craighead said. Having captured and drugged grizzlies before, both brothers knew how violent the bears could be upon awakening. In fact they'd experienced some close calls. Film of a later close call made it into a legendary *National Geographic* TV special: men in plaid collared shirts pulling away from a grizzly nicknamed Ivan the Terrible as it screams awake, then running for their station wagon as it smashes their equipment, then gunning the starter as it slams its shoulder into a passenger door, then backing away as it climbs atop the hood and aims a paw at the windshield.

This episode wasn't quite so dramatic. The scientists made it a safe distance away before the bear rose to its feet unsteadily. It ambled toward the woods. And although physically safe, the Craigheads were devastated. Unless Mike could receive a signal, all this work had come to nothing.

Then Mike's voice came across the walkie-talkie. "We've got it now! The signal's great!" While the bear was lying down, its body blocked the transmitter. Now that it was up and moving, the receiver emitted a series of beeps. The team allowed the bear to wander off, and then, following the beeps to climb a series of hills, found it again. For the first time in history, scientists gained the ability to track a wild animal wherever it went. Using the radio signals, members of the Craighead team could arrange to meet the bear when and where they wanted to. So long as they kept downwind, they could study a bear without it knowing they were there. To commemorate the occasion, they gave this bear not only a number, 40, but also a name, Marian, after the wife of the avionics engineer who designed her transmitter.

Even today, wildlife scientists stand in awe of the Craigheads' achievement. In the years since, radio transmitters have enhanced our knowledge of not only bears but also other species, from huge humpback whales to tiny honeybees. The Craigheads also pioneered efforts to concoct the best drugs for immobilizing grizzlies, ultimately performing 235 live-captures. And they used all of these innovations to generate nearly a decade's worth of groundbreaking longitudinal research, putting radios on twenty-four different grizzlies to learn about every aspect of how they lived. For example, before the Craigheads, nobody knew where any grizzlies hibernated for the winter. Nobody had ever seen a den. The Craigheads were able to track grizzlies to their dens—and even in later years crawl in to take mid-hibernation measurements. Before the Craigheads, the only way to estimate grizzly populations was to count grizzlies in a meadow, hoping that you weren't double-counting the same one twice. With the Craigheads' radio collars and colored ear markers, you didn't double-count. And because the Craigheads' study was longitudinal—they often re-collared a bear as its battery faded or a youngster's neck outgrew the collar—they were able to gather data on bear lifetimes: how often they reproduced, how their range changed, and how they died.

The Craigheads' techniques, and thus their insights, were leaps and bounds ahead of someone like Ernest Thompson Seton, whose observation was limited to his immediate senses. Through his curiosity and patience, Seton opened a window into animal life—but it was only a window, and that which he couldn't see he tended to cover up by assigning the bears sentimental human traits. With radio tracking, the Craigheads' observational universe grew exponentially. "We feel as if we now have a wide-screen view of grizzly behavior, whereas previously we had been peering at it through a keyhole," they wrote.[2] They regularly backpacked into remote areas, often in bad weather, sometimes staying long after their food ran out or intentionally going without sleep for days at a time so that they could spend all that time observing bear behavior in the wild, learning cub-rearing techniques, social dynamics, migration patterns, and eating habits.

The Craigheads' funding—more than a million dollars over the ten-plus years of their study—came from a variety of sources, with the National Park Service playing a relatively minor role. But the park benefitted hugely from their work. For example, when a ranger encountered a "problem bear," he would often call the Craigheads. The brothers taught rangers how to anesthetize bears for relocation away from people. If a bear was too ornery for rangers, the Craigheads were willing to subdue it themselves even if it wasn't associated with their study.

Furthermore, they were willing to provide management recommendations. Rather than a bear management policy, Yellowstone traditionally relied on ad-hoc problem solving. If a bear became a problem, it was killed or relocated. But with their improved knowledge, the Craigheads could offer policy advice. With science, humans could *conserve* grizzly bear populations. They could allow grizzlies to maintain their lifestyle in the wild, and thus prevent extinction without resorting to the zoo-like domestication strategies used with bison sixty years previously. Now, even in the face of human population growth, wildlife science could *save* species, rather than merely chronicle their demise. Unfortunately, however, it wasn't just a matter of accumulating data to the point where the Craigheads were ready to make policy prescriptions. They also needed people to listen.

Four hundred miles northwest of Yellowstone, Granite Park Chalet sits in the heart of that other triumph of the National Park system, Glacier. The chalet, a rough-hewn glorified bunkhouse ringed by mountains and snowfields, is perched on a mountainside more than four steep uphill miles from the nearest road. It's accessible only on foot or horseback, yet its bunks are regularly filled to capacity. These days, the main attraction is the scenery, with hikes to nearby knife-edge ridgelines that overlook year-round glaciers and jewel-like lakes. But in the 1960s there was another attraction: grizzly bears.

Three dozen overnight guests created a lot of garbage at the chalet, especially in an era before quality dehydrated food, when even dedicated backpackers typically chowed down on canned ravioli and Vienna sausages. Officially, the chalet had an incinerator for all of the garbage generated or brought into the site. But in practice, the incinerator was balky and ridiculously undersized. So the chalet regularly dumped its garbage in an open area well below the front deck, and most nights after sunset, guests were treated to a Grizzly Show. You could watch bears eat garbage, an activity that had first been popularized in Yellowstone in the 1910s and '20s, when the park constructed amphitheaters around garbage dumps so that tourists wouldn't have to crawl into the stench as Ernest Thompson Seton had.

The shows were hugely popular, attracting as many as 90 percent of Yellowstone's visitors.[3] But they were troubling for an institution that over the decades came to see itself as more nature than zoo. Having people watch "wild" animals eat table scraps felt too much like a spectacle. In 1931, officials closed the shows everywhere but Old Faithful and Canyon, with those two also closing in 1935 and 1942, respectively. The final closure didn't cause much controversy, in part because the nation's attention was diverted by the war, but mainly because the Yellowstone frontcountry was still full of black bears that you could feed by hand, a much more intimate encounter than watching a distant grizzly eat somebody else's garbage.

But with fewer bears in Glacier, a similar show became an unofficial tradition at the Granite Park Chalet. It was a bad idea from a visitor safety perspective. First, if something went wrong, the chalet was a long way from help. Second, hikers who couldn't fit into the chalet, or who wouldn't pay its $12.50 per night fee, were sent to camp in tents just below the feeding ground.

On the night of August 12, 1967, as a nurse from Kalispell, Montana, lay in her chalet bunk full of worry instead of sleep, she heard a scream. Her mind running, she wondered if a woman was being molested near the outhouse. She tried to rouse her husband but failed. Then several minutes later came another scream, unmistakable, distinct, shattering. It sounded like it was coming from much farther away than the outhouse. "Get out, get out, get away from me!" The nurse and her husband, now awake, raced out to the balcony. Silence, and then the voice clear and terrible: "God help me, he's stabbing me." It was coming from the campground. "God help me! Somebody help me!"[4]

No grizzly had ever killed a human in Glacier during its fifty-seven-year history, although nonfatal attacks had been increasing in the past decade. A conventional wisdom had arisen that as long as you weren't between a mother and her cubs, you shouldn't be in danger. "If there was one thing that was drummed into us," a teenager named Paul Dunn, who hiked that same night into Trout Lake, nine air miles and multiple mountain valleys from Granite Park, later told his parents, "it was that bears won't bother us if we didn't bother them. And we certainly weren't gonna bother them!"[5]

But in a gruesome coincidence, a grizzly bear did bother Dunn and his friends that same night. It walked into their camp and started poking their sleeping bags. Dunn and three comrades escaped only by violating the standard advice to play dead: they jumped out of their bags and ran away to climb trees. But a fourth comrade stayed put and was fatally mauled.

The situations were eerily identical. Both Michelle Koons, at Trout Lake, and Julie Helgeson, at Granite Park, were attacked in camp and dragged away to their deaths. (Helgeson survived long enough to be rescued, but perished while a surgeon—the no-longer-sleepy husband of the nurse who heard the scream—tried to save her life in an operation on the chalet's dining room table.) The park was understaffed in a heavy forest-fire season, and its leadership was confused by the grizzlies' behavior. Terror surged.

Four grizzlies were quickly killed, and the two identified as being responsible for the near-simultaneous attacks were both found to be injured and gaunt. The one at Trout Lake had been a nuisance all summer, but rangers hadn't gotten around to dispatching it.

The one at Granite Park had clearly been attracted by the chalet's practice of dumping garbage, an activity under a ban that rangers hadn't enforced.

Suddenly the entire National Park Service was panicked about grizzly bears. It wasn't just that Glacier's practices were lax. It was that leaders hadn't been terribly worried about enforcing those practices because they thought they knew how grizzlies behaved. It was a classic representation of the upheavals of the 1960s: What if everything we thought we knew was wrong? What if any garbage dump could turn any grizzly into a killer? What if the simultaneous attacks weren't coincidence but something suddenly snapping in the minds of grizzlies everywhere? What if this happened again?

Two years later, on September 6, 1969, a collection of big, big brass gathered for a meeting at Mammoth Hot Springs. Scientists and policymakers had flown in from all around the country to discuss data and viewpoints on bear management. After Labor Day, the crowds in Yellowstone thinned, so the park's administrative headquarters could start easing into offseason rhythms. In other words, people could go to meetings. This one was a formal information-gathering session for the secretary of the interior's Natural Sciences Advisory Committee, seeking to resolve disputes within the National Park Service (which was part of the Department of the Interior). And the disputes, in two years of post-Glacier concern about grizzlies, had become significant.

Thus the meeting's attendees were full of status. There was Yellowstone's relatively new superintendent, Jack Anderson, with his chiseled face and bushy eyebrows, and Anderson's chief biologist, Glen Cole, balding, with big ears, eyeglasses, and a mustache. There was the director of the entire Park Service, George Hartzog, along with his chief natural scientist and several other national-level executives. Also attending were four consulting scientists, including the Craighead brothers. The Craigheads had clashed terribly with Cole and Anderson, and what started as a scientific disagreement expanded into a bitter personality feud. They were fighting primarily over garbage.[6]

Yellowstone had ended the *public display* of grizzlies eating garbage, but not the practice. Since 1942 it had been trucking its garbage to two remote spots—Trout Creek in Hayden Valley and Rabbit Creek near Old Faithful—for the grizzlies to forage in privacy. Thus most of the bears that the Craigheads studied ate some garbage. After the Glacier attacks, this was a terrifying prospect, and all sorts of people wanted the dumps closed.

But to the Craigheads, science said something different. They argued that in Glacier, grizzlies became habituated to eating garbage in the presence of humans, and thus came to associate humans with food. But in Yellowstone, they said, these isolated dumps were simply another concentrated food source—they called them *ecocenters*.[7] To a grizzly, they said, a garbage ecocenter was little different from a salmon run, whale carcass, or berry patch. The remote dumps actually reduced the potential for conflict: they effectively zoned dangerous grizzlies away from human activity—an attractive notion in the 1960s, which were a high-water mark for community zoning regulations that kept dirty industries separate from healthy residences. If Yellowstone suddenly closed the dumps, the Craigheads said, it would cause the grizzlies to look for food anywhere, including campgrounds, picnic sites, and other places full of humans. There might well be loss of human life. And even if there wasn't, even if you could aggressively manage the problem bears before they became too much of a problem, that would result in more bears killed. The Craigheads' research into reproductive rates suggested that the bear population could not respond quickly enough to such losses. Yellowstone grizzlies would become extinct.

The counterargument involved both scientific and philosophical objections. Scientifically, Glen Cole disputed the Craigheads' belief that nearly all Yellowstone grizzlies ate at the garbage dumps. He believed there was an additional "backcountry population," unseen by the Craigheads, that would not be affected by the dumps' closure. Unfortunately Cole didn't have much data to back this assertion.

Philosophically, Cole and his superiors were hugely influenced by a 1963 document known as the Leopold Report. A blue-ribbon nationwide committee chaired by zoologist A. Starker Leopold was asked to look at the science behind wildlife management. (It was prompted by public outcry over the slaughter of forty-three hundred Yellowstone elk in 1961, killed by rangers concerned about overgrazing.) But the committee ended up going much further, writing an eloquent yet concrete meditation on ways to address the founding paradox of the National Park Service: to provide both recreation for today's tourists and preservation for the future. In the Leopold Report, for the first time, park managers felt like they had a unified set of principles to accomplish that goal.

One important principle was to use science within the Park Service. For example, rather than arbitrarily guessing at the number of elk that would overgraze the range, the Park Service should employ scientists who could provide an answer. To ensure that those scientists had enough internal clout to be listened to, they should be Park Service employees. The Leopold Report's call for increased science funding was hailed by scientists and policymakers alike. However, internalizing the science-management link also meant that outside scientists, such as the Craigheads, would provide data but not necessarily recommendations. National park managers had to listen to scientists, but only their internal people. In potential disagreements between internal and external scientists, only one side might be heard.

Another philosophical principle of the Leopold Report was that parks should strive to be a "vignette of primitive America."[8] Yellowstone should feel as "natural" as it had before Europeans arrived, and any artificial ways of achieving that feel shouldn't be easily observable. This philosophy had two huge flaws common to the era. First, it ignored the long-term presence of Native Americans in the parks and their significant and variable effects on "natural" conditions. Second, it assumed that the clock could be stopped, that the complex and dynamic processes of nature could somehow be dialed back to 1491 and held there forever. In constructing this vision, even scientists such as Leopold ended up adopting the nostalgic attitudes that had driven Larry Larom and the dude ranchers. They wanted Yellowstone to appear to be a Garden of Eden, where animals romped in the conflict-free way they presumably had before white people arrived to mess with them. For example, before white people arrived, Yellowstone bears didn't wear radio collars or colored ear markers, and they certainly didn't feed on tourists' garbage. As Cole and Anderson prepared for Yellowstone's 1972 centennial celebration, they interpreted the Leopold Report as demanding the elimination of both garbage dumps and marked animals.

Beginning in the summer of 1968, Yellowstone sharply reduced the amount of garbage made available to grizzlies at the dumps. And, Frank Craighead wrote, "The number of grizzlies captured in campgrounds during 1968 rose to about four times the average for the previous nine years."[9] Garbage-deprived bears were hunting for food closer to humans, just as he predicted. Cole and Anderson were curtailing the dumps for the purpose of reducing bear conflicts, but their action was actually having the opposite effect. If the Park Service wanted to close dumps, the Craigheads argued, closures should take place gradually, accompanied by the dumping of elk carcasses in remote areas to help wean the bears. But such mitigations were clearly artificial, violations of Leopold Report principles.

Fundamentally, Cole and other Park Service scientists believed that garbage-eating bears were problem bears. Feeding problem bears was bad; killing them solved problems.[10] And whatever happened to garbage-eating bears, the separate, non-problem, backcountry population would be unaffected. Yet the Craigheads said there was no such backcountry population. Their radio-collar data showed that several bears at the Trout Creek garbage dump migrated from far outside the park's boundaries. These bears had winter den sites and spring/fall ranges in outlying areas, and came to Trout Creek midsummer like a randy cowboy whooping it up on the Fourth of July. This was not a new idea—Seton claimed to have seen the grizzly Wahb both inside the park and near Triple-A Anderson's distant Wyoming ranch—but now it was backed by telemetry data. In their presentation to the Advisory Committee in Mammoth, the Craigheads argued that this data proved that there was only a single population of grizzlies, animals that ate garbage as well as many other food sources.

In an indication of just how contentious the situation had become, the Craigheads asked Park Service personnel to leave the room while they made their case to the outside experts on the committee. And in an indication of just how toothless such advisory committees can sometimes be, this one—chaired by Starker Leopold himself—wrote a report that included the ideas of both sides but didn't take much of a stand on them. Its bland language allowed Anderson and Cole to continue aggressively closing garbage dumps, ignoring the Craigheads' perspective.

Yet buried in the back-and-forth on this argument was a trans-formative ecological principle. The Craigheads' data showed that to a grizzly bear, the boundaries of Yellowstone National Park were ridiculously arbitrary. A grizzly lived in an *ecosystem*, a vast interconnected web of food sources, den sites, social gathering places, and remote spots to hide from enemies such as men with rifles. The ecosystem extended into the mountains and valleys of the surrounding National Forests and even onto private lands. In the same way we say that the Hayden/Moran or Washburn/Langford/Hedges expeditions *discovered* Yellowstone—because they were the first to alert the wider culture to this way of looking at a special place, in a format that the culture could understand—so too did the Craigheads *discover* the "greater Yellowstone ecosystem." Their science showed that the long-term protection of grizzlies or other animals was going to be not just about managing garbage in the park but managing habitat across that entire ecosystem's patchwork of public and private lands.

The bridge over the outlet from Yellowstone Lake is known as Fishing Bridge because it was once one of the easiest places in the world to catch fish. (With overfishing, populations of Yellowstone cutthroat trout became imperiled, and now the bridge is viewing-only.) East of the bridge is a tourist village: museum, gas station, store, and RV park. Behind the gas station, hidden between the RV park and the river, is a "utility area" including an employee dorm.

Six weeks after the Mammoth meeting, on Friday, October 10, 1969, a female grizzly bear and some yearlings were seen at the utility area. It was Marian, the bear that had received the Craigheads' first collar. Over the past eight years she had shown herself to be a remarkable animal, mating with dominant males, bearing several litters of young, and denning right there in the Hayden

Valley. Unlike some bears, she had a small range, centered on the Trout Creek dump. In 1968, with the dump curtailed, she had to travel farther to obtain the same amount of food. But it was a good year for berries and pine nuts, and she was mostly able to avoid food sources near humans, as she had her entire life so far. She made it through the summer of 1969 as well, but in a poor nut/berry year, by the fall her family was foraging in developed areas. That Friday, rangers trapped and transplanted two of her yearlings. The next Monday morning, a ranger saw a third yearling near a trap. He shot it with a drugged dart and moved in closer to finish the job with another dart. He got between mother and cub.

As Frank Craighead told the story, Marian charged out of the woods at full speed. Then, near the ranger, she paused. Perhaps it was a "bluff charge" of the sort bears have become famous for. Perhaps Marian, in her vast experience with men bearing drugged darts, was realizing that maybe the situation didn't require violence. She seemed "uncertain of her next move," Frank wrote. She turned toward her yearling, but then pivoted back toward the ranger. He was in danger. He used his .44 magnum to shoot Marian between the eyes.[11]

The Craigheads always tried not to be sentimentalists. They'd seen plenty of bears die. They'd even, before they fully understood the best drug dosages, caused some deaths themselves. But it was hard not to see Marian's death as symbolic of what would happen to Yellowstone grizzlies in general. Forced to range farther in search of food, the bears would end up in conflict with humans. For example, after Marian's death one of her yearlings traveled south toward Flagg Ranch, outside of the park on the road toward the Tetons. There, in November, he was killed by a poacher. The next spring, another of Marian's cubs moved west of the park, beyond the town of West Yellowstone, where he too was killed by a hunter, this one legal. Closing the dumps, Frank argued, pushed Marian's formerly nonmigratory family to the outskirts of the ecosystem, where wildlife protection was not as strong as it was inside the park. And while Marian's story was a striking anecdote, it was also representative of an overall trend.[12] In a sense, he was suggesting, humans were violating the "half-tame" compact of the Ernest Thompson Seton era. Although the park was still officially a refuge, the crowds diminished its protections, and the decrease in available garbage reduced the carrying capacity of its habitat. And so bears were forced out of the refuge into dangerous hunting territory. Yet now science could demonstrate that each bear death was not only an individual loss but also a collective one, because it contributed to possible extinction of the species.

Should the untimely deaths of Marian's cubs be considered in evaluating the Yellowstone grizzly population? To a scientist, the clear answer was yes. If Yellowstone-ecosystem grizzlies kept dying, the population would become extinct, and Yellowstone would have failed to preserve its natural conditions for future generations. But from a management perspective, a political perspective, how could one blame the Park Service for the hunting regulations and enforcement of the states of Montana and Wyoming, over which it had no control? As science edged into policy, the issues became complicated and political. And the roiling environment of the time—when everything from lunch counters to music to hair to sex had a powerful political overlay—made the issues incredibly hard to solve.

Although Old Faithful is Yellowstone's most famous attraction, it is just one of many thermal features in the area known as the Upper

Geyser Basin. Tourists who are willing to walk two or three miles on a network of dirt and boardwalk trails can see an astonishing array of bubbling and spouting water, steaming vents, and colorful pools. The basin's two square miles contain nearly one-quarter of all the geysers in the world. One trail leads to Grand Geyser, taller than Old Faithful but less regular, with eruptions every seven to fifteen hours. Behind Grand Geyser is a wooded hillside. And although it's less than a mile from the bustle of the Old Faithful village complex, between eruptions the area can be quite empty. In 1972 it was the sort of place where you might—if you were an antiestablishment young person who didn't want to camp with the regular tourists—sneak off the trail and set up a tent.

That's what 25-year-old Phillip Bradberry did on June 23 of that year. Tall and skinny, almost emaciated, with long and unruly red hair, he was nicknamed "Crow" because of his habit of flapping his arms on defense when playing basketball. Since returning from Vietnam, he'd been largely a drifter, and for this trip he'd convinced his Alabama high school friend Harry Walker to join him. Harry was also twenty-five, also tall and skinny, but more muscular and quicker to smile. Harry had spent years working hard on his family's small dairy farm and at off-farm jobs because money was tight. But in the past few months he'd suffered a debilitating elbow injury, become disillusioned with his National Guard service, and entered an early midlife crisis, of the sort that requires a road trip. Friends gave the boys a ride to Colorado, which Harry found beautiful, and then in search of more such beauty Harry and Crow hitch-hiked toward Yellowstone. From Livingston, Montana, they caught a ride with a girl who was working as a chambermaid at the Old Faithful Inn. When they arrived, rather than try to hitch another ride to the nearest campground at Madison Junction, sixteen miles away, they just set themselves down in a nearby, out-of-the-way place. (They actually thought they saw another camper's campfire about a quarter-mile away, but it turned out to be steam from a thermal feature.)

Harry developed a crush on the chambermaid. The next day, Friday, he and Crow kicked around the Old Faithful village until she got off work. Then they kicked around together and Harry walked her back to her dorm room, talking late into the night. Saturday was more of the same. In the evening the three of them laughed over drinks at the bar of the Old Faithful Inn, and as Harry walked her home, he got her permission to give her a kiss good-night. After midnight, Harry and Crow returned to their camp by flashlight, happily singing. They were only five feet away from camp when Harry's flashlight illuminated a four-hundred-pound bear eating their food.

The bear, apparently as surprised as the young men were, must have decided to defend its food source. It charged at them. Crow dove or fell to his left and rolled down an embankment. He heard Harry shouting, "Help me, Crow!" Then it was silent. Crow called back to Harry but got no response.[13]

Crow raced back to the Old Faithful Inn in a panic, somehow avoiding falling into any thermal pools in the dark. At the inn he collapsed on the floor, shouting, "Bear! Bear! Has my friend." (Experts later confirmed the wisdom of his choice—going for help was the best, the only way to try to save Harry's life.) Rangers quickly accompanied Crow back out along the boardwalk, but he could no longer find the site in the dark. They called to Harry but heard nothing, and dared not aimlessly wander the forest. They regrouped for a better-organized search party, and finally at 5:30 A.M. found Harry's body, about a quarter of it eaten by the bear. Five years after the Glacier incidents, the same thing happened at Yellowstone: a garbage-feeding bear attacked and killed a young victim in a terrifying early-morning episode. The next day officials killed a grizzly and identified it as responsible. The weatherbeaten twenty-year-old sow had been a regular at the nearby Rabbit Creek garbage dump before it was closed two years previously.

In the months afterward the Park Service received letters about the event by the dozen, almost all of them supporting the bear. The correspondents had contempt for Harry and Crow. Several pointed out that the boys were from Alabama—this during a time of palpable hatred for white Southerners. One correspondent wrote, "Some people have to learn the hard way"; another could "only wish the other intruder [Crow] had been attacked."[14]

But bigger than contempt for the victims was fury at the Park Service, because it killed a bear for an action that was not the animal's fault. "Why does the bear have to suffer?" one wrote.[15] It was almost too easy, in 1972, to see the two young men as lawless hippies, moochers, brazenly ignoring the rules of The Man, failing to grasp how those rules were designed for their own safety. It was almost too easy to jump from such condemnations to the view that the bear must have been the innocent victim of the man it had killed and eaten.

Few of the correspondents wrote out of any scientific knowledge. Many had seen a report on the network news, or read a wire-service story in a newspaper, and responded emotionally. Some were downright misinformed. One suggested that mouth-to-mouth resuscitation "has brought life [to people] after several years of burial . . . and should be attempted regardless of length of time in cemetery."[16]

Park officials responded politely to all but that last correspondent, seeing an opportunity to educate the public about bears and wildlife management. But Park Service press statements that continually emphasized how Harry and Crow *did everything wrong* may have contributed to the us–vs.–them mentality. Every argument in that era seemed to have a moral component, with young and old accusing each other of lacking basic values. And perhaps subconsciously, park officials must have known that they needed to portray Harry and Crow as ignorant at best—because the alternative was admitting that actual scientists, the Craigheads, had warned of an event just like this.

The United States Courthouse in downtown Los Angeles, a seventeen-story art moderne structure of pink terra-cotta walls on an oversized dark granite base, felt like the kind of courthouse you'd see in a movie. You could picture Clark Gable or Charlie Chaplin, during their real-life 1940s paternity cases, coming up the wide exterior stairs, through one of the five matching doorways set back in the rock, across the terrazzo floors of the entrance lobby, and past the ornate light fixtures and ornamentally painted ceilings.

In February 1975, Harry Walker's parents and sister made that same journey. His death was a personal tragedy, of course, and also an economic hardship, as he'd been expected to take over the dairy farm. In one sense, no amount of money could make up for their loss. But in another sense, precedent did exist for them to receive monetary compensation. After three previous Yellowstone bear attacks, in 1929, 1944, and 1958, Congress or the courts awarded money to the victims.

But now it was the 1970s. Park visitation had exploded. Issues of managing wildlife had become complicated and controversial. And political conflicts about Vietnam, drugs, sex, poverty, and race had divided the nation's population. So the Harry Walker lawsuit came to be about more than the tragic death of one young man. It became an exploration of the role of government in mitigating the risk of natural environments. As such it was also a debate about what constituted a natural environment, and what science said about how one should be managed.

The suit was an event that the Park Service had long dreaded. Although the Glacier attacks spawned plenty of press criticism and a best-selling book, *Night of the Grizzlies*, and although the official report on the Glacier incidents was generally seen as a whitewash, none of that ended up in court. Years later, after high-profile reconsiderations of grizzly policy, had anything changed?

An answer to that question would come here, in the second-story courtroom of Judge Andrew Hauk. The plush, warm room featured walnut wainscoting, fluted mahogany pilasters, and wooden pews over a red carpet. Its ceiling was two stories high, with the judge's seat of course elevated above the proceedings.[17] The setting felt imposing—until Andy Hauk walked in. The judge was so unpredictable that attorneys in civil lawsuits generally disliked practicing in front of him. Indeed, some thought he was crazy.

Andy Hauk was a short and stocky man, mostly bald. Though in his sixties, he was still athletic, an avid skier and tennis player. He'd learned to ski as a child in Colorado, worked as a naval intelligence officer, and after moving to Los Angeles helped found Mineral King and Mount Baldy ski areas and helped organize the 1960 Squaw Valley Winter Olympics. "Skiing is like being a judge," he once said. "You make quick decisions, and if you're wrong, they're brought up fast."[18]

But Andy Hauk didn't make decisions like a typical judge, reserved and dignified. He didn't have much of a filter between his brain and his mouth. Whatever he thought, he said, without pausing to consider if it might be irrelevant or offensive. Because of this habit, in a local bar association survey the following year, three-quarters of respondents said he was not temperamentally suited to his position. Over the course of his career, insensitive remarks accumulated—about minorities, women, homosexuals, and environmentalists—to the point where in 1994 colleagues barred him from hearing civil rights cases regarding police brutality, because his comments created too much controversy. But defense attorney Terry Amdur recalled that underneath the intemperate statements, Judge Hauk was kindhearted. "He had a soft spot for people in trouble," Amdur said, recalling that the judge gave a fair shake to his clients caught up in activities as varied as draft-dodging, fraud, and organized crime.[19]

So perhaps Judge Hauk felt a similar empathy for Harry Walker. The judge certainly worked hard to grasp the arguments and testimony. Because the lawsuit was a bench trial with no jury, the judge was free to question witnesses and argue with attorneys. The trial transcript shows that Judge Hauk wanted to fully understand the legal issues at stake—which Walker attorney Stephen Zetterberg portrayed as being primarily about grizzly bear science.

Zetterberg called Frank Craighead as a witness. Yellowstone management, Craighead argued, had ignored his science with devastating consequences. During Craighead's day and a half on the stand, Hauk seemed especially frustrated by the cross-examination of the government's attorney, William Spivak, because it strayed from this science. Exasperated with Spivak, at one point the judge even summarized Craighead's argument for him: "When they [Yellowstone officials] closed the dumps, it made it [the bear situation] even worse, because the animals did not have anything to eat, so they had to forage around and wham-o, the first thing you know they were in a campground and lost their respect or fear of humans, and then you had man-grizzly confrontations; is that right?"[20] His final question was for the witness, and Craighead agreed.

With this line of reasoning, Zetterberg argued that Yellowstone officials had put the public in peril. By closing the dumps at the same time they stopped radio-tracking grizzlies, they increased the potential danger to the public. And worse, they didn't let anybody know about it. Craighead testified that he'd camped informally all over Yellowstone, but by 1972, given what he knew about the garbage dumps, he wouldn't have camped where Harry and Crow did. But how could they have known how dangerous that spot was? Again the judge verbalized what he was learning: "[t]here should have been some signs down there [near where Harry and Crow camped] that say to the effect, 'Danger. Do not sleep or camp here. Regular campground one-half mile'—or two and a half miles, whatever it is—'Regular campground two and a half miles northeast' . . . and then have some markers up there that would show the way to a campsite that was patrolled, that was fenced in, perhaps, from those grizzlies."[21]

To advocates of parks and wilderness, the judge's attitude made no sense. First, the campground was in fact sixteen miles away. Second, all the fences and signs would detract from the visitor experience. As Yellowstone historian Lee Whittlesey later wrote, "the true resource of Yellowstone is *its very wildness*. When you take that away by sanitizing the place—whether by radio-collaring every bear, by putting up signs every ten feet, or by otherwise overdeveloping the place, you destroy its most important element: wildness."[22] But Craighead's point (which the judge exaggerated) was that he saw *no signs at all* in the boardwalk area to warn of the potential dangers from bears.

The early 1970s were a peak of *judicial remedies*, a period in which American courts frequently went beyond ruling on matters of law to actually overseeing implementation: taking over schools or prisons, assigning court-appointed masters, and even drawing up busing maps to desegregate schools. Judges saw such activism as a necessary response to bureaucracies that continually failed to properly enact the law. These bureaucracies grew through the 20th century to become remarkably independent of political processes— unaccountable. The most potentially treacherous ones were also in charge of a politically weak clientele, such as schoolchildren, prisoners, the disabled, or wildlife. When the entrenched bureaucracies were incapable of making decisions based on law or science, these clients needed the courts' full protection. Thus, in the view of many 1970s judges, a better option was to find someone more capable to do the bureaucracies' work for them—someone such as a judge himself. Judge Hauk seemed to be adopting this attitude as he talked to Craighead about radio collars. Shouldn't the bear that killed Walker—which Craighead believed had also been involved in a nearby unreported fatal attack two years previously—have been collared and tracked? In his navy days, Judge Hauk himself had marked the positions of nearby submarines on a glass board. After testimony was complete, as he advised the attorneys on what he wanted to hear in their concluding arguments, he asked about such a tracking system as a way of protecting the public. "Even today, wouldn't [a tracking system] be a wise thing? I do not know, but I want to hear argument on it. Wouldn't it be a wise thing for the Park Service to keep a plot like that? Wouldn't that be the best sort of patrol in the world? . . . What is the duty? Is there a duty to warn, and if so, what does that mean, warning that is not too expensive yet effective?"[23]

Such a tracking system was perhaps an idea ahead of its time. In a Los Angeles courtroom, a judge could not understand the scope of the Yellowstone wilderness. (Indeed on at least three occasions he slipped up and called it "Yosemite.") But his off-the-cuff comments made his desired remedy seem almost outrageous. He added, "If it can be done for four or five thousand dollars [then] in a sense—[and] I do not like to use this word—the *hell* with what the Sierra Club may say or those barefoot boys with environmental impact statements on their back." He continued, "As the Lord said, 'Use the mountains, use the land. Build upon it. Make it your home, dominate it.' That is what He told human beings. He did not tell grizzlies to dominate humans. He told humans to dominate grizzlies."[24]

Zetterberg succeeded in focusing the trial on public safety. He and Craighead used Harry Walker's death to point out problems with federal grizzly policy—they caused the trial to metastasize from one man's death to wildlife management to the philosophies of environmentalism and what God might have declared. Hauk awarded Walker's family more than $87,000, just one-fifth of their request but a sizable amount at the time. Yet focusing on public safety meant that the grizzlies themselves got nothing. The judge had no room to rule on how Yellowstone could remain a haven for imperiled bear populations, or a half-tame preserve for wild animals in general. Indeed the judge's remarks suggested that this might be the end of the road for the classic conflict inherent in the Park Service's mission: preservation (here, of wild uncontrolled ecosystems) versus public use. "It is ridiculous," Hauk said. "It is a fad, all this environmentalism, a big fad. One day it is going out the window. Why? Because we can use the wilderness, whether it be skiers, whether it be backpackers and whatnot, and use it safely, if those who run the wilderness will safely control the wilderness, so it does not injure us."[25]

The end of the story is anticlimactic. A three-judge appeals court panel overruled Andy Hauk, but with little of the pomp or drama of the trial. The panel simply appreciated defense lawyer Spivak's arguments in a way that Hauk had not. Rangers did warn every incoming tourist about dangerous wildlife, but Harry and Crow, riding in the car of an employee, cruised through the North Entrance without receiving that warning. Rangers did talk to Old Faithful visitors about dangers, but Harry and Crow, against the advice of their new friends, never spoke to one. Rangers did patrol campgrounds to spot bears and the foodstuffs that could attract them,

FIGURE 21: Larry Larom and other dude ranchers in the Cody, Wyoming, area rallied to support this Gertrude Vanderbilt Whitney statue of William F. "Buffalo Bill" Cody in their town. When superintendent Horace Albright spoke at the statue's 1924 dedication, he explicitly tied Yellowstone to the dude ranchers' frontier nostalgia. *Photo by the author.*

FIGURE 22 (LEFT): Horace Albright is shown here in about 1919, shortly after taking over as the first superintendent of Yellowstone to be employed by the new National Park Service. Albright, who had served as Stephen Mather's right-hand man during the service's 1916 establishment, gave Yellowstone patriotic associations when he consistently claimed that it was the setting for the invention of the very idea of national parks. *Library of Congress LC-USZ62-37302.* FIGURE 23 (BELOW): In 1870, the Washburn–Langford expedition camped at the confluence where the Firehole and Gibbon Rivers form the Madison. Here the scene is reenacted in an undated photo, part of the passion stoked by Horace Albright for this alleged birthplace of the "National Park Idea." *Courtesy of the National Park Service, Yellowstone history #09182.*

FIGURE 24: For Yellowstone's semi-centennial celebration in 1922, superintendent Horace Albright (left) put on a sort of Old Explorer's Reunion with 83-year-old Charley Cook (center) for the benefit of junketing journalists such as Anne Anzer of the National Editorial Association (right). Albright staged the ceremony at Madison Junction, to emphasize his story that the very idea of national parks was invented at this spot in the year following Cook's first visit. *Jack E. Haynes photograph courtesy of the National Park Service, Yellowstone National Park, YELL 106393.*

FIGURE 25 (ABOVE): Scientist and educator Hermon Carey Bumpus, left, poses with Rockefeller representative Kenneth Chorley (center) and architect Herbert Maier (right) in 1930. Bumpus had recommended that Yellowstone interpret its wonders for new automobile-based tourists with a series of rustic roadside museums—and the men stand in front of one being constructed with Chorley's funds, using Maier's design, at Madison Junction. *Courtesy of the National Park Service, Yellowstone National Park, YELL 44364.* FIGURE 26 (OPPOSITE): Photographer Ansel Adams, shown here with his camera and light meter probably in 1947, made his first trip to Yellowstone amid World War II gas rationing in 1942. *J. Malcolm Greany photograph via Wikimedia Commons.*

FIGURE 27: In Yellowstone, Ansel Adams found magnificent textures in the form of clouds and steam, as here at Fountain Geyser Pool. In a sense he was fortunate to make his first visit when crowds were diminished by the war, making unpeopled shots like this easier to capture. *Ansel Adams/National Park Service photograph via Wikimedia Commons.*

FIGURE 28: In portraying the vast expanses of Yellowstone Lake, with Mount Sheridan in the far distance, Ansel Adams emphasized solitary spirituality, a personal relationship to vast, unpeopled wilderness. *Ansel Adams/National Park Service photograph via Wikimedia Commons.*

FIGURE 29: Despite crowds in the frontcountry, Yellowstone still offers amateur photographers opportunities to mimic Ansel Adams in capturing the spiritual power of unpeopled wilderness, as in this author photograph of Heart Lake at sunrise. *Photo by the author.*

FIGURE 30 (ABOVE): After Ernest Thompson Seton hid himself in a garbage pit to observe bear behavior, the practice became formalized, with bleachers constructed for tourists to observe bear feeding shows. The shows were discontinued in the 1940s, shortly after this picture was taken. However, Yellowstone bears continued to eat garbage in privacy until the late 1960s. *Courtesy of the National Park Service, Yellowstone National Park, YELL 27353-07.* FIGURE 31 (BELOW): Many tourists enjoyed interacting with roadside bears as a highlight of their visit to Yellowstone into the 1960s. In this shot from 1940, tourists get dangerously close to two cubs near Isa Lake on Craig Pass. *Buffalo Bill Center of the West, Cody, Wyoming, USA. MS 089 Jack Richard Photograph Collection. PN.89.116.21435.19.*

FIGURE 32: Twin brothers Frank and John Craighead, shown here in 1966, pioneered the science of putting radio collars on grizzly bears. With increased scientific information they gained about grizzlies' lives came increased political debate about how to manage fragile bear populations. *Courtesy of the National Park Service, Yellowstone National Park, YELL 20481-1.*

HI KIDS!
Don't feed the bears.
Be sure Dad keeps the
car windows rolled up.

Over 40 people have been
hurt by bears this year.

FIGURE 33 (ABOVE): A grizzly bear feeds on garbage at the Trout Creek dump in 1963. The dumps' closure a few years later prompted a controversy, making Yellowstone the setting for an ongoing series of battles over environmental politics. *John Good NPS photograph 00036.* FIGURE 34 (LEFT): The Yogi Bear cartoon character, which debuted in 1958, familiarized "Jellystone" to children everywhere. In 1961 the Park Service tried, rather unsuccessfully, to co-opt Yogi for a "Don't feed the bears" message near the park entrance. *Courtesy of the National Park Service, National Archives Identifier 286013.*

FIGURE 35 (ABOVE) AND FIGURE 36 (BELOW): The Calfee Creek patrol cabin on the remote upper Lamar River, shown here in 1975, was one of the first structures threatened by the 1988 wildfires. Although the forest burned all around it, as shown in a 1998 photo, firefighters saved the cabin itself. *Chris Judson, National Park Service, photograph 03220 and Jim Peaco, National Park Service, photograph 15966.*

PRELIMINARY SURVEY OF BURNED AREAS:
YELLOWSTONE NATIONAL PARK AND ADJOINING NATIONAL FORESTS
GREATER YELLOWSTONE POST-FIRE RESOURCE ASSESSMENT COMMITTEE, BURNED AREA SURVEY TEAM

OCTOBER, 1988
(Burned areas as of Sept. 15, 1988)

COOPERATING AGENCIES

NATIONAL PARK SERVICE
Yellowstone National Park
Redwood National Park

FOREST SERVICE
Northern Region
Pacific Northwest Region
Pacific Southwest Region
Rocky Mountain Region
Intermountain Region
Geometronics Service Center
Nationwide Forestry Applications Program

NATIONAL AERONAUTICS AND SPACE ADMINISTRATION

MONTANA STATE UNIVERSITY

Legend:
- Forested: Canopy Burn; Moderate Soil Heating
- Forested: Surface Burn / Canopy Burn Complex
- Forested: Surface Burn; Low Soil Heating
- Nonforested: Low to Moderate Soil Heating Sagebrush, Shrubland, Grassland
- Nonforested: Low Soil Heating Sedge Meadows, Alpine Turf, Salix
- Slopes Greater Than 45%
- Forested: Unburned Yellowstone National Park
- Forested: Unburned National Forest
- Forested: Unburned Grand Teton National Park
- Nonforested: Unburned

FIGURE 37 (OPPOSITE): A map of the areas burned by the 1988 fires; the different colors reflect different types of burns (canopy, surface, etc.). Note the considerable burns south of Yellowstone Lake (where Grant Village is located), across western stretches of the park (Old Faithful, West Yellowstone, Norris, Mammoth), in wilderness near the eastern boundary (Calfee Creek), and at the Northeast Entrance (Cooke City, Silver Gate). *Greater Yellowstone Post-fire Resource Assessment Committee, Library of Congress 89691739.* FIGURE 38 (ABOVE): Lodgepole pines have evolved with wildfire, such that some of their pinecones open to release new seeds only in intense heat, as shown here in September 1988. The fires prompted widespread appreciation of these ecological effects, especially in an increasingly networked 1990s society. *Jim Peaco NPS photograph 13041.*

FIGURE 39: From Mount Sheridan, a vista stretches across the vast Yellowstone plateau, with Yellowstone Lake in the middle distance. This is the heart of Yellowstone's caldera, the collapsed center of the ancient volcano, a view that may prompt the question, "Will it erupt again?" *Photo by the author.*

but Harry and Crow, at an informal campsite that escaped detection, left out a bag of groceries and pots half full of leftovers.[26] Under Wyoming statutes, if the plaintiff contributed even ten percent to his own peril, he could not collect anything. And Harry could have done more to allow himself to be warned. (In his frustrating cross-examination of Craighead, Spivak was trying to get Craighead off his own science and onto Walker's actions, because that would get at Walker's culpability.) There was also a legalistic distinction with a deliciously opaque name, the *discretionary function exemption*, which said that closing garbage dumps was a *type* of management decision that was immune from lawsuits. In general, however, the appellate ruling shied away from both the rhetoric and content of big politics. And even it was not the final word. Zetterberg appealed to the US Supreme Court, which in 1975 declined without comment to hear the case. He then arranged for an Alabama senator to put the Walker family settlement into a 1978 congressional relief bill. But when the bill got irretrievably waylaid between a subcommittee and the Senate floor, the Walker family's quest was over.

The scientific story was similarly anticlimactic. In 1974 another blue-ribbon panel of independent ecologists—this one under the umbrella of the National Academy of Sciences—concluded that the grizzly population declined by one-third from 1967 to 1973, as the Craighead model would have predicted.[27] It criticized the Park Service's science. In his book *The Grizzly Bear*, writer Thomas McNamee called the panel's report "a nearly complete vindication for the Craigheads."[28] But for a battle so full of drama, victory was not exactly evident. Nobody was fired or went to jail. Indeed, several months later, the panel's chairman made other comments suggesting that he actually tended to believe the Park Service's estimates of grizzly populations rather than the Craigheads'.

The bureaucracy marched on. And in a sense that was its own resolution: Yellowstone was now so sophisticated a place as to have its own bureaucracy, its own established ways of doing things and people paid to be invested in those ways. It was a remarkable evolution from one hundred years previously, when the park had no paid staff at all.

But the grizzlies kept dying. In 1975 the species was listed as Threatened under the relatively new Endangered Species Act. This gave the U.S. Fish & Wildlife Service more say in bureaucratic arguments with the Park Service, thus giving the Craigheads another avenue to push their perspectives. But their triumph must have felt especially hollow: *yes, you were right that grizzlies would go extinct, and so now they are going extinct.*

Then, gradually, anticlimactically, grizzly populations stabilized. From 136 grizzlies across the Yellowstone ecosystem in 1975, populations declined to as low as 99 bears in 1990, before rebounding to approximately 800 today.[29] There is perhaps vindication for both sides of the debate: Cole was right that grizzlies could eventually be weaned off of garbage, but wrong about how quickly they could reproduce. The Craigheads were right about the importance of garbage as a food source—the fertility of Yellowstone grizzlies, and the park's carrying capacity, appear to be down slightly from the highs of the 1960s—but wrong about the continuing threats beyond park boundaries. The boom in population has come primarily because grizzlies now occupy much more land outside the park. Is that because they're no longer fed garbage inside the park? Because surrounding states tightened hunting regulations to comply with the Endangered Species Act? Because the bears could replace garbage in their diet with temporarily abundant whitebark pine nuts, which since the 2000s have become increasingly scarce? Because everyone involved now better understands the notion of an ecosystem?

These are hard questions, subject to disagreement, with very high stakes. Grizzlies in Yellowstone remain a hot political topic, as demonstrated by the trail of continuing litigation. The U.S. Fish & Wildlife Service removed Yellowstone-area grizzlies from Threatened status in 2007, and several environmental groups sued. In 2009, a federal judge agreed that potential loss of whitebark pine nuts warranted continued Threatened status, and a 2011 appeal upheld that decision. Since then federal scientists have continually recommended removal of Threatened status, and grizzly defenders have doubted the wisdom of those management recommendations. We have more science but no more collective certainty—only more data points to support our arguments.

Yet behind the political wrangling is the wonder of Yellowstone. This stretch of land, set aside for its geological curiosities, also happens to be the heart of the largest relatively intact temperate ecosystem in the world. It's capable of nurturing grizzlies, in an era when few other spots in America can. It boasts sufficiently diverse food sources, and sufficiently vast landscapes, to provide meaningful habitat for this rare creature, whose reclusive nature and man-threatening power make it unsuited to the typical forms of cohabitation with humans.

Yellowstone has provided the grizzly with a physical habitat and also a philosophical one. Managed as a preserve, with at least one of many goals being wildlife preservation, Yellowstone has been a place where scientists can come to study grizzlies. It's a place where the Craigheads, during the good years, found great cooperation from authorities and generated major scientific advances. And it's a place where, during the bad years, the Craigheads could rally public support for what might otherwise have been a rather obscure, impenetrable scientific disagreement. In the early 1970s, when America was arguing about *everything*, Yellowstone provided great material to argue about. (Note that in this era the typical dude ranch retreated from these political battles to become a sort of 1950s Hollywood-western theme park. Compared to Yellowstone, dude ranches didn't prompt the passions of hippies, scientists, or others—because they weren't offering as much to fight over.)

Yellowstone is a place where wildlife science has mattered enough that it *can* become political. Where tourists can become inspired enough to learn the science, where scientists can become impassioned enough to stick out their political necks, where bureaucrats can be called to task and judges can be tempted to wade in. And regardless of any past or future outcomes of those political debates, a place that inspires such a unique combination of intellect and emotional passion is a wonder indeed.

Advances in science showed how management decisions affected grizzly bear populations, thus affecting how Yellowstone looked and felt, indeed what it meant. This level of moral complexity enriched and complicated the value system embodied in national parks. Yet Yellowstone's evolving 20th-century reputation was also driven by the culture itself. Yellowstone had become such a celebrity—famous for being famous—that the fame started to take on a life of its own.

9
POPULAR

I n elementary school, Americans learn about pivotal episodes of our history, such as the Pilgrims, the Declaration of Independence, and Abraham Lincoln. We learn them as stories, burnished to a charming simplicity that conveys societal values, often wrapped up in iconic places such as Plymouth Rock or Gettysburg.

Historians sometimes complain about that simplification: maybe Paul Revere's fame owes more to Longfellow's rhyme about him than to his actual deeds; stories of Pocahontas, Betsy Ross, or Nez Perce chief Joseph may be better at form (appealing heroes, heartwarming values) than fact. But that art form—child-friendly stories with well-distilled values—is an honorable one, because the characters, lessons, and settings of kids' stories always reverberate well into adulthood.

Why is Yellowstone famous? Why is its name recognized by millions who have never even visited? Why does it seem to strike chords more widely than similar places such as Glacier or Grand Canyon? Because Yellowstone gains a step on most other places through these childhood resonances. Yellowstone, more than any other place in the country except those created by Disney, benefits from being the specific setting of a wildly popular tale for children. People around the world are predisposed to love Yellowstone because some of their earliest memories identify it as Jellystone, the home of Yogi Bear.

When Michael Keys was seven and eight years old, he spent most of his Saturday mornings sitting in his grandfather's lap in front of the television. It was the late 1970s, and his grandparents lived in a tri-level California home with a TV room down a few stairs from the front door. Grandpa had the latest, nicest, largest television available, along with a primitive video camera and one of the first VHS recorders ever marketed. Grandma would make toast and cereal and bring it in to the boys. "Grandpa and I just sat there, with me on his lap, for four hours. It was a kid's idea of heaven."[1]

They were, of course, watching cartoons. "We loved both Hanna-Barbera and Looney Tunes," Mike says. "His favorite was Road Runner and Wile E. Coyote, but my favorite was Yogi Bear."

Yogi was devious but jovial. A fun-loving bear, he wanted to be himself. His diminutive companion, Boo Boo, kept pointing out the rules. But Yogi thought rules were silly. Much better, he thought, to connive and scheme your way into stealing the tourists' "pic-a-nic baskets."

Mike responded to Yogi's character rather than to the quality of the animation. This resulted from conscious choices on the part of William Hanna (an outdoor-lover with a gift for timing and story), Joseph Barbera (a New York native with a talent for art and gags), and their employees. In their previous jobs at MGM, Hanna and Barbera produced the *Tom and Jerry* series, which, like Looney Tunes, was intended for movie theaters. Creating a new company, they produced a lot of original television programming. The small screen had an insatiable appetite for cartoons but tiny budgets. A typical ten-minute TV short might have only twelve hundred drawings rather than twenty-six thousand. That's why many Hanna-Barbera characters wore collars, often with neckties: because adding a neckline to a dog or a caveman allowed animators to move only the mouth when a character talked. Everything else, including the body, was a template.

Hanna and Barbera clearly also used cultural templates to develop their stories. In creating a bear hero, they modeled the name on Lawrence "Yogi" Berra, the baseball catcher and quotable sage. They modeled the voice ("Hey, Boo Boo!") on Art Carney's character Ed Norton on *The Honeymooners*. And they modeled the setting, Jellystone Park, on a famous place where people see bears.

When Yogi was first introduced in 1958, he, like Bugs Bunny, could live anywhere the story required. In the first episode to be aired, he was trying to escape from Jellystone, but the next four put him in varied settings: hibernating in a generic cave, outside a pie-baking home, quarreling with a bull on a farm, in the middle of a British-style foxhunt. In the 1959–60 season, Warren Foster was hired to write the stories, and gave Yogi a permanent base and a permanent adversary.[2]

Young Mike Keys was particularly fascinated by Yogi's relationship with Ranger Smith. "The ranger would always bust him, but then turn out to be his friend," Mike says. "I had trouble understanding that." In retrospect, Mike sees the relationship as modeled on that of a responsibility-burdened parent and a smarter-than-the-average-bear teenager. But at the time, as an oldest child, Mike hadn't witnessed anything like it. Indeed his deeply religious stepfather was quite strict—didn't even like cartoons—hence the role of Grandpa.

Ranger Smith and Yogi Bear enacted the kind of father-and-son dynamics that Mike wanted to experience in his California subdivision. As Ranger Smith attempted to both control and love his incorrigible teenager, Mike was thrilled: "That's how I thought the world should work: you try to get away with stuff, and people are nice when you're caught. But it sure wasn't the way my world worked," he says.

"As a kid, I was one of those who would always ask, 'Why?' So I was fascinated by characters like Yogi and Bugs Bunny, who would question authority or try to game the system," Mike says. He looks back on those mornings spent with Grandpa as islands of sanity, as guideposts to his future self. He would grow up to be a skeptic, whose impulse to question authority is deeply rooted in his personality. He suspects that he probably would have turned out this way anyway, but Yogi Bear was an early role model.

Yet the great thing about cartoons is how flexible they can be as role models, how you can see in them whichever values are important to you. For example, although young Mike's struggles with fathers and rules caused him to see Yogi as a teenager, others see the tie-and-hat-wearing bear as a bumbling blowhard father to Boo Boo. Some, with tongue presumably in cheek, have even claimed that the two pants-less bears sleeping together are gay lovers.[3]

When Mike was nine, his family moved to Oregon. It was the end of regular Saturdays with Grandpa, of cartoon role models, and of Mike's dreams for an idealized father-son dynamic.

The first time many Americans heard any kind of sound emanate from a bear, the sound was "I have had it, Boo Boo. I'm going to bust out of here." In "Yogi Bear's Big Break," the series's debut episode, a narrator explains that this "rugged individualist" is bored by the need to perform for Jellystone's tourists. Yogi says, "Every day, it's the same old thing. 'Lookit the bears, lookit the bears, lookit the bears!' Sheesh!"[4]

Yogi tries to elude the ranger and climb over Jellystone's mortared stone fence, but when he discovers that it's hunting season outside the park, he immediately races back to its cozy confines. The plot thus resembles a small child's first attempts to run away from home—but its portrayal of its cartoon hero is surprisingly bear-like. Mickey and Daffy aren't very mouse- or duck-like, respectively, but Yogi's antics in this episode capture the odd relationships among Yellowstone's wild bears, its parade of tourists, and the rangers responsible for all of them.

By the time Yogi Bear first debuted in 1958, feeding bears had long been officially illegal. After all, it is clearly unsafe. The National Park Service, as professionalized by Horace Albright, had to discourage feeding or else face liability for some incident where a bear drew blood from a taunting tourist. But Albright in particular knew how much people loved to feed bears. Indeed Albright himself loved to feed bears. So the law was rarely enforced.

A brief history of Yellowstone bear-feeding in some ways encapsulates the history of post–Industrial Revolution human relationships to wildlife. For example, in the exoticism-obsessed 1890s, bears were like sideshow freaks to be exhibited for tourists' fascination. One park concessionaire ran a zoo on an island in the middle of Yellowstone Lake featuring emaciated elk, bison, and bighorn sheep housed in filthy corrals. One year the zookeeper also petitioned to display, as part of his menagerie, an assemblage of Crow Indians. Luckily he didn't follow through, but the request indicated the imperialist attitude the zookeeper felt toward animals and even people that he and many of his contemporaries found inferior, though compelling. Wild animals were simply artifacts of a strange and rapidly disappearing lifestyle. Tourists in Yellowstone wanted to see them displayed, and between displays they should be warehoused as cheaply as possible. Although many complaints were registered about those conditions, the notion of captivity itself was rarely seen as a problem.[5]

By the 1920s, due in part to the animal portrayals of writers such as Ernest Thompson Seton, sympathies for the animals increased. The island zoo was long closed, and a new zoo at Mammoth Hot Springs treated its inhabitants more like pets. Juno and Pard, sibling black bears, had been born in captivity and sent to Yellowstone to be liberated. But "they did not want to be wild bears again. They were just like dogs," Albright wrote.[6] They were set free each winter, but were returned each summer to an enclosure where tourists could get close-up views of animals that represented nature's grandeur. In this era, the animals were the focus—not their setting. Even Yellowstone's head naturalist at the time kept a black bear cub in his home. In newsletters he discussed how it listened to opera, sucked a pacifier, and talked on the telephone. Like Yogi, the cub was portrayed as an endearing mix of human and bear characteristics.

People wanted to *see* bears, and even better to *interact* with bears. One of the era's biggest celebrities was a bear named Jesse James, who would step into the path of an oncoming car and rear up on his hind legs to stage a holdup for treats. Jesse James was never confined; he was free to travel where he wanted and eat what he chose. But he often chose candy—to the delight of humans. "Bears are no longer wild animals to us," Albright wrote in a book that then went on to offer instructions on the "right way" to feed a bear.[7]

President Warren Harding followed those instructions (don't tease the bears, don't feed directly from your hand) when in 1923 he fed a bowl of molasses to a bear named Max. Albright called what Max was doing a "performance," as if he were in a stage show or circus or cartoon. In truth that was how many Americans of the time experienced wildlife—as theater. And in retrospect, it's surprising how well the bears understood the theater's rules, how compliant and tame they were. By rarely attacking, and almost never fatally, they helped people's attitudes toward wildlife evolve: from freaks, to circus performers, to performers with more realistic backdrops such as a national park, and eventually to creatures whose natural setting was their defining characteristic.

But that evolution came unevenly. By the 1960s it permeated the educated classes and those who saw nature in spiritual terms. When those people found dignity in the bears' separation from human ways, they were discovering new territory: the idea of *wildness*. To feed candy to a bear was degrading because it took away the wildness that made the bear special. But affection for an idea, such as wildness, was learned behavior. The contrary, instinctive behavior was to feel affection for the animal right in front of you, and to express that affection by treating that animal as a pet. Yellowstone in 1958 was caught between these two behaviors. And Yogi Bear, the lovable but troublesome character who didn't like performing for tourists but loved eating their sweets, captured the essence of that contradiction.

The contradiction could stress Yellowstone's managers, but it juiced the park's appeal. Yellowstone was known nationwide as "the park with the bears." Feeding bears was a family tradition, something that many parents thought their children should experience, like a trip to Disneyland. In Yellowstone, the whole family could see extraordinary wildlife without getting out of the car. And at Yellowstone, to a far greater extent than any other place, they could interact with that wildlife and feel good about it. The idea that bears might be half tame (as discussed in chapter 2) meant that a black bear standing on her hind legs beside your car demonstrated your inherent goodness. *We* created this sanctuary for bears, *we* feed them these highly engineered modern foodstuffs, and *they* express their gratitude by repressing their instincts toward uncivilized, uncontrollable behavior. Their docile cuteness is our reward.

Other national parks didn't have this crowd-pleasing feature. Grand Canyon and Zion were geology parks, lacking much charismatic wildlife. Yosemite, Mount Rainier, and Rocky Mountain were too close to population centers to support animals on the scale of Yellowstone. And although Glacier had some bears, they weren't as well trained in roadside behavior. In Yellowstone, bears were numerous and well behaved.

On TV too: Even as Yogi Bear regularly outsmarted tourists, he did so in a nonthreatening way. He took their food, often against their will, but never harmed them. Furthermore, his public reputation could merge with that of other famous fictional bears: gentle and cuddly like Teddy, gentle and addicted to sweets like Winnie-the-Pooh, or gentle and benevolently public-spirited like Smokey.[8]

Yet behind the scenes, administrators were troubled. Bears *did* injure people. Despite what Albright had said, injuries could not always be blamed on feeding bears the wrong way. Was it dozens of people per year? Hundreds? The answer wasn't clear, in part because of low priorities placed on data collection. And here Yogi not only captured but also accentuated the cultural split. He made Yellowstone uniquely popular, but he also encouraged dangerous behavior. How should the park respond? One attempt was a humorous 1960 poster in which Yogi told tourists that Yellowstone's bears were potentially dangerous. But the conflicted message wasn't terribly effective. It suffered from another dichotomy of the Park Service mission: to educate the public or to please the public. The difficulty of that balancing act was exhibited in a response to a letter from a little boy to "Yogi Bear, The Cave, Jellystone National Park," which was delivered to headquarters at Mammoth: "Yogi" wrote back that rangers had been doing a good job of warning visitors about him, so he hadn't eaten many goodies recently.[9] To the extent that the boy must have been pleased to hear from Yogi, he probably didn't grasp the intended message that feeding bears was bad.

In short, the Park Service tried to co-opt Yogi but failed. This should not be surprising: the bureaucracy's job was to make and enforce rules, yet Yogi's personality was centered on skepticism about rules. Indeed, as latter-day interpreters look at Yogi, they tend to center less on pic-a-nic baskets and more on rules. For example, John Kricfalusi, the creator of the innovatively raunchy adult cartoon *Ren & Stimpy*, directed two Yogi Bear cartoons in 1999. Discussing a planned third one, he wrote, "Ranger Smith was always Man butting his nose into the wilderness and making its legitimate occupants obey unnatural laws. This basic conflict made the whole concept of the Yogi Bear show funny to me and your average Joes because we can all identify with the situation."[10] Kricfalusi, an incredibly talented animator, morphed Yogi and Boo Boo into characters closer to Ren and Stimpy. But that's the way cultural icons develop: they get reinterpreted in the face of changing cultural values.

And so what's particularly fascinating about Yogi Bear is that Yellowstone could boast such a cultural icon. No other national park is home to such a pop figure.[11] Yogi became yet another reason to visit Yellowstone. In addition to its natural wonders, patriotic associations, and architectural resources, it had a feature loved by children of all ages.

Even today, as the Park Service has taken a firm stand against roadside bear feeding, you can still see bears in Yellowstone, often from the safety and comfort of your own vehicle. You won't necessarily formally reenact a Yogi cartoon, but there's a deep and magnificent urge to say, "Lookit the bears, lookit the bears, lookit the bears!" If the bears are frustrated by this attitude, luckily there are no mortared fences locking them in.

Doug Haag was driving down a highway near Manitowoc, Wisconsin, in 1968. It was summertime and the vehicles around him were packed with families on vacation. Many of them were pulling camp trailers. As Doug looked at them, he was struck by a thought: these campers often ended up at a no-frills campground, little better than a parking spot alongside a busy highway. What if they had a nearby campground that could be its own destination, with opportunities to swim, play, and enjoy nature?[12]

It was not an entirely new thought. As a child, Doug spent summers in Door County, the forest-laden, beach-strewn peninsula that divides Green Bay from Lake Michigan. He so loved that outdoor life that he long figured he would go into the campground business someday. What was new for Doug now, in his late twenties, was the notion of the destination, plus his experience as an advertising executive. His clients included a shipbuilder and a toy company. He designed packaging for the world's largest manufacturer of that atomic-age wonder, the aluminum Christmas tree—complete with a base that rotated the tree while a color wheel spotlighted its branches.[13] But he still dreamed of campgrounds, and on this day he saw a way to make one thrive.

Doug and a friend purchased thirty acres in Door County. They secured financing to develop facilities: campfire rings and water and sewer hookups; a playground; a heated swimming pool; tennis courts and other sports facilities; a general store; billiard and ping-pong tables; and eighteen holes of mini-golf. And they also worked on a marketing plan.

Doug envisioned a nationwide chain of destinations. With all the amenities and family-friendly activities, his plans resembled a sort of Disneyland for the Midwestern camping market. Since 1955, Disneyland had been transforming the amusement park by tying it to characters from popular entertainment. In effect it turned those characters into *ideas*, which it then applied to rides and other amusements. Doug wanted to spur a similar transformation for campgrounds, and thus he too needed a popular character.

Doug recalled brainstorming potential ideas. "Paul Bunyan, Lewis and Clark, Hiawatha, Pocahontas, Robin Hood, sports stars, and historical figures. We went through them all, but nothing seemed to fit."[14] Then, on a cold, snowy January Saturday in 1969, he overheard a television set in another room playing cartoons for his three young children. "Hey Boo Boo, the campers are coming! Let's get the pic-a-nic baskets!"[15]

Doug made an appointment in New York with Screen Gems, the syndicator that owned the rights to Yogi Bear. "When I walked in there, my knees were shaking," Haag recalled. He had some hand-drawn sketches, a proposal to give Screen Gems 6 percent of his gross sales, and a lot of enthusiasm. But he was facing three stone-faced lawyers. One of the lawyers quickly questioned the idea's viability, noting that a recent Flintstones-themed campground had flopped. "The Flintstones don't belong in a campground," Doug replied. "Yogi belongs in a campground!"[16]

And so it was that "Jellystone Park" moved from a writer's satiric gag to an idea that fueled a full-fledged economic engine. Yogi and Boo Boo stepped out of their TV sets to give children interactive entertainment at a family-themed resort. Doug's goal was to create lasting positive memories, and bring families back year after year. The resorts went increasingly upscale, offering cabins, an outdoor theater, and waterparks that included a fountain called the "Old Faceful Geyser." Over the next six years Doug sold eighty-five franchises before burning out on all the travel and selling the company.

According to the company history, Doug's innovation was monumental: the invention of *destination camping*. Yet in a broader social history, we have to think of it as a *re*invention, because an earlier iteration of destination campgrounds was the national parks themselves. For almost one hundred years before Doug came along, parks such as Yellowstone offered family-friendly camping in a gorgeous setting with plenty of activities.

The trouble was, Yellowstone was remote. And by the late 1960s, it was increasingly difficult for middle-class Americans to get enough vacation time to drive all the way out to Wyoming. (Indeed, the desire to drive your own vehicle, rather than taking a train that could travel all night, increased the time required to get there.) Yellowstone was still incredibly popular—visitation surged year after year—but the population explosion of the baby boom meant that there was also plenty of demand for imitation-Yellowstones conveniently distributed throughout the country.

Of course they weren't exactly imitation-Yellowstones. They were imitation-Jellystones. They didn't highlight geology, frontier spirit, or patriotic history. Their goal was to entertain kids, in part through live appearances of characters seen on TV.

Jellystone reflected changing times. The franchise depended not only on the invention of television but also the invention of the *idea economy*, which fueled America's explosive economic growth in the second half of the 20th century. Fewer Americans worked with their hands, at farms or factories; more people worked in offices, manipulating ideas. Ideas were far more transferable. You could create value by applying an idea, such as Yogi Bear, to a traditional activity, such as camping. You could take the idea of Yellowstone and manipulate its famous characteristics into a similar (but privately trademarked) idea, Jellystone. And you could take an idea such as Jellystone and repackage it to be implemented in locations far from the original national park. Ideas were wonderfully manipulable, and transcended the distance constraints of real physical places. Best of all, they offered far greater economic rewards.

Of course, as physical places go, Yellowstone has long been tied to ideas as well as a specific landscape. The ideas were what made the place more memorable than the average lake, mountain, or canyon: scientific ideas behind the geysers, cultural ideas behind the architecture, and patriotic ideas behind the Campfire Myth. Indeed any attraction in Yellowstone was necessarily associated with the idea of a *national park*; by contrast, for example, the Devil's Slide, located five miles north of the park's boundary, never developed into the popular attraction that explorer Nathaniel Langford foresaw in 1870, perhaps because it lacked the backing of that idea.[17]

The ideas behind Yellowstone's landscapes were changing with the times. For example, as environmentalists including Ansel Adams associated *wilderness* with solitude rather than frontier adventure or scenic beauty, the idea of wilderness became a poorer fit with Yellowstone. Although the park contained plenty of solitude-enhancing backcountry landscapes, it was primarily known for its car-friendly, sometimes-crowded frontcountry. Thus through the 1950s and '60s environmental elites less frequently associated their ruling philosophies with Yellowstone, or with any national park.

For this audience, Yellowstone was an ironic victim of its own success, encapsulating the quote popularized by Yogi Berra: "Nobody goes there anymore, it's too crowded."[18] The Park Service understood the problem, and in an effort to manage the crowds in ways that would preserve the resource, it adapted itself to the new ideas sweeping postwar America. It went suburban.

After the success of Robert Reamer's hotel at Old Faithful and overhaul at Lake, Harry Child unleashed him on a third pillar of Yellowstone lodging: in 1911, the architect designed an overhaul of the hotel at Canyon. The result was another unique building with a special relationship to its surrounding environment. Perched on the edge of the canyon, the hotel's grand lobby allowed views of the sublime while nevertheless encasing the visitor in elegant refinement.

But by the 1950s the cultural context had changed. Yellowstone was about middle-class tourism rather than upper-class refinement; it was about appreciating wild places for themselves rather than as augmented by architecture. So the hotel was torn down, replaced by motel-style accommodations in an uninspiring location about a mile away. Canyon Village was the place where humans lived; the canyon rim would become more like untrammeled wilderness.

The change, part of the Park Service–wide infrastructure upgrade called Mission 66, was poorly received. The village was an uninspiring place to stay and required a car trip to the rim, where the collection of parking lots hardly felt untrammeled. The suburbs, it turns out, were what many people came to Yellowstone to escape. But as a way of manipulating the *ideas* behind Yellowstone in the face of changing popular tastes, the demolition of the Canyon Hotel wasn't much different from replacing a collection of huts with the Old Faithful Inn or creating a franchise of Jellystones scattered across the country. The big difference, really, was that Harry Child and Doug Haag gambled correctly—whereas the architects of Mission 66 gambled wrong—on which new ideas the public would love.

Like Mike Keys, Joyce Collamati loved Yogi Bear when she was seven to ten years old. She grew up in Bellingham, Massachusetts, in the late '60s and early '70s, and after school on weekday afternoons, she would do her homework while her mother cooked dinner. At least, she was supposed to be doing her homework. She was also trying to get in as much cartoon-watching as possible. "I remember *Dark Shadows* was on earlier in the afternoon, right after school. Then there was *Batman*, *Yogi Bear*, and *The Flintstones*, which was after my dad came home from work. We would watch it together."[19]

Joyce identified more with Boo Boo than Yogi. "I was the youngest. My sisters were seven and twelve years older than me. So I was the one who was always trying to get everyone together and keep them out of trouble. Following the rules is a key part of who I am, even today. Whenever I'm in a new situation, I first try to figure out: what are the rules?" Boo Boo knew the rules. Even today, in conversations with certain friends, Joyce often uses Boo Boo's tagline: "He's not going to like it!"

And like Mike, Joyce's memories of Yogi and Boo Boo are tied to memories of her life at that age. "It was a great time in my life when I was innocent and pure of mind," she says. She remembers a family trip in that era to Montreal, and nowadays a mention of Montreal triggers nostalgia. Joyce would love to go back to Montreal because it would feel like revisiting her eight-year-old self. Even though she's never been to Yellowstone, it triggers that same nostalgia.

Such attitudes could become self-fulfilling: if you *wanted to* experience nostalgia, you usually did. Thus many baby boomers entering Yellowstone felt a deep connection with their childhood, with the joy of unspoiled naïveté. It helped, of course, that Yellowstone changed little over the years, and that it was managed for a sort of pristine innocence. For managers, the point was to maintain the natural conditions that existed before Anglos arrived. But for many tourists, the nostalgia didn't have to go back that far.

They just needed Yellowstone to resemble the image they had of it as children.

Thus the primary genius of Yogi Bear was the way he captured timeless childhood desires. And so the fact that Yogi's creators hadn't been to Yellowstone wasn't a problem. They hadn't met Yogi Berra either and weren't constrained by facts. After all, they were creating a talking bear who stands on his hind legs and wears a hat and tie, so it missed the point to complain that Yogi's rhyme-speak lacked Berra's zen koans, or that his parklike setting lacked Yellowstone's expanse, geology, architecture, and unfenced borders.

The point was what Yogi did for Yellowstone: he secured it for the masses, even in an era when its appeal to the elites was waning. A national park was by definition a delicate balance between use and preservation, entertainment and education, relaxation and personal growth. The choice in 1872 to call Yellowstone a *park* rather than a *reserve* or *preserve* reflected a desire to create a space intended for all classes of people. It was not reserved for the benefit of wildlife, nor for a subset of the elite to appreciate preserved conditions. It would be more like a city park, full of activities to let working people let off steam. But a century of challenges to that balance swayed Yellowstone toward upper-class pursuits. First hunting was banned in favor of wildlife-watching. Then luxury hotels appealed to dudes who wanted to reenact the frontier. Steve Mather extolled the virtues of backcountry horsepacking trips while discouraging such plebian facilities as swimming pools, movie theaters, and mini-golf courses. Hermon Carey Bumpus enhanced the quality of the museum-like learning you could gain (. . . but what if you wanted just recreation?), and Ansel Adams helped people see how silent contemplation could lead to spiritual bliss (. . . but what if you wanted noisy fun?). Meanwhile, the midcentury innovations that improved lower- and middle-class life—from inexpensive fast-food franchises to televisions in motel rooms—were excluded.

The idea of traveling to a national park was increasingly coming to resemble the idea of giving your kids a college education: loved by all, widely seen as representing the best aspirations of America, without necessarily being something that every American would find rewarding, fun, or even possible.

And Yogi thwarted that trend. He made Yellowstone a park again. He told the world that it was a place full of activities that kids would enjoy. "For me, and every kid I knew, Yellowstone was an awesome, giant park. It was full of picnicking, woods, and bears, way up north where nobody lived," Mike Keys says. Indeed in the 2010 movie *Yogi Bear*, Jellystone's main attraction is a lake where people go swimming and waterskiing—city-park-type recreations, in contrast to the churchlike reverence favored by Ansel Adams.[20]

Yogi also helped people of all ages get back in touch with their childlike connection to all of God's creatures. A toddler who encounters an earthworm and a person may be equally fascinated by both. Thus in children's books and cartoons, animals can talk, having grown into verbalization the same way the kids did. As we age, we tend to limit our connections to domesticated animals, such as dogs and cats, because practicality requires control. But when we see kids engaging with Yogi on TV, we're inspired to try to reconnect with the truly wild, even at the risk of a ruined pic-a-nic.

Joyce and Mike each watched the show in reruns, a fact that would not have meant anything to them as kids, if they'd even noticed. But for kids on opposite sides of the country to be watching the same cartoons highlights another cultural development of the 1950s and early '60s: the rise of American monoculture. Television spread to nearly every household, broadcasting only three networks. Franchises such as McDonald's and Holiday Inn blanketed the nation's geography, while nationwide brands such as Wonder Bread and Twinkies gave the vast middle class a unified set of tastes. Air and highway networks reduced travel difficulties, and large corporations regularly transferred employees across the country. Regional differences faded.

In this atmosphere, Yellowstone could be a single national park for everybody. It was important for (white, middle-class) Americans of the time to feel commonality, to all share the same experiences. Yet such spectacular but one-dimensional places as the Grand Canyon, Glacier, or Gettysburg might not appeal to people who weren't into geology, mountain climbing, or Civil War history. Like a TV network, Yellowstone offered enough varied programming that almost everybody could find something valuable: wildlife, geysers, canyons, or forests. It had campgrounds, motels, and historic inns; indigenous, frontier, and patriotic history; drives, hikes, and fireside lectures. Different types of people could experience the same park, even if they did so in different ways.

Joyce Collamati has yet to experience Yellowstone in person. But for the past ten years she's been living in the Seattle area, pursuing a satisfying business career. She and her husband have visited some of the other national parks of the West, and as a group these have struck her as wonderful, elite natural places. Merely talking about Yogi Bear makes her eager to add to the list.

After high school, Mike Keys became a rock-climbing bum. He spent a fair bit of time in California's Yosemite, then bounced around a bit. In 1999 he moved to a small town outside of Yellowstone and really found himself. He loved being on the outskirts of the awesome, giant park. He loved the community of artists, skeptics, and freethinkers. He no longer watches much television. On Saturday mornings—actually, almost every morning—he and his wife sit in their outdoor hot tub and watch for wild animals to come down the hillside behind their house.

It's really quite extraordinary that a single place could have sufficiently captured and expressed so much diversity of American culture—much less continue to do so throughout the decades. Yellowstone was the ultimate national park for the baby boomers and post-boomers, just as it had been for previous generations, even though American culture experienced a century of change. Yellowstone could fill that role because it was big enough, and its landscapes diverse enough, to contain a wide range of ideas about America.

But there was a sense—especially for those who saw the park through Yogi's eyes—that the park was unchanging, unchangeable. Even if ideas evolved, the physical location would remain static. Outside Yellowstone's borders, cities might grow, economies might change, people might age. Inside its borders, the park would always be the sort of place where you could show your grandkids the same scenes that your grandparents had shown you. When change did come to Yellowstone, altering those scenes, it became a very big deal.

10
THREATENED

I n the summer of 1988, wildfires in Yellowstone dominated national headlines and TV news. Footage was compelling, and emotions strong. For much of the nation, it was a dramatic glimpse at a faraway place that many people cared about even if they had never been there. But what did it mean?

In the moment, the fires felt like a watershed. For people who lived even a thousand miles away, the freakish weather and smoky haze locked the summer in time like the Kennedy assassination or the 9/11 attacks. But in those other watershed events, a cultural meaning soon emerged: a loss of innocence, an ushering in of a new age. The previous massive wildfire in recorded Western history—the Big Blowup of 1910, which raged across eastern Washington, the Idaho panhandle, and western Montana—permanently shaped the character of the U.S. Forest Service, as historian Stephen Pyne wrote in *The Northern Rockies: A Fire Survey*. But Pyne wrote that memories of 1988 "left the interpretation of the [Yellowstone] fires—so vast they just had to mean something—unresolved."[1]

I first visited Yellowstone in the spring of 1988 but spent the next two years back east. When I returned to greater Yellowstone in 1990, I expected to learn the story behind the headlines in a way that I couldn't have grasped from a distance. But I didn't. People could share memories, often tied to still-raw emotions. And scientists could outline theories, which seemed distant from personal experience. All still struggled to fit the fires into a narrative that explained the place.

In these struggles, the fires were continually seen as an event happening in nature. They burned natural features—trees. But if Yellowstone's meaning isn't just nature, then the fires were also a cultural event that threatened a set of collective values. All of the traits that American culture had imbued upon Yellowstone—a place that people of 1988 saw as special, rugged, spiritual, blessed, and uniquely American—seemed imperiled.

This chapter quickly recaps the major events of the summer of fire, then tells more-detailed stories.[2] Unlike previous stories in this book, which showed Yellowstone gaining layers of meaning, the stories in this chapter show those layers under threat of being stripped off, burned away. These stories show that the 1988 fires were not only full of dramatic moments—they were an existential threat to what America saw in Yellowstone, and thus to the America that vision reflected.

After a wet April and May, thunderstorms in June of 1988 ignited wildfires across greater Yellowstone, as they do every year.

Consistent with a policy that had succeeded for fifteen years, the Park Service did not actively suppress remote lightning-caused wildfires that weren't endangering structures or people. And many of those fires indeed went out by themselves. But soon unusually hot, dry weather with incredible winds created dangerous conditions. Several fires burned uncontrollably, as ignitions continued both inside the park and across its wider ecosystem. Each fire was given its own name—the Shoshone, the North Fork, the Storm Creek, etc.—although fires also often merged, as when the Clover and Mist fires became the Clover-Mist.

On July 23, the Shoshone fire approached Yellowstone's Grant Village complex, prompting its evacuation and national media attention. Firefighters saved all buildings except for a campground restroom. By August 5, crisis apparently averted, Tom Brokaw announced on NBC *Nightly News*, "The danger from fires in Yellowstone National Park is over."[3] But in the backcountry, fires continued to ignite, blaze, merge together, and stymie suppression efforts. Containment lines failed. Fires jumped roads, rivers, and even the Grand Canyon of the Yellowstone. Rain never arrived. Experts' predictions of fire behavior proved laughably inadequate. On August 20, "Black Saturday," fires raged across more than 150,000 acres in a single day. Reporters returned, now sniffing for scandal. Was Yellowstone ruined? Who was responsible? Tensions resulted, especially on September 7, the day that the North Fork fire nearly burned down the Old Faithful Inn.

In mid-September the weather cooled. Snows put out the fires. The overall toll was amazingly light: two firefighters were killed in accidents outside the park, but none of the nine-thousand-plus deployed inside its boundaries. Surprisingly few animals died. Although the fires' perimeters included about 794,000 acres within the park—about 36 percent of its total area, less than initial estimates—most buildings were saved, including all of the architecturally important ones. The fires burned as much greater Yellowstone ecosystem acreage outside the park as within, including some private properties. But in the big picture, the "damage" was mostly burned trees. Compared to the expected potential—such as human casualties, wiping out animal populations, or the destruction of buildings or other economically valuable resources—the impact was far less than it might have been. However, that result was not foreordained, and the path to get there involved a great deal of drama.

From the helicopter, Dan Sholly watched a pine tree explode. He couldn't believe it. At one moment, it was a hundred-foot-tall tree near the upper Lamar River in the Yellowstone wilderness, forty miles east of Mammoth. Then *boom!* it was a swirling torch. In the dense forest, trees exploded one after another. Smoke rolled ahead of the inferno and rose twenty thousand feet into the sky. Just this morning—July 14, 1988—the three-day-old Clover fire had been lazily smoldering through about three hundred acres. Now it was at forty-seven hundred acres and hungry for more.[4]

"Dan! Straight ahead," the chopper pilot said, according to Dan's memoir. The pilot was pointing eastward, at an old cabin used by rangers on patrol. From the front fingers of the fire, the Calfee Creek cabin was less than a mile of ragged old forest away—it would burn in an hour or two.

The chopper circled around to take another look. "Do you think you could land a crew down there?" Dan asked. His mind was already racing: he intended to save the cabin.

Chief ranger Dan Sholly was a man of action. He wore a glass eye, after an injury in Vietnam, and rumor said the glass was etched with a Marine Corps insignia. With his one-eyed squint, cleft chin, and prizefighter build, he looked more like a horseman than a desk jockey. And he was comfortable on horseback, but almost more so in the helicopter that coworkers dubbed "Sholly's trolley." They also called him "Danbo," in reference to the movie hero Rambo.[5] But where Rambo was mostly a vigilante, Dan was dedicated to the National Park Service. His father had been chief ranger at Big Bend National Park. Dan himself rose quickly through the ranks to become chief of the nationwide ranger division. Then he gave up that Washington-based desk job to take this lower-paying job in Yellowstone, a park he'd fallen in love with while fixing trails as a teenager.

Dan's military background was appropriate to the duties of a 1980s Park Service ranger, which could be as humdrum and order-oriented as that of a policeman: controlling crowds and traffic around a bison or bear sighting, or issuing tickets for speeding or vandalism. But Dan's family Park Service background was especially valuable because he understood the point of all this enforcement: the natural wonders. Rangers' ability to balance the two had grown into a mythic image, one that the Park Service carefully stewarded. A park ranger was as rugged and honorable as a cowboy, as disciplined and devoted as a soldier, as knowledgeable and benevolent as a tour guide, and as fearless and cool in a crisis as the historic Texas Rangers they were named after. Following the political controversies of the 1960s and '70s, which tarnished the images of many so-called experts, park rangers were in some ways the last American heroes. Dan embodied all those traits, including an ability to make quick, self-confident decisions—ones that his critics argued bordered on recklessness.

To help save the Calfee Creek cabin, Dan had the chopper pick up a nearby three-person trail crew. But not all of the crew members had the right gear for fighting fires. This morning they'd been sent out to clear trails and prepare a patrol cabin for the upcoming backcountry vacation of Vice President George H. W. Bush. Jane Lopez, one of the crew members, twice told Dan that neither she nor Kristen Cowen had their fire shelters, the heat-resistant pup tents that firefighters could deploy as a last-ditch effort to save themselves from oncoming flames. Dan heard her and understood the gravity of asking a firefighter to work without the right safety equipment, but he decided that he couldn't wait for the equipment to arrive from Mammoth. He would soldier on. He told the pilot to let them out in a meadow a hundred yards north of the cabin.

But as the chopper tried to land, it suddenly rocked and pitched. Dan heard a sickening howl outside its frame. "Windstorm!" the pilot said. Forest fires often create their own crazy weather patterns, including unpredictable winds. And these winds were making the chopper, now full of people, too heavy to control. They backed off.

"What if we drop off one of the crew?" Dan asked. Jane was nominated. They flew to a ridge a few miles away; she disembarked and went to get her pack, which was tied beneath others outside the chopper.

"Leave it! There's no time!" Dan yelled, waving her away. The helicopter rose into the smoky sky.

Jane, now alone and vulnerable, had no fire shelter or any drinking water. She did have a radio, and one of her first calls was to the pilot of a plane coming to drop fire retardant. She wanted to make sure he didn't drop it on her.

By the time the chopper got back to the cabin, conditions were too smoky and windy to even attempt landing in the meadow. Instead they landed on a gravel bar in the river. Dan, Kristen, and John Dunfee quickly unloaded their equipment and hustled to the cabin. With the smoke, heat, and tension, for a moment Dan thought he was back in Vietnam.

The Calfee Creek cabin was classic 1920s parkitecture: large brown-stained logs, cut rough and laid in long overlaps with heavy chink. Even though most of the public never saw it, because it was almost ten miles from the nearest road and restricted to employee use only, it represented the essence of Yellowstone: historic, attractive, and informal; merging the man-made and the natural in a way that felt both beautiful and appropriate.

But like many of Yellowstone's buildings in 1988, it hadn't been fireproofed. Fireproofing is important because a forest fire seldom burns everything in its path. It burns whatever is easiest, whatever is driest, whatever is flammable enough to nurture shooting sparks, before moving on. A fire often leaves a patchwork, with some trees or even entire groves untouched. If a building doesn't provide the fire with opportunities to burn, it might survive while the fire passes around it. Thus the cabin's metal roof was invaluable to protect against falling sparks. But trees grew right up to its edge; firewood was stacked against its walls. The crew's first task was to toss that firewood as far away as possible. They chopped off tree branches that hung too close. They dug a scratchline, like a dry moat emptied of grasses or duff, to deter ground flames. And where sticks and pine needles were piled around nearby trees, Dan ignited a handheld flare to burn them off safely before the dangerous flames arrived.

The chopper waited on the gravel bar. The air was so smoky that the pilot could hardly see. But he could hear the sound of exploding trees continually growing closer. Finally trees started shaking around him as the fire crossed the river. He radioed Dan that he needed to leave. Didn't they want to come with him?

"Negative," Dan replied. If they left now, Dan figured, smoke would prevent them from returning for hours. They would lose the cabin. "Get out while you can. We'll be fine."[6]

After the chopper was gone, a gust of wind blew some embers into tall pines near the cabin's horse corral. Orange, yellow, and red: the crowns of the trees became a huge fireball. Flaming branches fell to the ground. Between the cabin and the river, all the trees were torching. The scene on the other side of the river, as Dan described it in his memoir, "was a seething black wall coming at us like an immense tornado." It was time for crew members to stop working and protect themselves.

Following plans, they hurried to the meadow where the chopper had first tried to land. They had two fire shelters for the three of them; Kristen crawled into one with Dan. This was her first fire. They lay on their stomachs, holding down the sides of the shelter with boot tips and gloved hands. They listened to the fire's roar, interrupted by sharp cracks as the wind blew limbs off trees, and deeper pops as boulders shattered in the heat.

They knew that the shelters were designed to withstand heat up to 1400°F. But the shelters felt so fragile, a mere membrane of foil, that firefighters nicknamed them Shake-and-Bakes. From the outside, Dan imagined, they might look like body bags. From the inside, there was no choice but to lie still. Ash pelted the walls. The heat and smoke sucked away oxygen. But Dan dared not lift up the shelter's edge, because the meadow itself could be on fire.

They had radios, and Dan tried to convey that they were okay, but he doubted that anyone could hear him above the fire's noise. In a plane far above them, park superintendent Bob Barbee could see the conflagration, the biggest fire he ever witnessed. "I thought Sholly was going to die," he said later. "I thought I was going to have to do the eulogy."[7]

Inside the shelter, Dan claims, he was not at all frightened. He'd been fully trained. He'd fought other fires. Indeed, he himself had torched thousands of acres of prescribed burns. Even though he was basically a cop—a "pine pig," in Park Service lingo, as opposed to a "fern feeler" on the interpretive side—he'd been required to learn the science of fires. So he was a strong believer in the revolution that had taken place over the previous twenty years, a new understanding of fire ecology.

From Anglos' arrival in the western United States, their dominant culture saw forest fires as unequivocally bad. Fires could be dangerous. They consumed trees that could otherwise be used for lumber. And they were difficult, if not impossible, to control. The best policy was not let them start in the first place. During World War II, it was rumored that the Japanese intended to use incendiary bombs to start fires in the Northwest, thus decimating industry. Later, Smokey Bear educated the public about how easily a fire could start from human carelessness.

But as scientists studied *ecosystems*—the interdependent web of nature in which grizzly den sites near Triple-A Anderson's Palette Ranch could be linked to grizzly food sources, such as garbage dumps, nearly a hundred miles away—they realized that fire could play a role too. From an ecosystem point of view, fire didn't destroy anything, it simply rearranged molecules. It returned nutrients to the earth, where new trees and shrubs could take advantage of them and begin new cycles of life. In the rainy ecosystems that Anglos were most familiar with, Europe and the East Coast, this function was performed by rot. But in the arid West, a dead tree would be too dry to quickly rot. It needed fire to complete its life cycle and allow the forest as a whole to continue living.

Such science had huge cultural implications: it meant that fire wasn't evil. Lightning had been sparking wildfires since long before humans came on the scene; wilderness ecosystems coevolved with fires. If a national park sought to honor ecosystems and let them play out their natural rhythms as much as possible, maybe there needed to be a role for wildfire.

Trained in the new philosophy, Dan could see how the trees around the Calfee Creek cabin were overmature. He could see how nature needed them to burn. As ecologists were fond of saying, nature was a process, not a painting. The purpose of Yellowstone was not to preserve a set of views in perpetuity—that was impossible. The purpose of Yellowstone was to preserve the natural processes that sustained such views. Knowing this, Dan said, gave him the peace of mind to wait calmly while a firestorm raged over his shelter.[8]

It took about forty minutes for the fire to pass through the meadow. The Shake-and-Bakes did their job. Meanwhile, the chopper picked up Jane, and the entire incident involved no casualties. Most amazingly, Dan's crew accomplished his goal—saving the Calfee Creek cabin. Some of the noises Dan heard during the heat of the fire made him fear that it was burning. But here it stood, barely scorched. Even the elk antlers hanging above the front porch were still in place.

Around the cabin, however, the scene was more extreme than Dan had expected. Spot fires flickered; smoke hung in the air. His nose was nearly overpowered by the smell of burned wood and grass. And the once-green curtain of pine trees was now full of charred skeletons. Some still stood, but others had been tipped over by the winds, their root systems looking like "crumbling tombstones in an ancient burial ground," Dan wrote.[9]

Compared to previous fires he'd seen, this one was more sudden and thorough. Rather than burning calmly, it was aggressively attacking trees and other fuels. It was ferocious. Such behavior might be understandable in late August, at the end of a hot, dry summer. Or in an area known to be especially dry, like southern

California. But this was Yellowstone in mid-July. Fires weren't supposed to act this way now. And so Dan started wondering: Was there something that their science hadn't taken into account?

Indeed, although debate was hushed at the time, even some fire professionals were concerned about how Yellowstone had translated fire science into policies. Its fire management plans were pretty good on choosing which fires to fight immediately: the human-caused ones and those that threatened people or developed areas. However, any plan is truly tested only in a crisis, when more difficult questions arise and managers face the need to change course. In the places where the Yellowstone fire plan could have identified specific triggers that might cause specific actions, it instead offered vague platitudes reaffirming fire's ecological value. It left too many decisions up to a fire management committee—and it gave that committee too few specific criteria to use, amid stressful situations, in deciding when, where, and how Yellowstone might choose to start fighting more fires.[10]

As chair of the committee, Dan called a meeting for 9:30 that very night, as soon as the chopper could get him back to Mammoth. The committee's decision did not come for a couple of days, and was not unanimous when it came. But it did decide to start moving away from the policy. Given the dry conditions that could lead to dangerous fire behavior, it concluded, Yellowstone should no longer allow natural fires to start in remote areas. It should try to snuff out all new fire starts, regardless of where they were located or how they had been caused.

In retrospect, the decision was wise, because conditions were indeed extraordinary, the driest summer on record in Yellowstone. Indeed in retrospect, perhaps the committee members who wanted to start fighting *all* fires—the ones that were already going in addition to the new starts—should have carried the day. Their view did not prevail until a week later, when continued dry, hot weather and ferocious fire behavior doubled the acreage being burned. But in retrospect it might not have mattered, because most firefighting efforts proved ineffective anyway. The 1988 fires were too ferocious to tame. They'd been started mostly by a natural process, lightning, and they could be stopped only by another, moisture falling from the sky.

At the time, however, the human decisions about firefighting policy, and the fire ecology revolution behind them, created tremendous controversy. The general public was unfamiliar with this new science, and ecologists and the press did a poor job of explaining it. After Vietnam, Watergate, the Arab oil embargo, and the seemingly ineffectual Carter presidency, the public was also skeptical about the government's ability to achieve its goals. When Yellowstone officials proclaimed that the regimen of heavily monitored burns in remote areas—what became known, to ecologists' frustration, as the "let-burn" policy—was the best thing for Yellowstone, anyone who remembered the wishful thinking and deceit surrounding previous government proclamations was hard-pressed to believe them. How did they know what was best? Wasn't it just best for their own careers? So many government officials had proven to be incompetent or self-serving or both. They would lie.

And thus the image of the honorable park ranger fell victim to the same disillusionment that tarnished America's other heroes. In the original *Yogi Bear* cartoons, for all of Ranger Smith's antagonism toward Yogi, he was a largely sympathetic character—Mike Keys thought of him as a father. The wise park ranger was part of Yellowstone's popular appeal as a sort of never-never-land of permanent escapism. But the fires revealed park rangers as a symbol of authority and government, corrupted by earthly politics and deserving of mistrust. The fires were threatening not only the hallowed ground of Yellowstone but also its value as a popular paradise.

Likewise, controversy over the "let-burn" policy challenged the idea that Yellowstone was a place where ecological science could lead to wise management. For a decade or two, the lesson of the Craigheads' experience was that scientists were usually correct. But those decades had also seen part of the *conservation* movement, with its focus on scientific conservation of natural resources, morph into the *environmental* movement, embracing a more spiritual relationship to perhaps-romanticized conditions of nature.

When ecologists said that Yellowstone's landscapes needed to burn, management listened. But with fires behaving more ferociously than ecologists expected, doubt crept in. Where did the science end and romantic desires begin? Even Dan Sholly, once he saw one of these fires up close, started wondering if the scientists yet knew enough to be making such radical political decisions. Scientists on his fire committee believed that any departure from ecological principles was a mistake, because in the long run fires didn't *destroy* forests, they *renewed* them. Yet when faced with the intensity and drama of a massive fire up close and personal, scientists' faith in these generations-long processes felt almost as naïve as the Leopold Report's faith in a mythical pre-Anglo stasis. What exactly did these processes look like, how did they interact with human civilization, and what was supposed to happen in the short run? Without answers to these questions, many people hesitated to continue trusting ecologists to make political decisions.

When Dave Poncin arrived at Grant Village, his blood ran cold. He was surrounded by smoke. Ash was falling on him. Clearly a major wildfire was approaching. Yet he was in the middle of one of the most urbanized developments in the park. And he could see fuels for the fire everywhere: old logging debris in huge piles on the ground, firewood stacked against buildings, and lodging units topped with cedar-shake roofs. On any given night, Grant Village brimmed with more than three thousand people, and many of its buildings might as well have been tinderboxes.[11]

It was July 22, and Poncin, the leader of one of the top fire-fighting units in the country, had been called in after another hot, windy day. At his home in northern Idaho, his phone had rung at 11:00 P.M. Within an hour he'd driven to Missoula for a predawn meet-up with his firefighting team. They'd flown to West Yellow-stone, eaten breakfast, and driven to Mammoth for a meeting with the fire committee. They'd learned their objectives: first save Grant Village from the Shoshone fire, then perhaps address a couple of other fires to the south. Then they'd driven to Grant Village, and Dave had gotten discouraged.

Grant Village, named after the president who signed the bill first making Yellowstone a national park, was perhaps the least-loved area of Yellowstone. It had first been proposed in the 1950s, as one of the suburban neighborhoods that might process large numbers of people more efficiently than quaint old structures such as the Old Faithful Inn. The Grant site was chosen not for scenery but for location, at the bottom of the figure-eight road system, closest to the Tetons. It was supposed to take pressure off more environ-mentally sensitive areas such as Fishing Bridge, but it sat in limbo for years when scientists discovered that constructing Grant would displace valuable habitat for grizzly bears. Finally the development was pushed through, likely in violation of environmental regula-tions, and the sprawling result was six two-story motel buildings, a restaurant, store, gas station, post office, visitor center, administra-tive facilities, employee housing, and 430 trailer-friendly campsites. Although many visitors appreciated its convenience, occasional lake views, and the mystique of Yellowstone as a whole, few insiders felt much affection for it.[12]

But you couldn't let it burn down. At the peak of the season, with other options already full, where else would its three thousand people go? Indeed this was a concern for even a temporary evacuation, although when Dave went out to the lakeshore, stood on a boat ramp, and looked back at the village and the fire behind it, he knew he had no choice. All these people had to leave.

Such extreme developments were a shock to everyone. "No one was believing this," Dan Sholly recalled. "People said, 'You've got to be kidding.'"[13] Poncin developed two firefighting plans. Plan A sought to stop the fire on the entrance road a quarter mile outside the village. One thousand firefighters cleared a six-mile-long containment line by hand. They set a backfire to reduce fuels outside the line, and dropped a thick pink retardant slurry on adjacent trees. It was a good plan, well executed. And the Shoshone fire tore through the canopy over the line. Dave had no choice but to fall back on Plan B.

In Plan B, purely defensive, firefighters scattered debris, ran hoses from hydrants, dropped retardant, and dumped buckets of water on the village itself. The few people remaining—those preparing dinner for the firefighters' lakeside camp—fled into the shallow waters of the lake. Firefighters turned the high-pressure hoses on the tree canopies, trying to force the fire down to the ground or off to the north, away from the village.

And they succeeded. The fire veered north. It devoured a restroom in the campground but left all other buildings untouched. But as with Dan's earlier victory, Dave's felt a bit hollow in the face of the fire's ferocious behavior. Dave couldn't remember the last time he'd seen such unusual fire behavior, a fire so erratic, hot, and dirty.

To know how to best win their battle, firefighters need to be able to characterize a fire's behavior, using adjectives that sound almost human. But when such descriptions leach out into the culture, they often acquire moral judgments. If a fire is erratic and dirty, if it's irrational, insatiable, and ferocious, it starts to sound evil. That's what Smokey Bear had been teaching as well: fire is evil. So as ecologists tried to reposition fire as simply a component of natural systems, no more "good" or "evil" than the eruption of a geyser or a streak of red on a cliff face, they faced ingrained cultural beliefs and habits.

But those beliefs were powerful because of the way the fires threatened another value the public had imbued upon Yellowstone: the notion of untouched spiritual beauty. When national TV networks broadcast the evacuation of Grant Village, their images of Yellowstone showed huge flames and charred areas covered in smoke. There were none of the distant vistas and clean lines of an Ansel Adams black-and-white photo. The fires suggested that unpeopled vastness was not necessarily benign: out of it could come supernatural, evil-sounding forces that would wreck your vacation.

Furthermore, the Park Service's early encounters with national broadcast media also demonstrated the failures of teachability. In a Hermon Carey Bumpus world, a wildfire would be an opportunity to teach the public about fire ecology. A roadside "shrine" would put somebody right next to a fire so they could see how it worked. Television cameras certainly had that quality of immediacy—but at the expense of the underlying message.

Throughout the summer, ecologists were appalled at media reports on the "let-burn" policy. The reports were often incorrect, failing to note that the park started moving away from the policy in mid-July. They weren't very in-depth, failing to present the story of long-term renewal. And they often gave equal weight to non-scientists—tourists or local businesspeople who were dismayed at the burning of the park's scenery. Reporters often referred to fires *destroying* so many acres of land, in the same way that an urban fire destroys a house—but the land still existed; its forests would use the ashes to grow again. In later years some broadcast journalists agreed that they did a poor job, in part because they struggled with new satellite uplink technology that improved their ability to quickly provide stunning video—and didn't give them enough time to do the research to support it.[14]

But dismissing 1988 as a "media failure" is too easy. Choosing not to fight some fires was indeed a radical (if fifteen-year-old) policy reversal that could indeed seem counterintuitive. In criticizing the policy, journalists might have also been picking up on the unspoken feelings of fire experts who were disappointed in Yellowstone's implementation of those ideals. Furthermore, the "let-burn" policy was part of a broader ecological philosophy of firefighting, some tenets of which *did* continue through the summer. For example, a primary method of fighting fires is building containment lines, which are fuel-free borders designed to stop a fire from advancing. To quickly build a wide containment line in National Forests, firefighters used bulldozers to scrape off topsoil. But Yellowstone leaders favored a "light hand on the land" approach that forbade bulldozers, allowing only hand tools. They argued that ecologically, the scar of a dozer line would last decades longer than the char of a fire. And practically, even the Lamar River (nature's version of a containment line, complete with running water) didn't stop the Clover fire that almost killed Dan. Conditions were too extreme for containment lines to work, regardless of how they were constructed. Intellectually, these arguments are compelling—but emotionally, at the time, the notion of placing ecological values above the latest technology felt new and different and deserving of media attention.

For most of the 20th century, American society prided itself on its increasing control over the natural environment. Now some government officials were willingly giving up control—but they hadn't spent enough time thinking about how to teach others that lesson. Yellowstone scientist John Varley later recalled that the public relations officer screened all the reporters: "Those that were hunting for the disaster-victim-villain story headlines, she sent this way or that, or over there. All of the reporters that I had to deal with were those journalists who wondered out loud to her about 'what might really be going on, what's this really doing to the park.'"[15] He was thankful that she sent him only people who were ready to learn, because Yellowstone didn't have the resources to try to teach everybody. In the 1920s, Horace Albright and Hermon Carey Bumpus overcame tiny budgets with appeals to philanthropists. But with a fire raging, there was no time to get a grant. And unfortunately, reporters who seemed less interested in learning ended up having a lot of clout. As Varley and other scientists watched in horror, Yellowstone became an opportunity not to teach but to misconstrue.

For example, one day plant ecologist Don Despain took a journalist along to some of his research plots. Despain, a Wyoming native with steel-gray hair and a toothy grin, had written the park's natural fire policy in 1972 and continued to be one of the policy's strongest advocates. "Fire is part of the system and therefore causes no damage to the system," he said. "In fact, it is fire suppression that causes damage by destroying the natural frequency of fire in the ecosystem."[16] He was fascinated by how plants and animals reacted to fire: how a burned forest would become home to wood-digesting fungi, which would be food for insects, which would be eaten by birds and bears. On this August day, his team set plots ahead of some flames near the Gibbon River. Recording all the vegetation in the plot, they marked it so that they could return year after year. At lunch, more quickly than expected, the fire advanced. Despain put on goggles and covered his nose with a kerchief. It was an exciting moment for him, the first time he was seeing one of the plots undergo its expected transformation. He verbalized that excitement: "Burn, baby, burn."[17]

In his *Denver Post* article, journalist Jim Carrier told the story with full context. But his editors used the quote alone as a headline. They knew, as perhaps Despain did not, that it had been made famous by the Black Panthers during arson-filled race riots in the 1960s. Using such a phrase suggested that Despain was eager for fires to consume the entire park, rather than merely transform his research plot. Indeed it suggested that Yellowstone administrators in general were too arrogant in their attitude toward natural fire. They seemed almost happy to let the park burn when they were supposed to be protecting it. Despain and his superiors were terribly hurt by the backlash. Of course they loved Yellowstone and wanted to protect it. They were victims of extraordinary circumstances—the fires were already far bigger than they had ever imagined. They had always intended to keep fires in the backcountry, away from tourists, and they would continue to do anything they could to protect people, buildings, and extraordinary features such as the Old Faithful Inn.

Yet that misunderstanding was rooted in the changing wider culture. In the 1920s and '30s, a middle-class society was hungry to learn the science that people were using to create so many new opportunities—science that they hadn't had a chance to learn in school. But by the 1980s a public scarred by Vietnam and Watergate wanted to learn about government scandals. Science had lost its luster, especially now that it was less about knowledge as control and more about our impotence in the face of ecological forces.

And in truth Yellowstone's administration made a good target, not because of corruption or incompetence or failures to effectively teach but because of that hidden mismatch of values. For ecologists, Yellowstone's most important resources were a set of natural processes, and the fires were part of those processes. But when *Newsweek* magazine referred to an "all-out war to save the park itself," it reflected a public view that the resources were the place itself, magical Yellowstone where you had opportunities to both learn and wonder, to activate the intellect and the spirit.[18] To the public, the fires' blackened landscapes were destroying those opportunities.

In another helicopter ride over a wilderness area in the park's northeast quadrant, in late August, Dan Sholly was again amazed at the fire's behavior. "I felt as though I were part of Armageddon," he wrote. As he flew over burned forests, he was reminded of napalm attacks he'd witnessed in Vietnam. Smoke ascended in a mushroom-shaped cloud. Sunlight was tinted red as blood. The air was hot, almost suffocating, and ash circulated like swarms of insects. He felt like he was witnessing the aftereffects of horror. "It was as if hell itself had spilled from the earth's bowels."[19]

His faith in nature was being tested. It had been easy to say "Nature is in control" as long as you still felt in control. For example, Dan's recollection of his childhood in Big Bend National Park was that his ranger father was "lord of his wilderness domain."[20] But no rangers could be lord over these fires. Dan was butting up against the limits of human control—a roadblock that society as a whole was facing as well. As America's military hegemony was tested by the Vietnam War and the Iranian hostage crisis, as its economic superiority wavered in a decade of dampened growth and raging inflation, so too was the nation surprised by crises in environmental management. From the Cuyahoga River fire and the Santa Barbara oil spill in 1970 to the Three Mile Island and Love Canal crises in 1978–79, America was besieged by environmental catastrophes, many of which resulted from human overreach. Believing that people had full control over nature, we pushed it too far, expected it to be more docile and less fragile. And now we were suffering the consequences of that hubris.

If facing a lack of control was hard for Dan, it was even harder for people who lived on the outskirts of the park. Cooke City, near the Northeast Entrance, was now potentially in the path of the Clover-Mist fire. Back in July, Dan had been surprised that Clover exploded from three hundred to forty-seven hundred acres in a day; now it had merged with another fire to grow to more than one hundred thousand acres. It would soon spill east into the Shoshone National Forest, despite firefighters' explicit goal to contain it within park boundaries, and it seemed likely to spill north as well. And where the danger to Grant Village had been destruction of dull government-owned buildings, now the fire might burn individuals' property.

When he'd seen enough of the fire from the helicopter, Dan instructed the pilot to fly to Silver Gate, a community of about 170 people adjacent to Cooke City outside the Northeast Entrance of the park. Silver Gate had called a community meeting at the Range Riders Lodge, an impressive 1937 rustic log structure built as a bar, gambling den, and whorehouse.[21] Its grand hall was filled with exposed beams rising to the two-story ceiling, a brick fireplace, antlers hanging from the walls, and log- and cowboy-flavored accents everywhere. It felt like the setting for a rugged sportsman's paradise vacation—but it was teeming with an angry crowd.

The chopper landed in a field, and Dan walked through smoke so thick that yard lamps were illuminated. He passed hard hats, shovels, hoses, and other firefighting implements. Ashes and dust blew in the hot wind. Pausing outside the lodge, he radioed head-quarters to get the latest facts. A young associate came out. "Dan, you better get in there." The meeting had been going on for a while, and the crowd, he said, was fighting mad. As Dan talked on the radio, the associate went inside and came back out again. "Dan, I think you better hurry. It's getting nasty."[22]

As he had at Calfee Creek, Dan took on the challenge. He strode into the maelstrom to put out the fire.

202

When he walked in, a congressman was excoriating the Park Service over the let-burn policy and wilderness regulations. Then a little old lady confronted the congressman: "What are *you* going to do about these fires coming at us?" And Dan felt the crowd turning. The congressman got into a lengthy argument with Hays Kirby, a scion of Texas oil barons who owned a local motel.

A hunter, aviator, and patriot, Hays had moved to Silver Gate because he saw it as a kind of cowboy heaven. "People hereabouts are like my people had been in Texas before they were changed by staggering amounts of money," he later explained. "Primitive people, in the best sense of the word. Mountain people. Ornery sons-of-bitches."[23] Hays believed in action rather than talk. So even though he agreed with the congressman that the Park Service was to blame, he didn't want to listen to any more talk. He wanted action. As Hays remembered the way he "made a goddamn fool of myself," his message was, "Don't you people understand that they're gonna burn you down! We need action! We need those fires put out *now*!"[24]

Dan was at the bar ordering a Coke. He took a deep breath and let it out slowly. In ranger training he'd learned how to splint a broken bone or rappel down a cliff, but not how to deal with an angry crowd. Some of these people, he felt, actively *hated* the Park Service. They believed that Yellowstone's administrators *wanted* the fire to burn down Silver Gate, to get rid of these pesky neighbors.

Finally the argument slowed and Dan was asked to report on the fire's conditions. Although it had grown, he said, "We are still confident it will *not* reach Silver Gate or Cooke City . . . If it goes anywhere, it should move off to the east, where we are building lines on the divide right now to keep it inside the park."

"Bull!" Hays shouted, according to Dan's memoir.

"Kirby, I was just up there. I know what I'm talking about."

"And so do I! I was just up there. Flew over in my plane, checked it out firsthand."

And so the argument continued. Dan tried to explain the science, and argued that the bald, rocky peak of Amphitheater Mountain would stop the flames. But when the crowd accused him of lying, he felt embarrassed. These flames had already jumped rivers, canyons, and meadows that scientists had said would stop them. So far fire science had been continually wrong.

Meanwhile Hays was standing up for "his people" against all forms of government authority. Hays in fact respected Dan, perhaps due to their shared military background. "The son-of-a-bitch was a likable man, a man who exercised power in an impressive manner." But higher-ups, Hays believed, were infected by a "political sickness" in which they paid too much attention to ecological goals.[25] It was a common sentiment. Another man at the meeting accused Dan of "just paying men to stand around and watch Yellowstone be destroyed! Why, you're nothing but a bunch of communists."

Dan responded with a litany he often used. All new fires were being suppressed immediately. Bulldozers were worthless when fires were throwing embers so far ahead, across the widest containment lines. And the big fires were so powerful that there wasn't all that much you *could* do to fight them. He hated to admit it. He wanted to ease the residents' minds. "It was never easy to think that you'd lost all control," he later wrote.[26]

The meeting ended uncomfortably. Dan felt like he'd been on trial. Hays believed it was already too late to save his community. Eventually Dan's prediction would come true: blocked by Amphitheater Mountain, the Clover-Mist fire instead moved east, sparing Silver Gate and Cooke City.

But the meeting demonstrated the breakdown of the Yellowstone patriotic ideal. Horace Albright had hammered home the selflessness and democratic spirit of that 1870 campfire gathering as a way to emphasize the patriotism of a national park and its employees. That mythology was now withering in the heat of the fires. Hays Kirby and other area residents believed that Yellowstone leaders suffered from a political sickness and too much power, and perhaps were even communists—in other words, the opposite of the patriotic ideal expressed in the National Park Idea. Conversely, many park employees saw Hays and other residents of gateway communities as basically doing what Cornelius Hedges, articulating that idea at the 1870 campfire, had sought to avoid: squatting on land close to the natural wonder in order to make a buck. The fires were burning the idealism associated with setting aside a park as a monument to selfless democracy.

The fires were also threatening the frontier mentality, the notion that we could tame the wildness of western landscapes sufficiently for society to exist. We'd tamed the menace from grizzlies and wolves, from marauding outlaws and Native Americans, from cold and heat and aridity and poor soil. Although Larry Larom's dude ranch ceased taking guests after he died in 1983, his promise had become part of the culture: you could come experience these landscapes, hunt and fish and ride horses, see amazing natural features and herds of wildlife, and do it all without the discomforts that plagued previous travelers. But the heyday of dude ranching—indeed the first seven and a half decades of the 20th century—happened to be a relatively fallow period in the history of Yellowstone-area wildfires.

It turned out that our success in conquering wildfire was an illusion—and one that was hard to shake. The refrain of many public meetings, as Dan phrased it about one in particular, was "Why in the hell don't you put the fires out? Why don't you just put them out!"[27] Residents couldn't believe that firefighters, rangers, administrators, and other experts didn't have the power to extinguish the fires. That disbelief led to conspiracy theories: it had to be possible for the fires to be put out, so there must be some other reason why they weren't being put out. The park staff *couldn't* be helpless—so they must be evil.

But the park staffers *were* helpless. And, because they were equally steeped in patriotic and frontier traditions, they were having just as hard a time admitting so.

The Holiday Inn in Bozeman, Montana, was a featureless conference center close to an interstate exit. Its best quality was its easy airport accessibility, as regional executives from both the Park Service and Forest Service flew in. On September 4 they gathered with Yellowstone superintendent Bob Barbee, five regional forest supervisors, and numerous other decision-makers.

The two agencies had struggled to get along all summer. Although the media reported primarily on fires burning within the national park, in fact fires also raged across the five separately-managed surrounding National Forests. When fires crossed boundaries, they presented coordination nightmares. To improve coordination, on July 23 the agencies had set up a jointly led Area Command, based in the Montana town of West Yellowstone. But Area Command struggled. Part of the problem was that its fire behavior models could not account for these fires' behavior. And in part the ad hoc group seemed to add another layer to bureaucracy rather than streamlining it. It was now on its fourth set of co-commanders; its staff had ballooned to more than two hundred people; its mission and authority weren't totally clear. What was clear was that few people were happy with Area Command, primarily due to lack of action. Incident commanders kept asking for more resources: more firefighters and retardant-dropping planes and bulldozers to take action against the fires.

Area Command rarely seemed to provide those resources quickly enough—and in this Bozeman meeting it was ready to admit why. The resources were tapped out.

Early in the meeting, one of the co-commanders summarized the statistics to date: across the ecosystem nearly a million acres had already burned. Firefighters had built more than 350 miles of containment lines, only 29 of which held. For the past nine days they hadn't bothered to create any new lines as they merely tried to hold the existing ones. Overall they'd conducted airdrops of 700,000 gallons of water and 1.2 million gallons of retardant. They'd deployed 9,600 firefighters, with an overall cost so far of $67 million. And still West Yellowstone, Cooke City/Silver Gate, and some smaller communities were in peril. There was nothing to be done in the face of this weather. Superintendent Bob Barbee later recalled "the single-digit relative humidity, and the explosively dry fuels, and then choreographed by the wind, the wind, the wind, the wind. That wind was incredible that summer."[28]

Crews were exhausted and demoralized. Some of them needed to go home. Others were needed elsewhere: it was a hot, dry summer throughout the West. Thus, although rain still hadn't come and the fires showed no sign of abating, Area Command announced that there were not enough resources to continue firefighting at current levels.

They had a plan: to shift from offense to defense. Instead of trying to contain a wildfire at its head, they would retreat to the essential communities: Cooke City, Silver Gate, and West Yellowstone (all outside the park); and Old Faithful and Canyon Village (inside the park). They would put all available resources into protecting structures. But the plan needed approval from the assembled bigwigs, in part because commanders of the individual fires hated it. The public was *really* going to hate it: indeed this was the very strategy that residents of Silver Gate had angrily accused

Dan of pursuing already. It felt like giving up. Few people wanted to give up.

But what other choice was available? As Ken Dittmer, one of the co-commanders, told the crowd, "We just can't fight everything. And we've got to realize that nothing is stopping these fires. Roads don't stop it. Rivers don't stop it. Wet meadows don't stop it. Young lodgepole growths with no ground cover don't stop it. Topographic features don't stop it. We cannot hold fire line."[29]

Because they indeed had no other choice, the assembled bigwigs approved the strategy. Ironically, it resembled the ecological approach that the Park Service had started with: let fires burn in the wilderness. Except that now the policy had been arrived at from a practical standpoint, from a lack of resources and a new appreciation of the fires' ferocity. Instead of saying, "We *won't* fight these fires," leaders were saying, "We *can't* fight these fires." Instead of an experiment in "natural regulation" derived from controversial new science, the policy was a practical necessity derived from availability of budgets and resources.

(Although fire management philosophies would become a political football for years to come, in retrospect the Bozeman compromise plus the experiences of Calfee Creek and Grant Village offered a kernel of hope. It turned out that defense was easier and more effective than one might think. Long before a fire arrived, you could create defensible space around important buildings by clearing brush and debris, by not stacking firewood against a wooden wall, and by installing metal roofs and sprinkler systems. Then if a fire did arrive, well-defended buildings faced a pretty good chance of surviving—with lower cost, not to mention less ecological impact, than trying to suppress every fire at its source.)

Lack of control was tough to accept: a complete breakdown of frontier ideals. But at the Bozeman meeting, Area Command presented even worse news. Over the next two days, forecasts predicted, northern winds from a Canadian cold front would push the Storm Creek fire into a timbered valley southwest of Cooke City and Silver Gate. (Storm Creek had burned innocuously for weeks deep in the Beartooth mountain wilderness north of the park and then suddenly made a surprise run, against prevailing winds, south to the park's border. Almost nobody worried about it all summer, and now it was a huge threat.) The winds would do the same thing to the North Fork fire at Old Faithful. The winds' effects would be the equivalent of loading two guns at the edge of two Yellowstone communities. Then after the cold front passed, predictions called for winds of 30 mph from the southwest, aiming the guns and pulling the triggers.

Jeff Henry climbed the intricate wooden stairway up, up, up through the seven-story atrium of the Old Faithful Inn lobby. He passed the lower floors and the lobby overlooks and the signs forbidding the public to climb any farther. He had a job to do up there. He was a seasonal ranger with the Park Service, but he was also a photographer, and once it became clear that this was going to be an unusual summer, his supervisors asked him to spend part of each workday documenting the fire and firefighting efforts. So he was headed to the roof.

It was Wednesday, September 7, yet another hot, smoky, windy day. Jeff had arisen early to drive from his base in Madison to Old Faithful. He was sure that the fire would arrive. In this view he hadn't always agreed with his superiors. The previous morning, as part of his ranger duties, he was asked to inform the various concessions in the Old Faithful village—a complex that contained more than four hundred buildings, including motels, shops, restaurants, and employee housing—of the official position that there was only a 33 percent chance that the fire would arrive. But Jeff's personal position was the opposite, because he could see the huge columns of smoke just a few miles upwind.

"Fire in town or at least on the outskirts of Old Faithful was all but inevitable, and probably imminent," Jeff wrote in his engaging, photo-laden memoir, *The Year Yellowstone Burned.*[30] Nothing could be done to stop it. He'd spent the last six weeks watching fire behavior up close, seeing the ferocity with which fires ruined plans to contain or divert the flames. He could feel the heat and the dry air, "almost as harsh as fine-grit sandpaper when it blew past my face."[31] And when he took a photo of a weathervane, it pointed directly at the column of smoke, with the wind meter blurry because it was spinning so fast.

The official message, Jeff and others believed, came from political pressure. Well-connected businesses inside the park and in the gateway communities didn't want to lose revenues from an evacuation. And politicians hated to admit a loss of control. Jeff could admit powerlessness, and much of greater Yellowstone's leadership had basically done so three days earlier in Bozeman—but Washington, D.C., thrived on a sense of American invincibility. After the frustrations of the 1970s, Ronald Reagan redefined the message of the Vietnam War: the problem was that we wouldn't *let* our soldiers win. We were invincible but too timid to take control. Applying Reagan's philosophy in Yellowstone would mean rejecting any admissions that we couldn't win—especially in an environment that reminded so many observers of Vietnam itself.

Wednesday morning Jeff handled some other ranger duties, and then he took his camera to the best vantage point in the area: a widow's walk atop the Old Faithful Inn, ninety feet off the ground. When he arrived he found two firefighters pointing infrared scopes at the smoke. In a wildfire, smoke dominates people's experiences. Smoke overwhelms your sense of smell, your lung capacity, and especially your view. Most of the time the flames themselves are enshrouded in their smoke. The infrared scopes allowed these spotters to see heat and thus understand where the fire was burning, how close it was coming.

Jeff took pictures of the smoky village: parking lots, other lodging facilities, and retail stores. By now everything was officially closed. During the morning visitors and nonessential employees had been evacuated; management accepted that the 33 percent chance had come true. But the evacuation wasn't very thorough. Many employees decided to stick around to see what happened. Some tourists were even taking pictures of the geyser's regular eruptions. And some people were—or believed themselves to be—stranded, as fires also threatened roads in and out of the village, with the result that they opened and closed in confusing fashion.

It was an epic day across the park. Total burned acreages were second only to Black Saturday. In Cooke City, a back-burn set to deprive the Storm Creek fire of fuel escaped its borders. It took out a shed on the outskirts of Cooke City and raced ahead to catch four cabins on the other side of town. (Astoundingly, most buildings in the town itself were spared.) In Crandall, Wyoming, twenty-five miles southeast of there, the Clover-Mist fire took out three privately owned cabins, a dozen trailers, and a store. Despite all this drama, the nation's eyes were on the imminent peril at Old Faithful. Journalists flocked to the village, because for many of them Yellowstone *was* Old Faithful, and a blaze here would be the climax of their summer's worth of stories.

On the fire front, helicopters dropped bucketfuls of water and airplanes dropped slurry, but they seemed to have no effect. Occasionally the curtain of smoke parted and Jeff captured flames dancing directly behind the village buildings. Eventually the two spotters' scopes became so bright with heat that they could no longer look through them. At that point they put on fireproof gloves and face masks. "While they were suiting up, both men resorted to nonstop strings of nervous profanity," Jeff wrote, "the meaning of which could be distilled down to their view that the Old Faithful area and most of the people in it were doomed."[32]

From the high vantage point, Jeff and others on the widow's walk believed, they had a better appreciation of the approaching danger than anyone below. Jeff tried to get on his radio to alert people, but there was so much chatter he could never find an opening. Another visitor to the widow's walk got on a fire-specific channel to issue a warning but was informed that other intelligence had determined the village was not at risk. At that moment the fire crested a ridge one and a half miles away, and Jeff could feel the increase in heat. Meanwhile, the hurricane-strength winds were continually knocking over his tripod. It was time to get off the roof.

Jeff wasn't afraid for his own safety—in part, he says, because he was young, macho, and naïve, but in part because he didn't put himself in situations from which there was no escape. But at this moment he felt a greater worry than he had all summer, a worry for the Old Faithful Inn itself. The old building, which he loved, had no escape route. It was a perfect pyre: its cavernous interior was filled with twigs and air. It was arranged like an oversized cone that you would use to start a campfire. Its cedar-shake roof would catch and torch any sparks. Robert Reamer had designed the building to merge perfectly with its surroundings—and now that the surroundings were burning, the landmark would too.

As Jeff roamed the grounds, he saw spot fires starting everywhere. The wall of flame tossed out embers and fireballs that the massive winds sent swirling throughout the complex. The wall itself, as it moved through trees in the forest, rose more than two hundred feet, twice the height of the trees. Flames reached so high that they were pushed forward by the wind—but on the ground, the inferno was sucking air inward, so the forward-leaning flames rolled over on themselves like crashing waves.

As the fires approached, the smoky air became tinted orange, then turned crimson, got ever-brighter, and then became black as night. The noise was as deafening as a fleet of jet engines. Jeff later realized that he and the others in the village probably got as close to the heart of a firestorm as anyone can possibly be and still live to tell about it.

It was terrifying, and some people cried or cowered in fear. Embers, and sometimes entire burning logs, flew past them—and many of the employees and visitors had no protective clothing or shelters. Rangers gathered most of these spectators in the massive parking lots behind the inn. With no trees or other fuels, an empty parking lot could not burn. As long as they could protect themselves from smoke and flying debris, people would be relatively safe here. The rangers told them to cover themselves with whatever they could find. A visiting elk researcher, who'd gotten bored sitting through meetings at Mammoth evaluating the park's fire policies and who had decided to see the front for himself, lay on his stomach as firebrands swirled over his head. He admitted that he was scared to death. (His name was Jack Ward Thomas, and in coming years he would serve as the head of the U.S. Forest Service in an era of increasing wildfires.)

However, the village was also filled with people who loved the place. The stories of the siege of Old Faithful include any number of little-remembered folks going above the call of duty to stamp out fires. For example, a maintenance supervisor put out a fire at a gas station before it could reach the thousands of gallons of stored fuel. A journalist found a cabin with its cedar-shingle roof on fire and put it out with a fire extinguisher.[33] A food and beverage supervisor, who'd driven to Old Faithful to remove the perishables from its newly closed restaurants but found his exit route blocked, stuck around to beat out spot fires near tourist cabins with a broom. And most heroically, several firefighters turned their hoses on the massive roof of the inn. Some of the firefighters did so while perched dangerously on the flat roofs of the inn's wings. Many spectators recalled at least one fire starting on the roof, and being put out by water from the firefighters and the inn's newly installed sprinkler system.

Finally the firestorm passed. It ignited a hillside on the opposite side of the village and continued on to the northeast. As people looked up, they saw the Old Faithful Inn emerging from the smoke, standing strong and dauntless. Although nineteen smaller buildings were burned, the firefighters and sprinklers saved the landmark. Once again a firefighting effort succeeded, although once again the victory felt dwarfed by the size and ferocity of the enemy.

With heroism and luck, people could save iconic structures. Geysers themselves, with their underground plumbing, were not really in danger. But a particularly devastating emotion at Old Faithful and everywhere that summer was the inability to do anything on behalf of that other great symbol of Yellowstone, the animals. Anyone who had seen the movie *Bambi* knew how terrifying a wildfire seemed to be for animals. That made it tough to accept ecologists' belief that, in general, nature should be allowed to take its course—that any interference could cause greater problems later. Ecologists believed that nutritious postfire new growths would contribute to the long-term overall health of animal populations. And some of them pointed out that *Bambi* was written by screenwriters, not scientists; actual animal behavior that summer differed from the fictional behavior portrayed in the movie. For example, Jeff took dozens of pictures of elk and bison grazing peacefully as flames danced a few yards away. Subsequent research demonstrated that animal herds, which coevolved with wildfire over centuries, were not widely hurt by the fires.

But at the time, it felt heartless to imagine individual animals getting scorched to death. It felt especially devastating to let this happen *in Yellowstone*, in the place we humans had set aside for those animals. We'd created a wildlife refuge and then allowed it to be consumed by—in the case of the North Fork—a human-caused fire. It felt like an abdication of a sacred responsibility, a threat to the age-old value of Yellowstone as half tame.

After the near charring of Old Faithful, the ultimate symbol of Yellowstone, anything else might feel like an anticlimax. But the fires were not done. Most amazingly, the North Fork fire, having loomed over Old Faithful, Madison Junction, Norris Hot Springs, and Canyon Village, and having turned back on itself to again threaten West Yellowstone and Island Park, Idaho, now marched in a new direction with a seemingly new target. It was headed for Mammoth Hot Springs, the park headquarters, where chief ranger Dan Sholly, scientists John Varley and Don Despain, superintendent Bob Barbee, and Yellowstone's other leaders worked and lived. You could almost imagine the fire as a supervillain, telling them, *You tried to put me down, so now I'm coming after your families.*

Varley lived in an eighty-year-old wooden house with a thirty-five-year-old shake shingle roof. He knew what he needed to do to save it: get it wet. So he took a lawn sprinkler and put it on the crest of the roof. When he turned on the water, he was amazed to see nothing drip off the roof's edges. There was no runoff. The shingles were so dry that they soaked up all of the water. They continued soaking it up for almost thirty minutes.[34]

With ash falling like snow in Mammoth, just breathing the air was like smoking four packs of cigarettes per day.[35] The sun was a tiny red dot. The whole park was now closed to overnight visitors, because the menace to its attractions and roads was so wide. Nevertheless, Dan Sholly hesitated to evacuate headquarters, believing that would send the worst signal yet.

Sholly was exhausted. Since July he'd been working past midnight and getting up before dawn. He barely saw his family. He had to work through his wedding anniversary. And the work sometimes seemed pointless. "I'd grown so tired of watching the black on the fire maps grow and grow each day as if none of us were doing anything," he wrote.[36] It was hard to give up control.

Even when he tried to sleep, he worried. Had he requested enough fire engines to save Mammoth? Would there be enough time to evacuate if the winds picked up? What would the national journalists say? Well after midnight on Saturday, September 10, he stumbled into bed and had a heartfelt conversation with his wife.

"What are you going to do?" she asked at one point, according to his memoir.

"About evacuating?"

"Yes. Are you going to do it?"

A window was open next to him, and through it he could hear the fire crackling one and a half miles away. "Yes, I'm going to evacuate," he told her. "But for now I'm going to rest my eye for about twenty minutes. Then I'll decide as to when."[37]

When Dan woke up, it was 3:30 A.M. and his body was telling him something was wrong. Maybe he'd gotten his twenty minutes; he hadn't looked at the clock before drifting off. But now he paused to figure out what had awakened him. He realized the crackling of the fire outside the window was louder than previously. He rushed into the kitchen and out the door. The fire sounded closer. It seemed to be encircling the village. There was only one unblocked route out, to the north, and he worried that the fire could cut it off.

He went back into the house to get dressed. His wife made him a sandwich. "The fire's gotten worse," he told her. "We're nearly surrounded, so I'm going to go ahead and evacuate." As he walked to the administration building, he passed the old Fort Yellowstone officers' quarters, built when the army had run the park a century before. Their windows were alive with reflected flames.

He issued the evacuation order at 5:00 A.M. A half hour later, the wind picked up. He gathered fire team leaders for a meeting. "Today could be the worst of the summer," he told them. An incoming cold front was likely to keep the smoke down close to the ground, so thick that helicopters would not be able to take off.

By noon the streetlights came on in the darkness. The incoming cold front had shifted the wind. Dan drove out to the edge of the fire and saw spot fires jumping down the meadows toward town. He stopped to talk to the firefighters, and when he got back into his car, he had to turn on the wiper blades to get the ash off the windshield. The ash smeared at first, taking several squirts of fluid to clear. Finally Dan turned off the wipers and put the car in gear. But suddenly he stopped, transfixed by what he now saw on the windshield.

Tiny clear blips appeared, dozens and then hundreds of them. It was raining.

Everyone had always known that rain would put out the fires—or more specifically, that the associated humidity would slow the fires' growth. Although less than four hundredths of an inch fell in

Mammoth that day, the fires' hunger was slaked.[38] The next several days brought continued moisture, reminding people of traditional August and September weather patterns. Within twenty-four hours Dan rescinded the evacuation order. And fire crews slowly shifted from defense back to offense, putting out spot fires within the mosaic of burns that covered so much of the park. They continued working into October, aided by the increasing snows of oncoming winter.

The political fallout continued much longer. There were bureaucratic reviews and congressional hearings. There was in-depth media coverage in which ecologists could finally explain in full the role of fire in rejuvenating an ecosystem. There was considerable debate about the "let-burn" policy and about coordination among agencies.

But in the moment, in mid-September, the main reaction around Yellowstone was "Finally."[39] Finally the long-expected rains had arrived, finally the fires were relenting, finally the period of panic was over. Some employees celebrated with parties, but others were simply too exhausted. They were relieved but not celebratory. For the few people remaining in Yellowstone National Park, even if the park felt symbolic of the rest of the country, it didn't feel at all special.

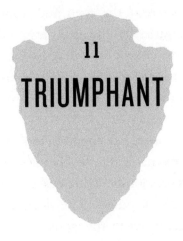

11
TRIUMPHANT

On September 10, 1988, ranger-photographer Jeff Henry was in Gardiner, Montana, at the house where he lived when he wasn't on duty in Madison. It was a Saturday, he wasn't working. Furthermore, if Mammoth evacuated, then Gardiner, just five miles away, would be next, and he would need to prepare. Then he awoke Sunday morning to snowflakes filling the sky. Weather had provided both moisture and cold. He knew the crisis was over; this storm would break the fires' back. He celebrated by going out to breakfast with friends.

Then he drove south through the park toward Madison. He drove past Mammoth, where the evacuation order was being lifted. Past Bunsen Peak, where a ranger friend had almost been stranded in the firestorm after getting her car stuck. Past Indian Creek campground, where Dan Sholly had spent his wedding anniversary setting a back-burn to save its scenic stand of pines. He drove into the burnscape.

Jeff saw some elk near the road and stopped to photograph them. He was intrigued by the geometry of the composition: windblown snow was falling on a diagonal, contrasting with the sharp verticality of the blackened lodgepole pines. Some spots on the ground were still smoldering, and steamed when the snow landed on them.[1]

Pleased with the image, Jeff stopped a few miles later for another photograph, of an area that had probably burned on Black Saturday, three rainless weeks previously. The trees' crowns were consumed. The understory was consumed. The duff was consumed. Logs lying higgledy-piggledy across the landscape looked like charcoal. It was a soot-drenched, monochromatic emptiness that the national press would soon dub a "moonscape." And yet: popping up behind a blackened log, he saw a sprouting tuft of grass. Just two dozen blades, less than two inches tall, but a symbol nevertheless. Like Noah on Mount Ararat, he could see the coming redemption. After the disaster, life would be restored.

In the long run, the ecologists were proven correct. Fire did not permanently destroy landscapes; rather, it was part of their natural evolution. Indeed the first ecological responses came almost more quickly than people expected. And with that rebirth came a rebirth in public affection, a resurgence in Yellowstone's popularity. Through September and October of 1988, until the park's roads were closed for the winter, residents of the surrounding area came to see Yellowstone for themselves. Like Jeff, they saw the wildlife apparently undisturbed. They saw sprouting grasses and forbs. A

Casper Star-Tribune reporter traveling from the East Entrance to Yellowstone Lake was surprised at how many living green trees he saw: because of the way any fire burns in a patchwork, areas were never as black as they were marked on the map.[2] It was fascinating, and maybe even a little beautiful. The following summer, tourism increased even more, and Yellowstone reestablished its core value of popularity.

With ecological science validated, park officials through the next five years were able to enact a long-contemplated ecological solution to one of their most vexing ecological problems. There were too many elk in the northern half of the park, and there had been for most of the century. They overgrazed the meadows, spilled into adjoining towns and ranches, and in harsh winters died of starvation by the hundreds. In the 1920s managers rounded up surplus elk and exported them to other regions, including Colorado's Rocky Mountain National Park. But then demand waned. In the 1960s rangers shot elk to thin the population. But the public was outraged. (The outrage helped prompt Starker Leopold's 1963 report advocating that the Park Service seek to preserve "natural conditions," as discussed in chapter 8.)[3] In the 1970s scientists hoped that the ecosystem would self-regulate, that whatever level at which elk populations naturally stabilized must be the right one. But eventually they realized that the ecosystem couldn't effectively self-regulate because it wasn't complete. It lacked the best regulating factor for elk populations: an apex predator.

Humans eliminated wolves from the park for the same reasons we suppressed fire: because we saw their actions as destructive, maybe even evil. But if humans were now going to honor Yellowstone as an ecosystem, we needed to stop manipulating it based on our own value judgments. Instead of suppressing wolves, we needed to support their role, and even help reintroduce them to the area. This view generated plenty of opponents, and wolf policy became a huge political controversy in the years both before and after their formal reintroduction in 1993. But that controversy itself demonstrated how Yellowstone had been reestablished as a place where management decisions were determined by ecological science, a place where the political implications of ecologists' opinions were paramount.

Opponents of wolves generally focused on practical matters, such as livestock depredations on ranches surrounding the park. They fulminated against the vagueness of the arguments offered by proponents, such as the unquantifiable value of an intact ecosystem. Yet since reintroduction, attempts to quantify that value—for example, by measuring the economic impact of increased tourism—have suggested that it's substantial.[4] Today wolf-watchers fill the Lamar Valley in the spring and fall, when hotel rooms in Cooke City, Silver Gate, and Gardiner might otherwise be vacant. They are drawn by a spiritual connection. For wolf-watchers, the thrill of seeing these mysterious creatures in the wild resembles the thrill that Ansel Adams's acolytes felt from those vast unpeopled landscapes. Here is the epitome of nature as a spiritual force. Although over the last twenty-four years wolves have slowly returned to many other areas of the northern Rockies, Yellowstone remains the easiest and best place to see them in the wild. Its calling card as the home of wilderness spirituality may thus be stronger now than at any point since the 1950s.

Whether tourists come to Yellowstone to see wolves, other creatures, or any of its other wonders, many of them are driven by intellectual curiosity—a curiosity that was likely heightened by news reports of the fires. By the early '90s, new roadside exhibits that focused on fire ecology greeted these tourists. For example, some exhibits explained how some lodgepole pinecones open to release their seeds only in extreme heat—the lodgepole has evolved to incorporate wildfire into its long-term reproduction strategy.

Immediately after the fires, such an exhibit in front of a moonscape might have seemed like wishful thinking. But soon many of those moonscapes became blanketed by tiny lodgepoles, often so thick that from a distance they looked like grass. On the side of the road, tourists experienced a teachable moment, and Yellowstone again became the perfect place to take advantage of that.

Such educational outreach took advantage of a huge trove of fascinating postfire ecological research. But postfire social research was perhaps more surprising. It showed that despite the televised firestorm, and despite the withering political criticism of Yellowstone management, the general public still loved the park, trusted its managers, and saw it as a symbol of American democracy. Even in 1989, 80 percent of the public believed that although there might have been problems in execution, fire policy in wilderness areas and parks was sound.[5] Over the past thirty years, a vocal minority has continued to mistrust Yellowstone leaders as much as they do any authority figures, but the general societal attitude, especially after 9/11, has been much more open to patriotic impulses. In 2012, as a postrecession Congress faced budgetary challenges that would eventually lead to the across-the-board cuts known as *sequestration*, a survey found that 95 percent of the public believed that protecting the national parks was an appropriate role for the federal government; 92 percent wanted park funding either kept the same or increased. The numbers, which held across political parties, demonstrated a patriotic appeal even among those who favored fiscal austerity, small government, and loosening environmental protection.[6] The public saw national parks—especially Yellowstone—as sacred, off-limits, because they were such a pure expression of the American ideal.

Americans could feel good about the national parks in part because they felt good about the economy. By the 1990s, technology was not only fueling economic growth, it was also changing the way people participated in that growth. Overnight delivery services, fax machines, and email were followed by increasingly sophisticated Internet tools to improve remote collaboration. Now many white-collar workers could live wherever they wanted to— and a large number chose the greater Yellowstone ecosystem. In these counties from 1970 to 2003, population, employment, and real personal income grew faster than the surrounding states or the nation as a whole.[7] By the mid-1990s the migratory influx was so noticeable that greater Yellowstone became a leading example of "the New West," and analysts pondered how new lifestyle accouterments such as mountain bikes and microbrews differed from those favored by previous area residents. Furthermore, the new attention to *networking*—the ways that New Westers could link to their remote coworkers, and more broadly the way that many companies interlaced their extended supply chains with globally networked connections—mirrored the new attention paid to the networks in ecosystems. People now celebrated how the presence of wolves in Yellowstone unleashed a *trophic cascade* that changed how elk browsed, which changed how aspens and willows grew, which changed how beavers built dams, which changed . . . And as they did so they were pondering their own role in an economy as complex and interdependent as that of a natural ecosystem.[8]

However, on another level the New West migration was far simpler. It was a collection of individuals choosing "quality of life," using the same factors that had driven Larry Larom, his contemporaries, and his dudes and dudines. Innovations made it easier to live in greater Yellowstone, made it less remote and less dangerous. Compared to their predecessors, both the dudes and the New Westers could more easily combine upper-class amenities with rugged outdoor activities. The New Westers were different from the dudes in the type of amenities they required: now, not only indoor plumbing but also a nearby Starbucks. Likewise they differed in their definition of rugged fun: now, not only hunting and horseback riding but also rock climbing and river rafting. But the desire for a rugged life, and the association of that life with Yellowstone, was reinvigorated.[9]

With new appreciation of rugged lifestyles came new appreciation of the informal architecture associated with them. The fires' threat to the Old Faithful Inn demonstrated what a national treasure it was. This was a message that some in the Park Service hadn't fully appreciated in previous years: during the modernist fad to build large, efficient structures located a safe driving distance from sensitive natural features, a 1955 long-range Yellowstone plan called for tearing down the inn.[10] But now its informal architecture, blending so well with the natural surroundings, could be appreciated as a wonder of its own. For the building's centennial in 2004, Yellowstone launched a major renovation to upgrade it: reinforce walls and roof with steel for seismic stability; improve electrical, plumbing, and heating systems. Yet it was a *historic* renovation, designed to make such supports nearly invisible, meanwhile restoring the lobby to more closely replicate Robert Reamer's original design.[11]

Appreciation of the importance of the Old Faithful Inn may have arisen from the way the national media focused on the 1988 fires' threat to it, as if the Old Faithful village comprised the entire park. The media also focused on imperiled animals, much to ecologists' aggravation. Yet the notion of Yellowstone as a *sanctuary*, as a place that humans created for the benefit of animals, continues to have a powerful hold on the public imagination. A bison or a bear wanders near a road, and people perceive it as "friendlier" than wildlife elsewhere. Sometimes, sadly, they approach too close and get mauled. But they continue to see Yellowstone as magical in part because they see it as a haven that humans created for animals—now including wolves. They again see these creatures as half tame.

If anything, the fires' threat to Yellowstone demonstrated how truly special it was. As a media event, it kept Americans glued to the TV all summer. "Part of our national heritage is under threat and on fire tonight," CBS's Dan Rather intoned on September 7.[12] A great deal of subsequent media criticism focused on whether wildfires were a threat or a natural process. But one thing the anchorman got right—and that even the most sensational coverage brought home—was Yellowstone's role in the national self-image.

Americans today more than ever believe that our country is special. The reasons differ: because of the Constitution or certain of its amendments, because of the economy or the military, because of racial diversity or in spite of its slow acceptance, because of the character of its people and/or the land we inhabit. And Yellowstone more than ever embodies those values in landscape. The reasons have multiplied: the geysers *plus* the wildlife, the informality, ruggedness, selfless patriotism, intelligent curiosity, spiritual depth, scientific integrity, and so on.

Yet what's truly special about Yellowstone—as about America— is the way these reasons change. America built 19th-century greatness on the back of incredible natural resources.[13] But when situations called for political leadership, military might, scientific innovation, or equal rights, the American character was deep and rich enough to respond effectively, if not always as quickly or completely as everyone might like. And with each change in values, America could look to this remote corner of the Rocky Mountains and find a feature in it to match those values. This landscape was so rich and deep, so varied and magnificent, that it could respond to society's needs. We may have first thought of it as a wonderland, a place of curiosities so different from the "real" world. But it's truly a wonderlandscape, a real place with nearly infinite capabilities to inspire that most gorgeous of human emotions, wonder.

EPILOGUE

A top Mount Sheridan, elevation 10,298 feet, my companions
gravitate to the sunny south side of the boarded-up-for-the-
season fire lookout. It's late September, but we've lucked into
perfect weather: no wind, bright sun, and skies finally cleared from
smoke of the summer's fires.[1] Mount Sheridan is the most prominent peak in the southern part of Yellowstone, and the views to
the south—of the Tetons and freshly whitened peaks in the nearby
wilderness—are spectacular. But I sneak off to the north side of the
lookout, stomping through snow sheltered by the building's shade.
I find a seat to perch on and look north to admire the vast expanses
of Yellowstone park itself.

Lakes spread out like blue jewels. Heart Lake, three thousand
feet directly downhill, cradles our campsite. Lewis Lake and

Shoshone Lake point off into the timbered flatlands of the park's western border. And from this high vantage I can finally appreciate the many tentacles of vast Yellowstone Lake: its incongruous West Thumb reaching out of the main lake toward Grant Village; the fantastical South and Southeast Arms ducking behind promontories to reach toward some of the most remote lands in the Lower 48, the hidden headwaters of the Yellowstone River itself. Beyond the lake to the east rise the high peaks of the Absarokas, far to the north the high plateau of the Beartooths, to the northwest the Madison and Gallatin ranges.

As my gaze moves from the mountains back to Yellowstone Lake, I suddenly realize what I'm looking at: the caldera. The sunken center of the ancient Yellowstone volcano. This broad plain is marked on maps handed out at park entrances, but it can be hard to get a sense of when you're in the middle of it. Mount Sheridan is, in effect, the highest point on its old rim, with the filled-in crater spilling out below me.

The realization of where I am in place prompts a second realization, of where I am in time. The Anglo history of the last 140-odd years is only a blip in the full history of humans in Yellowstone— and human history is only a blip in the geology of Mammoth's terraces. And yet even the deposition of those terraces, or the erosion of the canyon, is only a blip in the natural history of the earth itself. The volcano dwarfs us all.

And so, although my excursion to Mount Sheridan is vacation, I'm suddenly reminded of work. A question becomes paramount in my mind: *What on earth am I going to write about the supervolcano?*

Over the years that I have been researching and writing this book, I have known that its epilogue will need to look to the future. Specifically, given how much the meaning of Yellowstone has changed over its history, the end of the book is the time to ask:

What comes next? What meaning will America see in its signature national park in the coming decades?

At first I dreaded the question. I can research history, but I can't know the future. I'm a storyteller, not a fortune-teller. But as I laid out the story, I realized that the story itself was answering the question. What will society value about Yellowstone in the future? It depends on society's values. That's the way it has always worked. What Americans value in our society—what we celebrate, struggle with, seek to ponder or question—becomes what we highlight in Yellowstone. Whether America wanted to understand why it was special, protect its wild animals, mourn its frontier, celebrate its democracy, educate its masses, locate individual spirituality, or appreciate community networks, it saw those ideas playing out in Yellowstone. We have continually interpreted this iconic landscape as a representation of ourselves. And what's amazing about Yellowstone is that it is so rich and varied that it keeps presenting a meaningful mirror, keeps showing us something powerful and new.

Predicting what Yellowstone will mean in the future involves predicting what America will value in the future. And although lacking a crystal ball, I do see some possibilities.

First is climate change. It's likely to be the biggest ecological story of the 21st century, yet it's so long term and all-encompassing that it's difficult for everyday folks to get a handle on. How are we going to understand what is happening to the earth around us?

Well, for more than a century Yellowstone has been helping us understand an even slower natural process: geology. Perhaps if society sees understanding climate change as an imperative, it will turn to national parks, including the soon-to-be-glacierless Glacier, to serve that function. And actually, when you think about it, it turns out that for the past three decades Yellowstone has been offering us opportunities to improve that understanding, opportunities that we've generally ignored.

In retrospect, the 1988 fires were a signal event for global warming. That same summer, a NASA scientist first testified in Congress about the "greenhouse effect," but almost nobody made the connection to the wildfires. By any measure—firefighters deployed, firefighting budgets, acreages burned, or media coverage—1988 felt like an outlier, an anomaly, a once-in-a-lifetime summer. But nationwide, half of the summers since then have burned equivalent acreages and higher budgets.[2] The summer of 1988 was in fact a *new normal*, a preview of what the American West could look like in a hotter century.[3]

To know how to respond, we need ecological research. Yellowstone provides an opportunity to answer questions about how a relatively untouched natural system responds to climate change. Do warmer winters lead to higher populations of mountain pine beetles, and does their diet of whitebark pine trees affect grizzly bear food sources?[4] Do warmer summers send heat-averse pikas to higher elevations, and if so, what happens to those populations when they reach the top of a mountain?[5] Do the natural schedules of wildfires change, for example from once every three hundred years to once every thirty to fifty years in certain forest types, and if so, how does that affect the plants that thrive in those regimes?[6] Such questions currently fascinate ecologists, and if that fascination spreads to the wider population, Yellowstone becomes a laboratory and classroom for learning how natural and human systems can best adapt to a world with a changing climate.

Which leads to the second possibility: a change in America's view of its relationship to nature. Among environmental scholars and activists, one of the most hotly debated subjects of the past few decades has been the idea of *wilderness*. Does it really make sense to draw boundaries around areas "untrammeled by man," given what we now know about how ecosystems extend across boundaries and how they are affected by external factors, including climate change?

Was the creation of wilderness areas, in retrospect, just another way of dispossessing Native Americans? Did it favor the leisure activities of the rich over the subsistence activities of the poor? And doesn't a wilderness area suggest that nature is something over there, in a box, that we drive to—when it should be part of our everyday world?

Yet if you accept these arguments and stop advocating for wilderness, won't materialist culture overtake everything? Where will be the places for grizzly bear habitat, or for the sort of spiritual retreat that Ansel Adams so effectively articulated?

The debate is only slowly seeping into public consciousness. Many books have been written, but few have been best sellers. Televised documentaries have not approached the popularity of, say, Ken Burns's series on the national parks. Cheryl Strayed's popular memoir, *Wild*, speaks to the transformative power of nature without dwelling much on the political designations of the land she traverses, and the movie version doesn't mention wilderness at all.[7] Between the wilderness debate's lack of visibility and its lack of resolution, I can't say whether it will have any effects on broader national culture.

But let's imagine it does. Let's imagine that a new generation of nature-lovers devises new ways of articulating the role that human beings play in natural systems. These new thought patterns might even do better than our current ones at incorporating natural beauty into everyday lives. In this yet-to-be-articulated vision, Yellowstone could play a powerful role. After all, Yellowstone is known as a place to experience nature—but it accommodates four million visits per year. It's a place of nature *and* people. It's a place where one of the world's most extraordinary natural features, the Old Faithful geyser, erupts adjacent to an extraordinary man-made work of art, the Old Faithful Inn. And when people visit, they like both, see them as complementing each other. What could be a better representation of humans living in concert with nature? The natural glory of the geyser spurred the creativity of Robert Reamer and the Childs, with a result that enhances your ability to experience both wonders. A society more focused on incorporating nature into everyday life would find much inspiration here.

Which leads to the third possibility: an increased reverence for Yellowstone's ancestral cultures. I was pained to spend so little of this book discussing Native Americans. But I was looking at what the wider culture had valued through American history, and it had not valued indigenous people.[8] Nineteenth-century explorers encountered Crow, Bannock, Flathead, Pend d'Oreille, Kiowa, and Nez Perce in the lands surrounding Yellowstone; all of them knew and used the park. These tribes and others had names for the region, such as the Blackfeet "Many Smokes" or Crow "Land of Steam." Yet somehow there arose among Anglos a crazy idea that Indians were "afraid" of the geysers.[9] It was not true; rather, many native tribes saw Yellowstone as a wondrous but everyday place. As Oglala Lakota chief Luther Standing Bear said, "Only to the white man was nature a 'wilderness' and only to him was it 'infested' with 'wild' animals and 'savage' people. To us it was tame. Earth was bountiful and we were surrounded with the blessings of the Great Mystery."[10]

On a very basic level, a society that honored Native Americans in part by trying to treat nature the same everywhere—a society that didn't zone landscapes into wilderness areas versus oil fields—would take some inspiring lessons (far different from the lessons that today's society takes) from the human history of Yellowstone.

Indeed a society that honored Native Americans would likely dig deeper into the native history of Yellowstone and find even greater tragedy. Although most of the tribes cited above used the park only seasonally, one tribe did live here nearly full-time—but its members have been aggressively erased from the records. They were a Shoshonean band known as the Sheepeaters.

Before the arrival of Anglos, bighorn sheep were far more numerous than they are today. The Sheepeater diet centered on bighorns, while also including fish, smaller game, wild root vegetables, berries, seeds, and pine nuts. From the sheep's hides they made elaborate clothing and blankets; from the sheep's horns they made bows for their arrows. These bows, strengthened by deer or elk sinew, were the most powerful ever made, stronger than those of any other tribe, and arguably stronger even than English crossbows. Shaping the horns into the bow required repeated soakings in hot water, which the Sheepeaters could easily find in Yellowstone. For the arrowheads, obsidian represented the sharpest, cleanest edge in the world—and it was in rich supply in their homeland.

Bighorn sheep commonly escape enemies by running up rocky hillsides, to places where wolves, for example, can't follow them. So the Sheepeaters would chase the sheep up hills—past blinds where they could be shot, or into traps where they could be clubbed. The process did not require horses. Indeed the horse was not very useful amid long winters and rocky terrain, where its grass-based diet was often unavailable. So when horses became available in the 18th century, the Sheepeaters saw no need for the new technology. They were like Manhattanites who don't drive. Plains Indians, including the Sheepeaters' close relations, the Eastern Shoshone, needed horses not only to chase bison but also to make war with other tribes chasing bison. But the Sheepeaters had a unique niche that didn't require making war. On the rare occasions when they faced an aggressor in their homeland, they could rely on their superior knowledge of the crazily rugged mountain terrain. There were plenty of sources of obsidian, plenty of bands of sheep. They could run away and live to thrive another day.

The invasion of colonials brought domestic sheep to the periphery of bighorn territory, carrying diseases against which bighorns had no defense. Bighorn populations plummeted. (Although in 1836 trapper Osborne Russell regularly encountered thousands of bighorns, in his entire 1897 visit Ernest Thompson Seton encountered zero.) Meanwhile other game was decimated by hunters for mining camps, and fish were poisoned by pollution or blocked from the high country by dams. Although early trappers had been impressed with the wealth and self-confidence of Sheepeaters, later explorers claimed to find them starving and miserable. They were easily rounded up and exiled to the Fort Hall (Idaho) and Wind River (Wyoming) reservations, where they mixed with other bands of Shoshones, Bannocks, and Arapahos. Few of their stories made it into the national consciousness. And so they became known for the prejudices of those late encounters: *They were starving. They ran away. They didn't even have horses.* The Sheepeaters became known as the lowliest form of Indians: dirty, poor pygmies lacking status, wealth, pride, or beauty.[11]

Yet in fact, as far as we can tell, the Sheepeaters had developed a remarkably sustainable way of life. They didn't insist on using horses simply because horses worked well elsewhere, or because horses enhanced the masculinity of their riders. They chose their tools and strategies to maximize the value of the surrounding landscape. They found a home and a lifestyle that allowed them to live as relative pacifists.

American society is becoming more multicultural. As it does so, it is also becoming more attuned to the unique advantages offered by specific micro-landscapes or communities. A society that fully embraces those visions could celebrate the way Yellowstone's Sheepeater culture maximized the advantages, while gracefully acknowledging the limits, of the very specific and special place where they lived.

Wouldn't that passage have made a great ending to the book? Three hopeful visions for the future, with links to future visions of Yellowstone. But when I looked up from my fascinating sources, I found Yellowstone not yet really moving in any of these directions. Instead, I found a lot of talk about a supervolcano. For example, in the summer of 2014 a series of videos purporting to show animals fleeing Yellowstone in advance of an alleged volcano eruption went viral, being viewed more than 1.5 million times.[12] Although their specifics were discredited—for example, the animals were actually running *toward* the park—the videos dominated social media because they captured the zeitgeist. Indeed as I told people I was writing a book about Yellowstone, many responded with some variant of *And will you end with the supervolcano? When do you think it's going to blow?*

It felt like one of those nightmares where I was taking a fiendish professor's final exam. I was alone in a classroom and required to distill all that I'd learned by answering a question totally out of left field. I felt pressure: if I flubbed this, it meant my grade for the whole course—in this case, whatever I came up with on the supervolcano was going to be the only thing you would remember about this book. It almost made sense for the nightmare to end with the supervolcano destroying the world as we know it, such that nobody would be able to read the book and I'd be spared their scorn. (Plus, being dead, I'd be largely beyond embarrassment.) Luckily, however, I found that I could click my heels three times and repeat, "It's only a dream! Maybe you could do some research!"

I turned first to the science. A volcano is "super" when it has the potential to eject more than 240 cubic miles of magma, which is a scale not known to recorded history. Yellowstone is indeed earth's largest known supervolcano. If it blew all at once, the eruption would be eight thousand times bigger than that of Mount St. Helens in 1980. It could well bury hundreds of square miles of the surrounding area in ash, killing me and everyone in my town. It could furthermore disrupt infrastructure, climate patterns, and food systems across the continent and even around the world. Indeed it would be so cataclysmic that it's hard for anybody to understand exactly what would happen or how ecosystems or societies would react.

However, all the science I've read says that I will not die tomorrow. Although it's true that the Yellowstone supervolcano erupted 2 million, 1.2 million, and 640,000 years ago—in other words, historical math says we might be due—the U.S. Geological Survey (USGS) has done a more sophisticated mathematical analysis of that data. It estimates that the probability of a mega-eruption in any given year is 1 in 700,000, about the same as that of an asteroid hitting the earth. And when USGS scientists examine scientific factors, not just historical math, they aren't even convinced that it will *ever* erupt again. It certainly might, but if and when it does, the eruption would almost surely follow noticeable warning signs. The rising magma would first rupture geologic plates, creating earthquakes. It would then leak out in tiny spurts, creating nonexplosive lava flows. We would know something was coming, perhaps months and maybe even decades in advance. No such warning signs are currently evident.[13]

The threat of the supervolcano isn't imminent—nor is it new. We've known for a long time that Yellowstone sits precariously atop a gigantic pool of magma. That's what heats the water to create the geysers and other thermal features. Although scientists have recently improved their estimates of the size of a lower magma chamber, the overall picture hasn't much changed in decades.

Instead, what's changed is the values of the wider culture. In the 2010s we've reached a relative apex of apocalyptic fantasies. There have been movie series such as *The Hunger Games* and *Divergent*, as well as TV shows such as *The Walking Dead, Black Mirror,* and *The Leftovers.* In popular media, it sometimes seems that you can't swing a dead cat without hitting a zombie.

Granted, the end of the world has long been a popular plot for stories, from *Dr. Strangelove* all the way back to the Book of Revelation. But until recently, such stories were created for the purpose of moralistic prophecy. Their authors had firm ideas about what needed to change to achieve salvation and/or avoid the end of the world. The point of a science fiction book or art-house movie was to be thought-provoking. Conversely, today's apocalyptic stories tend toward disposable entertainment. Even with all the nihilism and sadistic violence, they can be told as broad comedies (Seth Rogen's *This Is the End*) or teen fiction (Scott Westerfeld's *Uglies*).[14]

Here's the hopeful way to look at the trend: the postapocalyptic landscape has become allegorical. It's a widely understood setting in which we can tell stories that work through big societal issues that are too emotionally fraught to address head-on. In the 1950s, Americans debated the news through Western movies: *High Noon* was all about McCarthyism, *Rio Grande* mirrored the moral choices involved in the Korean conflict, and *Shane* represented the sacrifices required to preserve the sense of domestic order that suburbanites then so cherished.[15] Today, postapocalyptic landscapes function similarly: as imaginary places where we can ponder troubling issues such as all-encompassing surveillance, income inequality, the dehumanizing (zombifying) effects of consumerism, or the dystopian experience of high school.

However, when you spend so much time discussing apocalypses, the traditional nuclear Armageddon can get to feel a bit stale. There's value in creativity, in predicting unusual triggering cataclysms. Indeed part of the horror of the terrorist attacks of September 11, 2001, was the emotional shock of how surprising they were, how poorly they'd been predicted. So today, when Americans tell stories about *unexpected* devastating events such as a zombie apocalypse, on some level we're processing that horror in a relatively safe space. In that sense, imagining an extinction-level volcanic eruption in Yellowstone becomes a kind of public service. The supervolcano is the zombie apocalypse wrapped in mostly-legitimate science.

After all, the science doesn't tell us that an eruption is *impossible.* In some ways, these are the "right" lessons to have learned from Yellowstone's history. The 1988 fires taught us that nothing is permanent. Yellowstone will change. So why wouldn't it change suddenly and explosively, with devastating consequences for not only the cultural values we place on the park but also humanity's entire existence?

From an emotional perspective, for Yellowstone to erupt and destroy the world would be a satisfying mirror of the story of the Garden of Eden. We perceive the park as a wondrous place where all creatures live in harmony. Yet we are continually confronted with a sad truth: things that inspire wonder—such as air travel or the World Trade Center—can become instruments of horror. (There's a fascinating parallel to 19th-century *sublimity*, although with the power now resting as much with technology as with God.) So it would feel tragically appropriate if Yellowstone would also turn out to be the source of worldwide devastation.

I think people fascinated by the supervolcano are layering this meaning on top of everything else in Yellowstone. They are once again seeing the park as a wonderlandscape. They are repeating the historical pattern: The culture develops a new fascination. People seek to apply it in the nation's signature landscape. And miraculously, Yellowstone reveals itself to contain previously underappreciated wonders that fulfill and expand upon that cultural need.

Yellowstone has always acted as a reflection of American society. It is now acting as a reflection of American society. And—well, I was going to write *it always will*, but in the unlikely event that the supervolcano does indeed explode the very essence of American society, that certainly would provide a dramatic end to the story.

ACKNOWLEDGMENTS

Yellowstone is big. Not only geographically, at two million acres, but also in the mind and the heart. It cradles lots of big stories. So my first acknowledgment is to all the people—artists, activists, and administrators; scientists and historians; wanderers and wonderers—whose stories I haven't included here. Not because they aren't important but because they didn't fit the narrative I chose to tell.

This book is a work of nonfiction. All its characters are real; nothing has been altered or embellished. Where I have used dialogue, it is based on the recollection of at least one participant, as documented in the endnotes. I've built on the scholarship and experiences of hundreds of wonderful people, and I thank them for their work and their stories.

ACKNOWLEDGMENTS

Thanks to the Yellowstone National Park library, museum, and archives in Gardiner, Montana—Colleen Curry, Anne Foster, Jackie Jerla, and their colleagues. Also the libraries and archives at Montana State University-Bozeman, the University of Montana-Missoula, the Center for Creative Photography and the University of Arizona in Tucson, the Montana Historical Society, Montana State University-Billings, Northwest (Wyoming) College, Park County (Wyoming), and cities of Billings and Red Lodge, Montana. Special thanks to the Buffalo Bill Center for the West in Cody, Wyoming, which gave me a small fellowship to spend a week in its McCracken Research Library; I appreciate the support there of John Rumm, Chuck Preston, Mary Robinson, Char Gdula, Nicholle Gerharter, and Marguerite House. And thanks of course to the many people who have accompanied me on excursions in and around Yellowstone over the last almost-thirty years.

From my earliest conceptualizations of this book, support came from many friends and family members, especially Charlie Mitchell, Kari Mitchell, Cathy Clayton, Luca Macchiarulo, and Paul and Jackie Clayton. (By the way, my conceptualizations often start with other books, so I'd like to honor William Cronon's *Nature's Metropolis* and Hal Rothman's *Neon Metropolis*; my quest to write a book halfway as good as those even included a Yellowstone-as-metropolis theme, until Jeff Speck wisely talked me out of it.) Lee Nellis, Charlie Mitchell, Gary Ferguson, Steve Pyne, Kim Anderson, and Ken Egan helped me hone ideas. Lee Whittlesey, Dave Stauffer, Charlie Mitchell, Lee Nellis, Gary Ferguson, Jackie and Paul Clayton, and Stephen Wilcox read drafts of the entire manuscript, and Amy Hyfield, Tom Rea, Allen Jones, Kevin Kooistra, Chuck Preston, John Rumm, Phil Brigandi, Terry Amdur, Mike Keys, Joyce Bileau, Mark Robertson, and "Yowp Yowp" read sections. All of these people provided valuable input that saved me from factual and rhetorical errors; of course all errors that remain are my own responsibility.

Portions of chapter 7 were previously published in *Big Sky Journal* as "Ansel Adams in Yellowstone." Portions of chapter 10 and the epilogue appeared, in very different form, in *Points West*. My research into Robert Reamer, Steve Mather, Howard Eaton, and others found expression in articles for *Magic (City)* magazine, my research on dude ranches at www.wyohistory.org, and my research on the Hayden expedition in the anthology *Unearthing Paradise: Montana Writers in Defense of Greater Yellowstone* (Elk River Books, 2016). So I'd like to thank editors Allyn Hulteng, Brenda Maas, Tara Cady, Tom Rea, Marguerite House, Marc Beaudin, Max Hjortsberg, and Seabring Davis for the opportunities. But I'm especially appreciative of Allen Jones, editor of *Big Sky Journal*, who not only embraced the Ansel Adams story but also helped me redo my book proposal.

My agent, Laura Wood, knew just what to do with that proposal. Thanks to Bill Steigerwald, who connected us, and Tony Martin and John Dvorak, for encouragement. At Pegasus Books, Jessica Case was a wonderful host and champion, who thankfully edited my prose with more rigor than any of my previous book editors. Copyeditor Judy Gelman Myers and proofreader Mary O'Mara made many more great textual improvements. Maria Fernandez designed the interior, Michael Fusco designed the cover, and Katie McGuire and Katie Cahill-Volpe aided early marketing efforts.

I had an idiosyncratic passion. All of these people, and many more who aren't mentioned here, came together in support of me, and the result of their efforts was the book you hold in your hand. My gratitude is—well, I'm not sure it could be as big as Yellowstone, but it's pretty darned big.

NOTES

PROLOGUE

1. Lynn Ross-Bryant, *Pilgrimage to the National Parks: Religion and Nature in the United States* (London: Routledge, 2013), 2.
2. In *Wilderness and the American Mind* (New Haven: Yale University Press, 1967; fifth edition 2014), Roderick Nash argued that "civilization created wilderness" (p. xx). See also William Cronon, "The Trouble with Wilderness; or, Getting Back to the Wrong Nature" in William Cronon, ed., *Uncommon Ground: Rethinking the Human Place in Nature* (New York: W. W. Norton & Co., 1995), 69–90.

CHAPTER I: SPECIAL

1. A note on terminology: Both "Anglo" and "white" are potentially problematic ways to refer to *descendants of colonizing northern European cultures*, because "white" includes Hispanics while "Anglo" might exclude people whose language or bloodlines are French or otherwise not-English. But more-correct alternatives (such as the italicized phrase above) are wordy and awkward, and realistically, neither of the problems is much of a factor when discussing Yellowstone since

1870. So with this caveat, I use "Anglo" and "white" interchangeably, in their commonly-accepted meanings.

2. A good discussion of Colter's trip, and the way later writers burnished his legend, is in George Black, *Empire of Shadows: The Epic Story of Yellowstone* (New York: St. Martin's, 2012), 33–35.

3. Aubrey L. Haines, *Yellowstone National Park: Its Exploration and Establishment* (Washington: U.S. National Park Service, 1974), 21.

4. The most common definitions of *discover* involve *finding* or *becoming aware of*, usually associated with a notion of being the first. A secondary definition, which Oxford calls archaic, is to *divulge* (a secret) or *display*, as in "with what agility did these military men discover their skill in feats of war." The 1870 and '71 explorers were certainly not the first to find, become aware of, show an interest in, or recognize the potential of Yellowstone, but because they were the first chroniclers of the place that wider American society listened to, one could argue that they were the first to divulge the existence of Yellowstone and its wonders. Certainly at the time they got credit as discoverers. See https://en.oxforddictionaries.com/definition/discover, accessed November 19, 2016.

5. The early Yellowstone expeditions have been well documented by historians, especially Aubrey Haines in *Exploration and Establishment* and *The Yellowstone Story: A History of Our First National Park* (Yellowstone Library and Museum Association, two volumes, 1977). They were chronicled in magazine articles at the time. For perspective and interpretation, this chapter also relies generally on Anne F. Hyde, *American Vision: Far Western Landscape and National Culture 1820-1920* (New York: NYU Press, 1990) and Thurman Wilkins, *Thomas Moran: Artist of the Mountains* (Norman: University of Oklahoma Press, 1998).

6. Hayden quoted in Philip Fradkin, *Sagebrush Country: Land and the American West* (Tuscon: University of Arizona Press, 1989), 160. To judge from the rugged, unsettled Uintas today, you might say Hayden failed.

7. See generally Marlene Deahl Merrill, ed., *Yellowstone and the Great West: Journals, Letters and Images from the 1871 Hayden Expedition* (Lincoln: University of Nebraska Press, 1999). This excellent book corrects previous misperceptions that Moran joined the others at Virginia City.

8. All of Langford's quotes are from Nathaniel Pitt Langford, "The Wonders of the Yellowstone," *Scribner's Monthly* 2 (May 1871): 1–16.

9. Peter H. Hassrick, *The Rocky Mountains: A Vision for Artists in the Nineteenth Century* (Norman: University of Oklahoma Press, 1983), 13, 195.

10. Ferdinand Hayden, "The Wonders of the West II: More about the Yellowstone," *Scribner's Monthly* 3 (February 1872): 388–396. Albert Peale quoted in Marlene Merrill, ed., *Seeing Yellowstone in 1871: Earliest Descriptions & Images from the Field* (Lincoln: University of Nebraska Press, 2005), 33.

11. Ross-Bryant, *Pilgrimage*, 28.

12. F.V. Hayden, "Preliminary Report of the United States Geological Survey of Montana and Portions of Adjacent Territories being a Fifth Annual Report of Progress" (Washington: U.S. Department of Interior, 1872), 84.

13. Rudyard Kipling, *American Notes* (Boston: Brown and Company, 1899), 88.

14. Hayden, "The Wonders of the West II," 392.

15. Thomas Moran to Ferdinand Hayden, March 21, 1872, quoted in Nancy K. Anderson, et. al., *Thomas Moran* (Washington: National Gallery of Art in association with Yale University Press, 1997), 89.

16. Wilkins, *Thomas Moran*, 3; Jno. [John] R. G. Hassard. "The New York Mercantile Library," *Scribner's Monthly* 1 (February, 1871): 353–367. Clinton Hall has since been torn down.

17. Technically, Congress could have granted the park to one or more territories, and indeed some Montanans argued for such a solution (as further discussed in chapter 5). But would the rudimentary Wyoming government administer this land from distant Cheyenne? Or would it be taken from Wyoming and given to Montana? A national park was the more practical solution. See Haines, *Exploration and Establishment*, 111.

18. "Notes from Washington," *The Ladies' Repository: Universalist Monthly Magazine* 48 (July 1872): 158–159.

19. Richard Watson Gilder quoted in Wilkins, *Thomas Moran*, 100.

20. Moran quoted in Wilkins, *Thomas Moran*, 100. The Clinton Hall exhibition did not accomplish Moran's goal of selling the painting, but a later exhibition in Washington led to its purchase by Congress.

21. For related discussions, see generally Andrew Wilton and Tim Barringer, *American Sublime: Landscape Painting in the United States 1820-1880* (Princeton: Princeton University Press, 2002) and Alison Smith, "The Sublime in Crisis: Landscape Painting after Turner," in Nigel Llewellyn and Christine Riding (eds.), *The Art of the Sublime* (London: Tate Research Publication, January 2013).

22. Anne Morand, Joni L. Kinsey, and Mary Panzer, *Splendors of the American West: Thomas Moran's Art of the Grand Canyon and Yellowstone* (Seattle: University of Washington Press, 1990), 34.

23. Albert Peale's diary for August 4, 1871, in Merrill, *Yellowstone and the Great West*, 147.

24. W. H. Jackson interviewed for the monthly Yellowstone superintendent's report for August 1937, which is reprinted at "Old Report Describes Photographer W. H. Jackson's Return To Yellowstone National Park At The Age Of 94," *National Parks Traveler*, August 28, 2014. However, Peale's diaries (in Merrill, *Yellowstone and the Great West*, 131, 161) and the Barlow-Heap report (J.W. Barlow and D.P. Heap, *Report of a Reconnaissance of the Basin of the Upper Yellowstone in 1871* (Washington: U.S. Army Corps of Engineers, 1872) do indicate a bear and two or three cubs being killed near

Mammoth, and another seen near Lake. Perhaps Jackson himself never saw a bear, and in old age recklessly expanded that perspective to the entire party.

CHAPTER 2: HALF TIME

1. Todd Wilkinson, "Bison Calf's Death Shows Dangers of People in Yellowstone," nationalgeographic.com, May 17, 2016.

2. Deby Dixon, "The Real Story About The Bison Calf That Took A Ride In The Car," *National Parks Traveler*, May 22, 2016. Associated Press, "Tourists Defend Loading Yellowstone Bison Calf into Vehicle," June 3, 2016.

3. Many of today's Yellowstone bison trace to a herd assembled in 1902 from northwest Montana via North Dakota and Texas. See Michael Punke, *Last Stand: George Bird Grinnell, the Battle to Save the Buffalo, and the Birth of the New West* (Washington: Smithsonian, 2007), 219–223.

4. In addition to the Setons' own writings, this chapter is indebted generally to H. Allen Anderson, *The Chief: Ernest Thompson Seton and the Changing West* (College Station, TX: Texas A&M University Press, 1986).

5. Ernest Thompson Seton, *Trail of an Artist-naturalist: The Autobiography of Ernest Thompson Seton* (New York: Scribner's, 1948), 6.

6. Ernest Seton Thompson, "Elkland," *Recreation* 7 (1897): 199.

7. See Richard Slotkin, *The Fatal Environment: The Myth of the Frontier in the Age of Industrialization, 1800–1890* (New York: Atheneum, 1985), 80–106.

8. Seton deserves credit for training kids on nature skills through positive depictions of indigenous people, although by today's standards his understanding of Native traditions was badly garbled. See H. Allen Anderson, *The Scout*, 128–165.

9. Seton himself estimated 75 million, a number that was accepted for many years. Modern estimates range from 25 to 40 million. See Andrew C. Isenberg, *The Destruction of the Bison: An Environmental History, 1750–1920* (Cambridge: Cambridge University Press, 2000), 24–25.

10. Early explorers mischaracterized the red streak as being caused by mercuric sulphide, or cinnabar, and gave that name to an adjacent town site. Ferdinand Hayden identified the red as iron oxide, but allowed the site name to remain. See Lee Whittlesey, *Gateway to Yellowstone: The Raucous Town of Cinnabar on the Montana Frontier* (Helena: TwoDot, 2015), 8–9.

11. Rudyard Kipling, *From Sea to Sea; Letters of Travel*, vol. 2. (New York: Doubleday, McClure, 1899), 67–68.

12. Carl E. Schmidt, *A Western Trip* (Detroit: Herold Press, c. 1904), 59–63.

13. Ernest Seton Thompson, "Elkland II: The Beaver Pond," *Recreation* 7 (1897): 289.

14. Ernest Seton Thompson, "Mammals of the Yellowstone National Park," *Recreation* 8 (1897): 365–371.

15. Dialogue recorded in Ernest Thompson Seton, *Wild Animals at Home* (New York: Grosset & Dunlap, 1913), 205.

16. Ernest Thompson Seton, *Krag and Johnny Bear: With Pictures* (New York: C. Scribner's Sons, 1906), 99. All Seton quotes use his original spelling and capitalization preferences, such as "Blackbear."

17. Ernest Thompson Seton, *Krag and Johnny Bear*, 100.

18. Ernest Thompson Seton, *Krag and Johnny Bear*, 96. Seton's personification of the animals—giving them names and portraying them as grumbling or whining, as if in need of a spanking—got him in trouble with scientists. Today, some experts dismiss his works as children's storybooks: more useful in getting kids excited about nature than in explaining how nature really works. Because the Setons' books are our only sources for his episode in the garbage pit, we may want to use that skeptical lens in considering his descriptions of the bears' and his own actions.

19. The dialogue and descriptions of this episode are recorded in Grace Gallatin Seton, *A Woman Tenderfoot* (New York: Doubleday, Page, 1900), 210–213.

20. For biographical information on Anderson, see the A. A. Anderson vertical file, McCracken Research Library, Buffalo Bill Center of the West, Cody, Wyoming. Anderson's nickname "Triple-A" is referenced in a clipping from www.plantingfields.org/collec/cody_connection.htm, accessed April 22, 2008.

21. See generally A. A. Anderson, *Experiences and Impressions* (Freeport: Books for Libraries Press, 1933).

22. The Setons' activities with A. A. Anderson are documented in H. Allen Anderson, *The Chief*, 40, 82–85, 275. See also Grace Gallatin Seton, *A Woman Tenderfoot*, 185–209.

23. Grace Gallatin Seton, *A Woman Tenderfoot*, 185.

24. Starting in the 1960s, science suggested that it might indeed be possible for grizzlies to travel such great distances, as discussed in chapter 8. But my point is that our heroes loved the legends.

25. Grace Gallatin Seton, *A Woman Tenderfoot*, 190.

26. For photos of the Palette Ranch, see records P87-05-002 through P87-05-006, and P90-33-038, at the Park County Historical Archives, Cody, Wyoming. Other area descriptions are from my visit to the valley in July 2014.

27. The legend of Warhouse Creek is discussed (although not well documented) at http://www.wyomingtalesandtrails.com/cody4.html, accessed November 17, 2016.

28. Jeremy M. Johnston provides background to the novel in the introduction to a recent reissue: Ernest Thompson Seton, Jeremy M. Johnston, ed., and Charles R. Preston, ed., *Wahb: The Biography of a Grizzly* (Norman: University of Oklahoma Press, 2015).

29. A. A. Anderson, *Experiences and Impressions*, 186–194; "'Wab,' Wisest of Bears, Falls Victim to Anderson's Rifle After Many Years of Defiance," *Park County Enterprise*, September 22, 1915, 1.

30. Ernest Thompson Seton, *The Biography of a Grizzly* (New York: Century, 1900), 126.

31. For records, see Alice Wondrak Biel, *Do (Not) Feed the Bears: The Fitful History of Wildlife and Tourists in Yellowstone* (Lawrence: University of Kansas Press, 2006), 25. Seton was incorrect: Bears *had* attacked people, including incidents documented by Lee Whittlesey in *Death in Yellowstone: Accidents and Foolhardiness in the First National Park* (Boulder: Roberts Rinehart, 1995), 37–38.

32. Scientist John Burroughs later targeted Seton as part of his 1903 crusade against "nature fakers" whose compassion for animals led them to purposeful fabrications. The two men then made up, with Burroughs admitting that Seton didn't fabricate actions as aggressively as some of the other fakers did, and Seton admitting that the anthropomorphism in some of his early stories may have gone too far. More broadly, some criticism of Seton may have come because he violated *Christian* (as opposed to scientific) views of the animal world. See Ralph H. Lutts, *The Nature Fakers: Wildlife, Science & Sentiment* (Charlottesville: University of Virginia Press, 1990), 33, 47, 93, 161–162, and 178.

33. H. Allen Anderson, *The Chief*, 55–57.

34. Biel, *Do (Not) Feed the Bears*, 7–8.

35. H. Allen Anderson, *The Chief*, 104. The Roosevelt angle on the invention of Teddy Bears is true; see National Park Service, "The Story of the Teddy Bear," http://www.nps.gov/thrb/learn/historyculture/storyofteddybear.htm, accessed November 18, 2016. The link to Seton, however, deserves skepticism.

36. Ernest Thompson Seton, *Wild Animals at Home*, 210.

37. Ernest Thompson Seton, *Lives of the Hunted* (New York: C. Scribner's Sons, 1912), 187–191. Given Seton's reputation, we should interpret the Little Johnny stories more for what they say about cultural values than for any literal truth.

38. An example of that evolving science: given what we now know about the evolution of human morality as an outgrowth of our social nature, scientists are increasingly willing to consider ascribing emotions to canines as well. See Dan Flores, *Coyote America* (New York: Basic Books, 2016), 92–94.

39. The bison recovery story—the first-ever effort by humans to save an animal from extinction—is well told in books such as Punke's *Last Stand*.

40. Richard West Sellars, *Preserving Nature in the National Parks: A History* (New Haven: Yale University Press, 2009), 78.

41. Ernest Thompson Seton, *Wild Animals at Home*, v–vi.

CHAPTER 3: INFORMAL

1. Park Service personnel refer to this contrast as *natural* vs. *cultural* resources. See Sue Consolo-Murphy, "Integrated and Equal?" *Yellowstone Science: A Quarterly Publication Devoted to the Natural and Cultural Resources* 8, no. 3 (Summer 2000): 1.

2. This chapter relies generally on Ruth Quinn's extraordinarily well-researched book *Weaver of Dreams: The Life and Architecture of Robert C. Reamer* (Gardiner: Leslie and Ruth Quinn, 2004). See also Ruth Quinn, "Overcoming Obscurity:

The Yellowstone Architecture of Robert C. Reamer," *Yellowstone Science* 12(2), Spring 2004, 23–40. Among her other credits, Quinn uncovered the Reamer–Child connection at the Hotel del Coronado.

3. For Harry and Adelaide Child, see Bertie Charles Forbes, "Harry W. Child," in *Men Who Are Making the West* (New York: B. C. Forbes, 1923), 322–343; Mark Barringer, *Private Empire, Public Land: The Rise and Fall of the Yellowstone Park Company*, a 1997 PhD thesis available in the park library and archives; and especially Harry W. Child II, *Montana Pioneers: the Huntley, Child & Dean families: Yellowstone Park*, an unpublished manuscript available in the park library and archives. This recollection by a great-grandson says that Adelaide, who was called Addie, originated the plans to build the Old Faithful Inn.

4. Thomas Morrow, et. al., *Hotel del Coronado* (Coronado: Hotel del Coronado, 1984).

5. Helena, in an oft-quoted but hard-to-document story, boasted 50 millionaires in 1888. The most authoritative source I could find for this claim: Gordon Morris Bakken, ed., *Encyclopedia of Immigration and Migration in the American West* (Los Angeles: Sage Publications, 2006), 383.

6. Richard A. Bartlett, *Yellowstone: A Wilderness Besieged* (Tucson: University of Arizona Press, 1985), 174. See also a photograph of Child in Quinn, *Weaver of Dreams*, 8.

7. Quoted in Robert Shankland, *Steve Mather of the National Parks* (New York: Knopf, 1970), 118.

8. Unidentified acquaintance quoted in Barringer, *Private Empire, Public Land*, 36.

9. Both quoted in Quinn, *Weaver of Dreams*, 74.

10. Concession manager J. H. Dean quoted in Quinn, *Weaver of Dreams*, 44.

11. Babcock quoted in Quinn, *Weaver of Dreams*, 6.

12. Jane White quoted in Quinn, *Weaver of Dreams*, 171.

13. Babcock quoted in Quinn, *Weaver of Dreams*, 172.

14. Charles Francis Adams quoted in Bartlett, *Wilderness Besieged*, 181–182.

15. For the characteristics and influence of the Old Faithful Inn, see David Naylor, "The Old Faithful Inn and its Legacy: The Vernacular Transformed"; "Historic Structure Report, Historical Data Section, Old Faithful Inn, Yellowstone National Park, Wyoming"; and Laura E. Soullière Harrison, *Architecture in the Parks: National Historic Landmark Theme Study* (Washington: National Park Service, 1987). All of these documents are available in the park library.

16. For femininity, see Sarah Bonnemaison and Christine Macy, *Architecture and Nature: Creating the American Landscape* (London: Routledge, 2000), 76–97.

17. Harrison, *Architecture in the Parks*, 68.

18. *Western Architect* and Pitcher quoted in Quinn, *Weaver of Dreams*, 11–12. Adams quoted in Bartlett, *Wilderness Besieged*, 183.

19. For example, see H. L. Mencken, *The American Language*, (New York: Knopf, 1919), 361: "Despite the contrary examples of Mark Twain and [William Dean] Howells, all of the more pretentious American authors try to write chastely and

elegantly." Mencken also famously said, "Henry James would have been vastly improved as a novelist by a few whiffs" of the Chicago stockyards.

20. Merrill Ann Wilson, "Rustic Architecture: The National Park Style," *Trends,* (July August September, 1976): 4–5.

CHAPTER 4: RUGGED

1. Theodore Roosevelt, Gardiner, Montana, April 24, 1903, quoted in Lee H. Whittlesey and Paul Schullery, "The Roosevelt Arch: A Centennial History of an American Icon," *Yellowstone Science* (Summer 2003): 14–15. Emphasis added.

2. For Howard Eaton, see generally Tom Ringley, *Wranglin' Notes: A Chronicle of Eatons' Ranch* (Greybull.: Pronghorn Press, 2012). See also Lee Silliman, "'As Kind and Generous a Host as Ever Lived': Howard Eaton and the Birth of Western Dude Ranching," *American West* 16 (July/ August 1979): 18–31, and Carter G. Walker, "Eatons' Ranch," *Big Sky Journal* (Spring 2006): 112–117. For background, see John Clayton, "Romancing the West: Dude Ranching in Wyoming," at www.wyohistory.org (2014), and Lawrence R. Borne, *Dude Ranching: A Complete History* (Albuquerque: University of New Mexico Press, 1983).

3. Silliman, "'As Kind and Generous a Host,'" 18, and A. A. Dailey, "Uncle Howard Eaton," *Outing* 76 (July-August 1920): 200–201.

4. For Larom, see generally W. Hudson Kensel, *Dude Ranching in Yellowstone Country: Larry Larom and Valley Ranch, 1915–1969* (Norman: Arthur H. Clark Co., 2010).

5. See photos of Larom in Kensel, *Larry Larom,* and in the Charles Belden Collection at the American Heritage Center of the University of Wyoming in Laramie, Wyoming.

6. After buying the Valley Ranch from James and Jennie McLaughlin, Larom hired them the first summer, but never again. In 1917 James died of syphilis in Los Angeles at age 54. See Kensel, *Larry Larom,* 36–50.

7. For Burt, see generally Maxwell Struthers Burt, *The Diary of a Dude-wrangler* (New York: Scribner, 1924, 1938); Hal K. Rothman, *Devils Bargains: Tourism in the Twentieth-Century American West* (Lawrence: University Press of Kansas, 1998), 128–140; and National Park Service, "Grand Teton Historic Resource Study, Chapter 14: The Dude Wranglers," http://www.nps.gov/parkhistory/online_books/grte2/hrs14.htm, accessed November 20, 2015.

8. See, for example, "Bar BC Ranch (Landscapes of Loss)" http://jacksonhole history.org/bar-bc-ranch-landscapes-of-loss/, accessed November 19, 2015.

9. For Rooseveltian masculinity, see, for example, Richard Slotkin, *Gunfighter Nation: The Myth of the Frontier in Twentieth-century America* (Norman: University of Oklahoma Press, 1992), 29–62, and Edmund Morris, *The Rise of Theodore Roosevelt* (New York: Modern Library, 2001), especially 199–201 and 272–273.

10. Larom quoted in Kensel, *Larry Larom,* 63.

11. Burt, *The Diary of a Dude-wrangler,* 50.

12. This fascinating conundrum is highlighted in Rothman, *Devils Bargains*, especially 120–142.

13. For example, see generally Robert W. Righter, *Crucible for Conservation: The Creation of Grand Teton National Park* (Boulder: Colorado Associated University Press, 1982).

14. John Clayton, *The Cowboy Girl: The Life of Caroline Lockhart* (Lincoln: University of Nebraska Press, 2007), especially 122–123 and 170–182.

15. Emma Hayden Eames Yates, *70 Miles from a Lemon* (New York: Houghton Mifflin, 1947), 156.

16. Scattered counterexamples to this assertion rely on the vague distinctions between "ranch," "hunting camp," and "dude ranch." See Clayton, "Romancing the West."

17. Doris Whithorn, "Wrangling Dudes in Yellowstone," *Frontier Times*, November 1969, 18–22.

18. These are basaltic columnar joints, a product of volcanic cooling. Beth Taylor, "Inside Yellowstone: Sheepeater Cliff" [video], https://www.nps.gov/media/video/view.htm?id=007BBFE1-155D-451F-6779FB37D3D5BC36, accessed November 19, 2016.

19. Albright quoted in Liza Nicholas, *Becoming Western: Stories of Culture and Identity in the Cowboy State* (Lincoln: University of Nebraska Press, 2006), 61.

20. Today Sheepeater Cliff is picnicking only, no camping. But I recommend a dinner picnic there, a leisurely riverside evening followed by a short drive to your campsite or hotel room.

21. "Old West Dinner Cookout: An evening you won't soon forget," http://www.yellowstonenationalparklodges.com/things-to-do/summer-things-to-do/wild-west-adventures/old-west-dinner-cookout/, accessed November 24, 2015.

22. In fairness, I should note that the Park Service requires the activities to be factually authentic. So movie clichés are banned and attendees learn instead about the early days of the park and pioneers such as Uncle John Yancey, whose Pleasant Valley Hotel was nearby. My objection, then, is less to the cookout itself and more to the impulse to which it's marketed—for example, this is the only section of the concessionaire's website to use the dropped *g*'s of the Hollywood-cowboy drawl.

CHAPTER 5: PATRIOTIC

1. Anne-Gerard Flynn, "Ken Burns talks about new PBS series 'The National Parks: America's Best Idea,'" *Springfield Republican*, September 26, 2009. Dayton Duncan, Ken Burns, et. al., *The National Parks: America's Best Idea,* episode 1 (Arlington: PBS Home Video, 2009).

2. This interesting period is addressed in Bartlett, *Wilderness Besieged*, 233–255, and Haines, *The Yellowstone Story,* vol. 1, 261–326.

3. The best account of the development of the Campfire Myth and the National Park Idea is Paul Schullery and Lee H. Whittlesey, *Myth and History in the Creation of Yellowstone National Park* (Lincoln: University of Nebraska Press, 2003), from which this chapter draws generally. See also Lee H. Whittlesey, "Loss of a Sacred Shrine: How the National Park Service Anguished over Yellowstone's Campfire Myth, 1960–1980," *The George Wright Forum* 27, no. 1 (2010): 94–120.

4. For Mather, see generally Robert Shankland, *Steve Mather of the National Parks* (New York: Knopf, 1970).

5. A popular story is that Mather wrote directly to Interior Secretary Franklin Lane because they were friends from college, and that Lane responded, "Dear Steve, If you don't like the way the parks are being run, come on down to Washington and run them yourself." Horace Albright disputed the story, saying that the two men didn't know each other until 1914, and that a series of correspondences involved several intermediaries. See Shankland, *Steve Mather*, 7, and Horace M. Albright and Marian Albright Schenck, *Creating the National Park Service: The Missing Years* (Norman: University of Oklahoma Press, 1999), 30–35.

6. Albright and Schenck, *Creating the National Park Service*, 230.

7. For Albright, see generally Donald Swain, *Wilderness Defender: Horace M. Albright and Conservation* (Chicago: University of Chicago Press, 1970) and Albright and Schenck, *Creating the National Park Service*.

8. Struthers Burt, "A Certain Mountain Chief," *Scribner's* (June 1929): 621.

9. Albright and Schenck, *Creating the National Park Service*, 239.

10. Horace Albright to Stephen Mather, May 22, 1922, Semi-centennial file, YELL 203324 Series 4, file 1.02, Management and Accountability Records, Yellowstone National Park Archives (National Archives Affiliate), Gardiner, MT (hereafter YNPA).

11. William Chauncy Langdon, "America, Like England, Has Become Pageant Mad," *New York Times*, June 15, 1913, 37. See generally David Glassberg, *American Historical Pageantry: The Uses of Tradition in the Early Twentieth Century* (Chapel Hill: UNC Press Books, 1990).

12. Albright to Mather, May 22, 1922.

13. Stephen Mather to Horace Albright, May 27, 1922, Semi-centennial file, YELL 203324 Series 4, file 1.02, Management and Accountability Records, YNPA.

14. Unidentified "friends" quoted in Haines, *The Yellowstone Story*, vol. 1, 94.

15. All of Langford's quotes are from Nathaniel Pitt Langford, *The Discovery of Yellowstone Park: Journal of the Washburn Expedition to the Yellowstone and Firehole Rivers in the Year 1870* (Lincoln: University of Nebraska Press, 1972), 117–118.

16. Catlin quoted in Haines, *Exploration and Establishment*, https://www.nps.gov/parkhistory/online_books/haines1/iee0.htm, accessed November 20, 2016, emphasis in original. Catlin did not see Yellowstone. His proposal addressed the then wildlife-drenched Dakotas.

17. Francis Kuppens quoted in Haines, *The Yellowstone Story*, vol. 1, 90. Kuppens's memoir dates from 1897, so may deserve as much skepticism as Langford's story.

18. Cook speech, July 14, 1922, Semi-centennial file, YELL 203324 Series 4, file 1.02, Management and Accountability Records, YNPA. Cook emphasized that he never used the phrase "national park."

19. Albright speech, July 14, 1922, Semi-centennial file, YELL 203324 Series 4, file 1.02, Management and Accountability Records, YNPA.

20. All quoted communications from the Semi-centennial file, YELL 203324 Series 4, file 1.02, Management and Accountability Records, YNPA.

21. Semi-centennial file, YELL 203324 Series 4, file 1.02, Management and Accountability Records, YNPA.

22. Yellowstone historian Aubrey Haines made the first factual challenges to the campfire myth in the 1960s, but acceptance of his view required a transformation of underlying Park Service values toward a more science-based approach that favored facts over myths. See Whittlesey, "Loss of a Sacred Shrine."

23. See generally Phil Brigandi, *Garnet Holme: California's Pageant Master* (Hemet: The Ramona Pageant Association, 1991).

24. Jack Haynes to Ansel Hall, February 22, 1926, and Garnet Holme [pageant script cover letter], Feb. 3, 1926, Box K15, 139.91, Interpretation and Education Records, YNPA.

25. Horace Albright to Garnet Holme, February 9, 1926, Box K15, 139.91, Interpretation and Education Records, YNPA. All script quotes are from Holme, [pageant script,] February 3, 1926, Box K15, 139.91, Interpretation and Education Records, YNPA.

26. Phil Brigandi, personal communication, June 26, 2016.

27. Horace Albright to Garnet Holme, July 19, 1926, Box K15, 139.91, Interpretation and Education Records, YNPA.

CHAPTER 6: TEACHABLE

1. Visitation data from https://irma.nps.gov/Stats/SSRSReports/Park%20 Specific%20Reports/Annual%20Park%20Recreation%20Visitation%20 %281904%20-%20Last%20Calendar%20Year%29?Park=YELL, population data from http://www.census.gov/population/estimates/nation/popclockest. txt, both confirmed November 29, 2015. Note that raw visitation continues to rise, but we're comparing it to the nation's population as a whole. The graph covers only 1904 to 2000 because that was the span of the most easily accessible datasets—as I said, it was a crude chart.

2. Hermon Carey Bumpus, Jr., *Hermon Carey Bumpus, Yankee Naturalist* (Minneapolis: University of Minnesota Press, 1947), 11.

3. Bumpus quoted in Ralph H. Lewis, *Museum Curatorship in the National Park Service 1904-1982* (Washington: Department of the Interior, 1993), 32.

4. Colleague quoted in Bumpus, Jr., *Hermon Carey Bumpus*, 58.

5. The World's Work quoted in Bumpus, Jr., *Hermon Carey Bumpus*, 68.

6. Sherman Langdon, "The New Museum Idea," *The World's Work* 12 (1906): 7711.

7. Langdon, "The New Museum Idea," 7711.

8. Kiki Leigh Rydell and Mary Shivers Culpin, *Managing the "Matchless Wonders": A History Of Administrative Development In Yellowstone National Park, 1872–1965* (Yellowstone National Park, WY: National Park Service, Yellowstone Center for Resources, YCR-2006-03, 2006), 100.

9. Bumpus's trip is detailed at great length in a memorandum from J.E. Haynes to Stephen T. Mather, September 10, 1925. Box K-18, files 154.3 and 833.05 and 702.133. This fascinating account is my major source for this chapter.

10. You don't hear the chemical theory much today; the cap's shape is believed to be caused by the configuration of the spring's plumbing. See "Mammoth Hot Spring Terraces Tour: Liberty Cap," http://mms.nps.gov/yell/features /mammothtour/librtcap.htm, accessed December 16, 2015.

11. Haynes to Mather, September 10, 1925, 1.

12. Jones probably played a smaller role than people of the 1920s believed. See Paul Schullery, "'Buffalo' Jones and the Bison Herd in Yellowstone: Another Look," *Montana: The Magazine of Western History* 26:3, summer, 1976, 40–51.

13. Lawrence L. Loendorf and Nancy Medaris Stone, *Mountain Spirit: The Sheep Eater Indians of Yellowstone* (Salt Lake City: University of Utah Press, 2006), 134, and https://www.nps.gov/yell/learn/historyculture/obsidiancliff.htm, accessed November 18, 2016.

14. Ross-Bryant, *Pilgrimage*, 7.

15. Yellowstone National Park, *Yellowstone Resources and Issues Handbook 2014* (Yellowstone National Park, WY: Yellowstone National Park), 15.

16. Haynes to Mather, September 10, 1925, 2.

17. Haynes to Mather, September 10, 1925, 3.

18. Stephen Mather, "Annual Report of the Director of the National Park Service," October 3, 1925, 10.

19. Haynes to Mather, Sept. 10, 1925, 5.

20. Laurence Vail Coleman, *The Museum in America: A Critical Study,* vol. 1 (Washington: American Association of Museums, 1939), 56.

21. Harrison, *Architecture in the Parks*, 13.

22. Ethan Carr, *Wilderness by Design: Landscape Architecture and the National Park Service* (Lincoln: University of Nebraska Press, 1998), 277–296.

23. Coleman, *The Museum in America*, 56.

24. Horace Albright to Stephen T. Mather, September 10, 1925. Box K-18, files 154.3 and 833.05 and 702.133; Box K-15, file 152, YNPA. Bumpus's other suggestions are scattered through his correspondence in Box K-18.

25. Bumpus, Jr., *Hermon Carey Bumpus*, 103.
26. Mather quoted in Rydell and Culpin, *Matchless Wonders*, 100.

CHAPTER 7: SPIRITUAL

1. Ansel Adams to Nancy Newhall, June 11, 1942, Ansel Adams Archives, Center for Creative Photography, Tucson, Ariz. (hereafter AAA), AG31:1:1:46. My thanks to archivist David Benjamin.
2. Ansel Adams to Alfred Stieglitz, July 7, 1942, AAA, AG31:1:1:79.
3. Ansel Adams and Mary Street Alinder, *Ansel Adams: An Autobiography* (Boston: Little, Brown, 1996), 76.
4. See generally, for example, Alfred Runte, *National Parks: The American Experience* (Lincoln: University of Nebraska Press, 1997).
5. See generally, for example, Paul Sutter, *Driven Wild: How the Fight against Automobiles Launched the Modern Wilderness Movement* (Seattle: University of Washington Press, 2005).
6. Jonathan Spaulding, *Ansel Adams and the American Landscape: A Biography* (Oakland: University of California Press, 1998), 256.
7. Adams and Alinder, *Ansel Adams*, 235.
8. "Old Faithful Geyser, Yellowstone National Park," Ansel Adams Photographs of National Parks and Monuments, 1941–1942, National Archives Identifier: 520017.
9. Adams to Newhall, June 11, 1942.
10. Ansel Adams to Newt Drury, January 22, 1952, AAA, AG31:2:15:3. Italics added.
11. Yellowstone National Park Lodges, "Services and Amenities," http://www.yellowstonenationalparklodges.com/lodging/services-and-amenities/, accessed Sept 5, 2016.
12. Ansel Adams to Horace Albright, July 11, 1957, AAA, AG31:1:1:4. Although Albright left the Park Service in 1933 for a business career, he remained keenly interested in park issues for another 54 years.
13. Ansel Adams, *My Camera in the National Parks* (Yosemite National Park: Virginia Adams, 1950).
14. Adams to Albright, July 11, 1957.
15. Spaulding, *Ansel Adams and the American Landscape*, 324. Italics in original.
16. Kevin DeLuca, "Environmental Movement Media," in John D. H. Downing, ed., *Encyclopedia of Social Movement Media* (Thousand Oaks: Sage, 2011). The context of that sentence was Carlton Watkins at Yosemite, but it clearly also applies to other photographers and places.
17. Spaulding, *Ansel Adams and the American Landscape*, 189.
18. Adams and Alinder, *Ansel Adams*, 155.
19. Ansel Adams, "The Meaning of the National Parks," *Living Wilderness* 43 (March 1980): 14–15.

20. Ansel Adams, *Ansel Adams in the National Parks: Photographs from America's Wild Places* (Boston: Little, Brown and Company, 2010).

21. Ansel Adams to Nancy Newhall, August 21, 1948, AAA, AG31:1:1:47. The dude ranch they were visiting was the 9 Quarter Circle on the Taylor Fork south of what is now Big Sky, Montana.

22. Adams to Newhall, August 21, 1948.

23. For fascinating discussion of these issues see generally Ethan Carr, *Mission 66: Modernism and the National Park Dilemma* (Amherst: University of Massachusetts Press, 2007).

CHAPTER 8: POLITICAL

1. This episode, including all dialogue, is taken from Frank C. Craighead, jr., *Track of the Grizzly* (San Francisco: Sierra Club Books, 1979, 1982), 15. Much of the background for this and other episodes in this chapter comes from Jordan Fisher Smith's excellent book *Engineering Eden: The True Story of a Violent Death, a Trial, and the Fight over Controlling Nature* (New York: Crown, 2016).

2. Craigheads quoted in Smith, *Engineering Eden*, 86.

3. Biel, *Do (Not) Feed the Bears*, 18–20.

4. Jack Olsen, *Night of the Grizzlies* (New York: G.P. Putnam's Sons, 1969), 134. This dramatic book is my primary source for the Glacier incidents.

5. Olsen, *Night of the Grizzlies*, 128.

6. The meeting and underlying debate are described, from varying perspectives, in Frank Craighead, *Track of the Grizzly*, 203–204; Paul Schullery, *The Bears of Yellowstone* (Worland: High Plains Publishing Company, 1992), 114–148; Biel, *Do (Not) Feed the Bears*, 86–112; and Thomas McNamee, *The Grizzly Bear* (New York: Knopf, 1984), 99–120.

7. John J. Craighead, et. al. *The Grizzly Bears of Yellowstone: Their Ecology in the Yellowstone Ecosystem, 1959–1992* (Washington: Island Press, 1995), 321–344.

8. A. Starker Leopold, et al., "The Goal of Park Management in the United States" in *Wildlife Management in the National Parks* (Washington: National Park Service, 1963).

9. Frank Craighead, *Track of the Grizzly*, 196; Smith, *Engineering Eden*, 161–182.

10. Biel, *Do (Not) Feed the Bears*, 92.

11. Frank Craighead, *Track of the Grizzly*, 232.

12. Seventeen Craighead research bears (forty-nine grizzlies total) were euthanized by rangers or killed by hunters by the end of 1971. See Smith, *Engineering Eden*, 208.

13. Bradberry quoted in Whittlesey, *Death in Yellowstone*, 45, and Smith, *Engineering Eden*, 218–228.

14. Correspondence in Box RG02, Series 3, box 4, file A7623, Protection and Safety Records, YNPA.

15. Correspondence in Box RG02, Series 3, box 4, file A7623, Protection and Safety Records, YNPA.

16. Correspondence in Box RG02, Series 3, box 4, file A7623, Protection and Safety Records, YNPA.

17. Author Jordan Fisher Smith has conducted admirably comprehensive research into the Walker trial, including portraits of the victim's family, in *Engineering Eden*.

18. Russ Tiffany and Catherine Ohl, "Remembering A. Andrew Hauk," Pacific Rim Snow Sports Alliance, http://www.pacificrimalliance.org/F.PublicAffairs /SkiHistory/FWSA/AndyHauk.htm, accessed April 22, 2015.

19. Telephone interview with Terry Amdur, Pasadena, CA, April 21, 2015. Many thanks to Mr. Amdur.

20. Transcript, Dennis G. Martin, as Administrator of the Estate of Harry Eugene Walker, Deceased, Plaintiff, v. United States of America, Defendant, YNPA. Although it had not been catalogued during my visit, I was fortunate to read the full trial transcript (thanks to Jordan Smith for help in arrangements). Many of the best passages are quoted in Whittlesey, *Death in Yellowstone*, 44–49, but the transcript also shows the judge fully grasping the science at issue.

21. *Martin* trial transcript, YNPA.

22. Whittlesey, *Death in Yellowstone*, 48–49. Emphasis in original.

23. *Martin* trial transcript, YNPA.

24. Hauk quoted in Whittlesey, *Death in Yellowstone*, 48.

25. Hauk quoted in Whittlesey, *Death in Yellowstone*, 48.

26. There is disagreement about the camp's cleanliness. Whittlesey writes that the investigating ranger told him the camp was "as dirty as any he'd ever seen" (*Death in Yellowstone*, 44–45). But Frank Craighead testified that the campers had taken "reasonable" precautions, not too dissimilar from what he himself might have done.

27. See Frederic H. Wagner and Joseph L. Sax, *Wildlife Policies in the U.S. National Parks* (Washington: Island Press, 1995), 65, and James A. Pritchard, *Preserving Yellowstone's Natural Conditions* (Lincoln: University of Nebraska Press, 1999), 247.

28. McNamee, *Grizzly Bear*, 116. For the Craigheads' detailed numbers, see John Craighead, et. al., *Their Ecology*, 370–381 and 438–440.

29. Today's most definitive population estimates are at the National Park Service's "Grizzly Bear Ecology" page at https://www.nps.gov/yell/learn/nature /gbearinfo.htm, accessed September 5, 2016. The figure of 99 in 1990 is from Smith, *Engineering Eden*, 316. For more detailed discussion of bear population trends, see John Craighead, et. al., *Their Ecology*, 386–390 and 445–456.

CHAPTER 9: POPULAR

1. Interview with Mike Keys, May 26, 2015.

2. Personal communication with "Yowp Yowp," author of the informative blog yowpyowp.blogspot.com, which covers the early cartoon era, May 17, 2015.

3. For example, see Daniel Best, "Yogi Bear's Sexuality Explained," http://oh dannyboy.blogspot.com/2004/03/yogi-bears-sexuality-explained.html, accessed

October 29, 2016. Analyses of "gay Yogi"(and even, if Boo Boo is seen as a child, "predator Yogi") are generally satiric, but after televangelist Jerry Falwell claimed Teletubbies cartoons were "modeling the gay lifestyle," the line between satire and reality became blurred. See Leonard Pitts, Jr., "Fred? Barney? Yogi? You Just Never Know" in *Forward From this Moment: Selected Columns, 1994–2009* (Evanston: Agate Publishing, 2009), 132–134. Hat-tip to Amy Hyfield.

4. "Yogi Bear's Big Break," http://www.dailymotion.com/video/xy25b0_yogi -bear-01-yogi-bear-s-big-break_fun, accessed May 28, 2015.

5. Biel, *Do (Not) Feed the Bears*, 7–12. Biel's great book is a source for many of the facts in this section.

6. Albright quoted in Biel, *Do (Not) Feed the Bears*, 16.

7. Biel, *Do (Not) Feed the Bears*, 10, 22–24, 77.

8. Despite his Park Service–style flat hat, Smokey was created by its rival, the U.S. Forest Service. But public imagination often merged them, as when a 2013 skit on Jon Stewart's *Daily Show* incorrectly identified Smokey as a "National Parks employee" being interviewed in Yosemite (http://thedailyshow.cc.com/videos /lmoqh1/shutstorm-2013--america-sits-on-its-balls---smokey-the-bear, accessed May 28, 2015).

9. Biel, *Do (Not) Feed the Bears*, 68–75

10. John K[ricfalusi], "The Lost Ranger Smith Cartoon," January 7, 2009, http://johnkstuff.blogspot.com/2009/01/lost-ranger-smith-cartoon.html, accessed June 2, 2015.

11. Bugs Bunny's archenemy, the hot-tempered, gunslinging prospector Yosemite Sam, is almost never shown in his namesake habitat. If you believe Wikipedia, he was almost named Texas Tiny, Wyoming Willie, or Denver Dan.

12. Leisure Systems Inc., "Company History," http://www.jellystonefranchise.com /about/, accessed May 29, 2015.

13. Jeni Sandberg, "History Lesson: The Aluminum Christmas Tree," https://blog.etsy.com/en/2013/history-lessons-the-aluminum-christmas-tree/, accessed May 29, 2015.

14. Leisure Systems, "Company History."

15. Jenny Callison, "Yogi makes Jellystone sweet," *Cincinnati Enquirer*, December 5, 2002. Leisure Systems quotes Haag's recollection of the line as, "OK, Boo Boo, let's get our pic-a-nic baskets ready, the campers are coming!" but Callison's version sounds more like Yogi to me.

16. "Doug Haag Describes Jellystone's Origins," http://www.woodallscm.com /2014/12/doug-haag-describes-jellystones-origins/, accessed May 29, 2015.

17. Langford wrote of the Devil's Slide, "In future years, when the wonders of the Yellowstone are incorporated into the family of fashionable resorts, there will be few of its attractions surpassing in interest this marvelous freak of the elements." ("The Wonders of the Yellowstone," 7). Today, although it has a roadside shrine, the pullout is frequently empty.

18. Berra was pretty sure he'd once said it, but he wasn't the first. See http://quote investigator.com/2014/08/29/too-crowded/, accessed October 25, 2016.
19. Telephone interview with Joyce Collamati Bileau, May 29, 2015.
20. Eric Brevig, dir., *Yogi Bear*, 2010.

CHAPTER 10: THREATENED

1. Stephen J. Pyne, *To the Last Smoke: The Northern Rockies: A Fire Survey*, vol. 3 (Tucson: University of Arizona Press, 2016), 111. See also Stephen J. Pyne, *Fire in America: A Cultural History of Wildland and Rural Fire* (Princeton: Princeton University Press, 1982), 239–259.
2. To research this chapter, I studied 1988 print media at the McCracken Research Library as a Research Fellow at the Buffalo Bill Center for the West in Cody, Wyoming; thanks to the Center for the fellowship. There are innumerable scientific and policy publications about the fires, but the books I generally relied on included Jeff Henry, *The Year Yellowstone Burned: A Twenty-Five-Year Perspective* (Lanham: Rowman & Littlefield, 2015); Dan R. Sholly with Steve M. Newman, *Guardians of Yellowstone: An Intimate Look at the Challenges of Protecting America's Foremost Wilderness Park* (New York: William Morrow and Company, 1991); Hal K. Rothman, *A Test of Adversity and Strength: Wildland Fire in the National Park System* (Washington: National Park Service, 2006); Karen Reinhart and Jeff Henry, *Yellowstone's Rebirth by Fire: Rising from the Ashes of the 1988 Wildfires* (Helena: Farcountry Press, 2008); Jim Carrier, *Summer of Fire* (Salt Lake City: Gibbs Smith, 1989); and Micah Morrison, *Fire in Paradise: The Yellowstone Fires and the Politics of Environmentalism* (New York: HarperCollins, 1993).
3. Brokaw quoted in Conrad Smith, *Media and Apocalypse: News Coverage of the Yellowstone Forest Fires, Exxon Valdez Oil Spill, and Loma Prieta Earthquake (Contributions to the Study of Mass Media and Communications)* (Westport: Greenwood Press, 1992), 46.
4. My primary source for the Calfee Creek incident, including Sholly's thoughts and all of the dialogue below, is Sholly's memoir, *Guardians of Yellowstone*, 205–219. I've supplemented it with the story of Jane Lopez from Reinhart and Henry, *Yellowstone's Rebirth by Fire*, 70–72, and additional context from Rocky Barker, *Scorched Earth: How Fires in Yellowstone Changed America* (Washington: Island Press, 2005), 193–198, and Morrison, *Fire in Paradise*, 3–19.
5. Henry, *The Year Yellowstone Burned*, 45–46.
6. Sholly, *Guardians of Yellowstone*, 212. In the past 25 years, firefighting ethics have evolved to focus more on firefighter safety than when Sholly was making these decisions, or unapologetically telling this story in 1991.
7. Barbee quoted in Barker, *Scorched Earth*, 196.
8. This may sound exaggerated, but Sholly wrote, "I knew I should have been more worried . . . But a wildfire normally did not frighten me nearly as much as

it did others," as his introduction to a discussion of fire ecology. *Guardians of Yellowstone*, 214.

9. Sholly, *Guardians of Yellowstone*, 216.

10. For criticism of the Yellowstone fire plan, see Pyne, *The Northern Rockies*, 146–150. Today we know Pyne as a MacArthur Award–winning fire historian, but in his transition from firefighter to writer, he spent some time writing and editing national park fire plans, including Yellowstone's in 1985. In *A Test of Adversity and Strength*, 196–202, Rothman summarizes Pyne's critique and does little to rebut it.

11. The Grant Village evacuation, including Dave Poncin's recollections, are well covered by Carrier, *Summer of Fire*, 24–50, and Morrison, *Fire in Paradise*, 63–87.

12. The development of Grant Village is detailed in Alston Chase, *Playing God in Yellowstone: The Destruction of America's First National Park* (Boston: Atlantic Monthly Press, 1986), 197–231. Chase's scathing critique of the Park Service is disputed by park advocates to this day, but in 1988 provided a framework for journalists seeking controversy and scandal behind the fires.

13. Sholly quoted in Carrier, *Summer of Fire*, 32.

14. Smith, *Media and Apocalypse*, 37–76.

15. John Varley, "Science and the Media," *Yellowstone Science*, 17, no. 2 (2009): 16–17. "We were not really prepared for that kind of media triage," Superintendent Bob Barbee later admitted (Rothman, *A Test of Adversity and Strength*, 193).

16. Despain quoted in Morrison, *Fire in Paradise*, 31.

17. The well-known story is told in Carrier, *Summer of Fire*, 42, and Barker, *Scorched Earth*, 210–211.

18. *Newsweek* quoted in Chris J. Magoc, *Yellowstone: The Creation and Selling of an American Landscape, 1870–1903* (Albuquerque: University of New Mexico Press, 1999), 174.

19. Sholly, *Guardians of Yellowstone*, 11.

20. Sholly, *Guardians of Yellowstone*, 19.

21. Vranna Sue Hinck, "Images of the West: From Prostitutes to Polkas," *Big Sky Journal*, July 2014.

22. The dialogue and Sholly's thoughts are from *Guardians of Yellowstone*, 11–25. Sholly does not identify the Congressman or the date, although Morrison suggests that it may have been August 20, "Black Saturday."

23. Morrison, *Fire in Paradise*, 121–122. See also Allan Turner, "Hays Kirby, scion of prominent Houston family, dies," *Houston Chronicle*, Saturday, December 19, 2009.

24. Morrison, *Fire in Paradise*, 122.

25. Morrison, *Fire in Paradise*, 122.

26. Sholly, *Guardians of Yellowstone*, 23.

27. Sholly, *Guardians of Yellowstone*, 15.

28. Barbee quoted in Rothman, *A Test of Adversity and Strength*, 204.

29. Morrison, *Fire in Paradise*, 170. Morrison's account, based on a videotape of the meeting, is compelling.

30. Henry, *The Year Yellowstone Burned*, 217. This engaging book is my primary source for the Old Faithful siege story.

31. Henry, *The Year Yellowstone Burned*, 218.

32. Henry, *The Year Yellowstone Burned*, 225.

33. Barker, *Scorched Earth*, 216.

34. Varley, "Science and the Media," 15.

35. Sholly, *Guardians of Yellowstone*, 240.

36. Sholly, *Guardians of Yellowstone*, 243.

37. The Mammoth evacuation story, including all dialogue and Sholly's thoughts, is told in *Guardians of Yellowstone*, 244–255. In this particular quote, recall that Sholly had only one eye to rest.

38. Sholly, *Guardians of Yellowstone*, 255.

39. Henry, *The Year Yellowstone Burned*, 266–272.

CHAPTER 11: TRIUMPHANT

1. Jeff Henry, *The Year Yellowstone Burned* (Lanham: Taylor Trade, 2015), 265–266.

2. Paul Krza, *Casper Star-Tribune*, October 20, 1988. McCracken Research Library, Buffalo Bill Center for the West, MS 21, box 6.

3. Bartlett, *Wilderness Besieged*, 388.

4. See, for example, John Duffield, Chris Neher, and David Patterson, "Wolves and people in Yellowstone: Impacts on the regional economy" (Bozeman: Yellowstone Park Foundation, 2006).

5. Barry Davis, Shoshone National Forest, presentation notes for a speech about the fires at a conference in April of 1989. McCracken Research Library, Buffalo Bill Center for the West, MS 21, box 1, folder 15.

6. Hart Research Associates and North Star Opinion Research, "Strong Bipartisan Support For National Parks" (Washington: National Parks Conservation Association and National Park Hospitality Association, July 2012). Hat-tip to George Black.

7. Ray Rasker, et. al., "Gateways to Yellowstone: Protecting the Wild Heart of Our Region's Thriving Economy" (Helena: National Parks Conservation Association, Northern Rockies office, 2006), 15. By many measures, greater Yellowstone outperformed even areas around other Western national parks.

8. See, for example, Daniel Fortin, et. al., "Wolves Influence Elk Movements: Behavior Shapes a Trophic Cascade in Yellowstone National Park," *Ecology* 86 (2005): 1320–1330, doi:10.1890/04-0953. Recently some scientists have criticized the popularized version of trophic cascades as a dangerous oversimplification (see Arthur Middleton, "Is the Wolf a Real American Hero?" *New York Times*, March 9, 2014). Regardless, what fascinates me is its *appeal* in a networked Internet age.

9. As something of a New Wester myself, I've given these migrations some thought. See John Clayton, *Stories from Montana's Enduring Frontier* (Charleston: The History Press, 2013), 115–122.

10. It would have been replaced by "Firehole Village," a suburban development similar to today's Grant Village. Carr, *Mission 66*, 95–96.

11. Yellowstone National Park, *Resources and Issues Handbook 2014*, 39.

12. Rather quoted in "Summer of Fire," *Retro Report*, September 2, 2013.

13. See generally William Cronon, *Nature's Metropolis: Chicago and the Great West* (New York: W. W. Norton, 1992).

EPILOGUE

1. It was 2015, a year of few fires within Yellowstone, but considerable smoke from some of the largest wildfires on record in Washington state.

2. National Interagency Fire Center, "Federal Firefighting Costs (Suppression Only)," https://www.nifc.gov/fireInfo/fireInfo_documents/SuppCosts.pdf, accessed October 27, 2016.

3. Todd Wilkinson, "Fires of '88 were just a warming warning," *Jackson Hole News & Guide*, August 2013. I relied on the profound, under-appreciated perspective offered by Wilkinson and Rocky Barker in that article for my own essay, "Understanding the 1988 Yellowstone Fires: Part II," *Points West*, spring 2016.

4. The issues are far more complex than this question suggests, but see, for example, Cecily M. Costello, et. al., "How Important is Whitebark Pine to Grizzly Bears?" *Yellowstone Science* 23, no. 2 (2015): 12–16.

5. The Craighead Institute conducts this research; see http://www.craighead research.org/pika.html, accessed November 19, 2016.

6. Anthony L. Westerling, et. al., "Continued warming could transform Greater Yellowstone fire regimes by mid-21st century," PNAS, www.pnas.org/cgi /doi/10.1073/pnas.1110199108, accessed November 19, 2016.

7. Cheryl Strayed, *Wild: From Lost to Found on the Pacific Crest Trail* (New York: Knopf Doubleday, 2012); Jean-Marc Vallée, dir., *Wild*, 2014.

8. I was also pained, for similar reasons, to spend so little time talking about women. For some great stories about women in Yellowstone, see Elizabeth Watry, *Women in Wonderland* (Helena: Riverbend, 2012). And the same holds for people of color. See Ross-Bryant, *Pilgrimage,* 220, and Joe Weber and Selima Sultana, "Why Do So Few Minority People Visit National Parks? Visitation and the Accessibility of 'America's Best Idea,'" *Annals of the Association of American Geographers* 103, no. 3: 437–464.

9. Lee H. Whittlesey, "Native Americans, the Earliest Interpreters," *The George Wright Forum* 19, no. 3 (2002): 40–51. See also generally Peter Nabokov and Lawrence Loendorf, *Restoring a Presence: American Indians and Yellowstone National Park* (Norman: University of Oklahoma Press, 2004).

10. Chief [Luther] Standing Bear, *Land of the Spotted Eagle* (Boston: Houghton Mifflin, 1933), xix. As an Oglala Lakota, Standing Bear (1868–1939) would not have been speaking specifically of Yellowstone. And the tribes that used the area, who came from many different backgrounds, may have had varying philosophies. But as a widely traveled educator and author, Standing Bear was comfortable speaking of how pan-Indian attitudes differed from Anglo ones. Hat-tip to David Moore.

11. Loendorf and Stone, *Mountain Spirit*, especially pages 58–59, 106–107, and 137. I highly recommend this fascinating book. See also Haines, *Exploration and Establishment*, https://www.nps.gov/parkhistory/online_books/haines1/iee1d.htm, accessed November 18, 2016.

12. George Black, "The Yellowstone Supervolcano Goes Viral," Newyorker.com, September 4, 2014.

13. USGS, "Questions About Supervolcanoes," http://volcanoes.usgs.gov/volcanoes/yellowstone/yellowstone_sub_page_49.html, accessed June 4, 2015. See also USGS, "Steam Explosions, Earthquakes, and Volcanic Eruptions—What's in Yellowstone's Future?" http://pubs.usgs.gov/fs/2005/3024/.

14. Steve Almond, "The Apocalypse Market Is Booming," *New York Times Magazine*, September 27, 2013; Laura Miller, "Fresh Hell," *New Yorker*, June 14, 2010; Mike Mariani, "Apocalypse Now: How Television's Boldest Sci-Fi Shows Are Tackling Contemporary Injustice," *Pacific Standard*, October 21, 2016. Hat-tip to Charlie Mitchell.

15. Slotkin, *Gunfighter Nation*, 351–365 and 391–400.

BIBLIOGRAPHY

ARCHIVES

American Heritage Center, University of Wyoming, Laramie, Wyoming.

Ansel Adams Archives, Center for Creative Photography, Tucson, Arizona.

McCracken Research Library, Buffalo Bill Center of the West, Cody, Wyoming.

Merrill G. Burlingame Special Collections of the Montana State University Library, Bozeman, Montana.

Montana Historical Society research center, Helena, Montana.

Park County Historical Archives, Cody, Wyoming.

Yellowstone National Park Archives (National Archives Affiliate), Gardiner, Montana.

BOOKS, ARTICLES, VIDEO, WEBSITES

Adams, Ansel, *Ansel Adams in the National Parks: Photographs from America's Wild Places* (Boston: Little, Brown, 2010).

———, *My Camera in the National Parks* (Yosemite National Park: Virginia Adams, 1950).

———, "The Meaning of the National Parks," *Living Wilderness* 43 (March 1980): 14–15.

Adams, Ansel, and Mary Street Alinder, *Ansel Adams: An Autobiography* (Boston: Little, Brown, 1996).

Albright, Horace M., and Marian Albright Schenck, *Creating the National Park Service: The Missing Years* (Norman: University of Oklahoma Press, 1999).

Almond, Steve, "The Apocalypse Market Is Booming," *New York Times Magazine*, September 27, 2013.

Anderson, A.A., *Experiences and Impressions* (Freeport: Books for Libraries Press, 1933).

Anderson, H. Allen, *The Chief: Ernest Thompson Seton and the Changing West* (College Station: Texas A&M University Press, 1986).

Anderson, Nancy K., et. al., *Thomas Moran* (Washington: National Gallery of Art in association with Yale University Press, 1997).

Associated Press, "Tourists Defend Loading Yellowstone Bison Calf into Vehicle," June 3, 2016.

Bakken, Gordon Morris, ed., *Encyclopedia of Immigration and Migration in the American West* (Los Angeles: Sage Publications, 2006).

Barker, Rocky, *Scorched Earth: How Fires in Yellowstone Changed America* (Washington: Island Press, 2005).

Barlow, J.W., and D.P. Heap, *Report of a Reconnaissance of the Basin of the Upper Yellowstone in 1871* (Washington: U.S. Army Corps of Engineers, 1872).

Barringer, Mark, "Private Empire, Public Land: The Rise and Fall of the Yellowstone Park Company" (PhD. dissertation, Texas Christian University, 1997).

Barringer, Mark Daniel, *Selling Yellowstone: Capitalism and the Construction of Nature* (Lawrence: University Press of Kansas, 2002).

Bartlett, Richard A., *From Cody to the World: The First Seventy-Five Years of the Buffalo Bill Memorial Association* (Cody: Buffalo Bill Historical Center, 1992).

———, *Nature's Yellowstone* (Albuquerque: University of New Mexico Press, 1974).

———, *Yellowstone: A Wilderness Besieged* (Tucson: University of Arizona Press, 1985).

Best, Daniel, "Yogi Bear's Sexuality Explained," http://ohdannyboy.blogspot.com/2004/03/yogi-bears-sexuality-explained.html, accessed October 29, 2016.

Biel, Alice Wondrak, *Do (Not) Feed the Bears: The Fitful History of Wildlife and Tourists in Yellowstone* (Lawrence: University of Kansas Press, 2006).

Black, George, *Empire of Shadows: The Epic Story of Yellowstone* (New York: St. Martin's, 2012).

———, "The Yellowstone Supervolcano Goes Viral," Newyorker.com, September 4, 2014.

Bonnemaison, Sarah, and Christine Macy, *Architecture and Nature: Creating the American Landscape* (London: Routledge, 2000).

Borne, Lawrence R., *Dude Ranching: A Complete History* (Albuquerque: University of New Mexico Press, 1983).

Brevig, Eric, dir., *Yogi Bear*, 2010.

Brigandi, Phil, *Garnet Holme: California's Pageant Master* (Hemet: The Ramona Pageant Association, 1991).

Bumpus, Hermon Carey, Jr., *Hermon Carey Bumpus, Yankee Naturalist* (Minneapolis: University of Minnesota Press, 1947).

Burt, Maxwell Struthers, *The Diary of a Dude-wrangler* (New York: Scribner's, 1924, 1938).

Burt, Struthers, "A Certain Mountain Chief," *Scribner's* (June 1929): 621.

Calkins, Frank, *Jackson Hole* (New York: Knopf, 1973).

Callison, Jenny, "Yogi makes Jellystone sweet," *Cincinnati Enquirer,* December 5, 2002.

Carr, Ethan, *Mission 66: Modernism and the National Park Dilemma* (Amherst: University of Massachusetts Press, 2007).

———, *Wilderness by Design: Landscape Architecture and the National Park Service* (Lincoln: University of Nebraska Press, 1998).

Carrier, Jim, *Summer of Fire* (Salt Lake City: Gibbs Smith, 1989).

Cassidy, James, *Ferdinand V. Hayden: Entrepreneur of Science* (Lincoln: University of Nebraska Press, 2000).

Chase, Alston, *Playing God in Yellowstone: The Destruction of America's First National Park* (Boston: Atlantic Monthly Press, 1986).

Chittenden, Hiram M. *The Yellowstone National Park: Historical and Descriptive.* (Cincinnati: R. Clarke, 1895).

Clayton, John, *The Cowboy Girl: The Life of Caroline Lockhart* (Lincoln: University of Nebraska Press, 2007).

———, *Stories from Montana's Enduring Frontier* (Charleston: The History Press, 2013).

———, "Romancing the West: Dude Ranching in Wyoming," at www.wyohistory.org (2014).

———, "Understanding the 1988 Yellowstone Fires," *Points West*, spring and summer 2016.

Coleman, Laurence Vail, *The Museum in America: A Critical Study,* vol. 1 (Washington: American Association of Museums, 1939).

Consolo-Murphy, Sue, "Integrated and Equal?" *Yellowstone Science: A Quarterly Publication Devoted to the Natural and Cultural Resources* 8, no. 3 (Summer): 2000, 1.

Costello, Cecily M., et. al., "How Important is Whitebark Pine to Grizzly Bears?" *Yellowstone Science* 23, no. 2 (2015): 12–16.

Craighead, Frank C., Jr., *Track of the Grizzly* (San Francisco: Sierra Club Books, 1979, 1982).

Craighead, John J., et. al., *The Grizzly Bears of Yellowstone: Their Ecology in the Yellowstone Ecosystem, 1959–1992* (Washington: Island Press, 1995).

Cronon, William, *Nature's Metropolis: Chicago and the Great West* (New York: W. W. Norton, 1992).

———, "The Trouble with Wilderness; or, Getting Back to the Wrong Nature" in William Cronon, ed., *Uncommon Ground: Rethinking the Human Place in Nature* (New York: W. W. Norton, 1995), 69–90.

Culpin, Mary Shivers, "The History of the Construction of the Road System of Yellowstone National Park 1872–1966" (Washington: National Park Service, 1994).

————, *For the Benefit and Enjoyment of the People: A History of Concession Development in Yellowstone National Park 1872–1966* (Yellowstone National Park, WY: Yellowstone Center for Resources, 2003).

Dailey, A.A., "Uncle Howard Eaton," *Outing* 76 (July–August 1920): 200–201.

Daugherty, John, et. al., *A Place Called Jackson Hole: A Historic Resource Study of Grand Teton National Park*. (Grand Teton National Park and Grand Teton Natural History Association, 1999).

DeLuca, Kevin, "Environmental Movement Media," in John D. H. Downing (ed.), *Encyclopedia of Social Movement Media* (Thousand Oaks: Sage, 2011).

Demaray, Jane Galloway, *Yellowstone Summers: Touring with the Wylie Camping Company in America's First National Park* (Pullman: Washington State University Press, 2015).

Dixon, Deby, "The Real Story About The Bison Calf That Took A Ride In The Car," *National Parks Traveler*, May 22, 2016.

"Doug Haag Describes Jellystone's Origins," http://www.woodallscm.com/2014/12/doug-haag-describes-jellystones-origins/, accessed May 29, 2015.

Duffield, John, Chris Neher, and David Patterson, "Wolves and People in Yellowstone: Impacts on the Regional Economy" (Bozeman: Yellowstone Park Foundation, 2006).

Duncan, Dayton, Ken Burns, et. al., *The National Parks: America's Best Idea*, episode 1 (Arlington: PBS Home Video, 2009).

Ferguson, Gary, *Hawks Rest: A Season in the Remote Heart of Yellowstone* (Washington: National Geographic, 2003).

————, *Walking Down the Wild: A Journey Through The Yellowstone Rockies* (New York: Simon & Schuster, 1993).

Flores, Dan, *Coyote America: A Natural and Supernatural History* (New York: Basic Books, 2016).

Flynn, Anne-Gerard, "Ken Burns talks about new PBS series 'The National Parks: America's Best Idea,'" *Springfield Republican*, September 26, 2009.

Forbes, Bertie Charles, ed. "Harry W. Child," in *Men Who Are Making the West* (New York: B. C. Forbes, 1923), 322–343.

Fortin, Daniel, et. al., "Wolves Influence Elk Movements: Behavior Shapes a Trophic Cascade in Yellowstone National Park," *Ecology* 86 (2005): 1320–1330, doi:10.1890/04-0953.

Foster, Mike, *Strange Genius: The Life of Ferdinand Vandeveer Hayden* (Boulder: Roberts Rinehart, 1994).

Fradkin, Philip, *Sagebrush Country: Land and the American West* (Tucson: University Arizona Press, 1989).

Glassberg, David, *American Historical Pageantry: The Uses of Tradition in the Early Twentieth Century* (Chapel Hill: UNC Press Books, 1990).

Haines, Aubrey L., *Yellowstone National Park: Its Exploration and Establishment* (Washington: U.S. National Park Service, 1974).

————, *The Yellowstone Story: A History of Our First National Park* (Yellowstone Library and Museum Association, two volumes, 1977).

Hales, Peter Bacon, *William Henry Jackson and the Transformation of the American Landscape* (Philadelphia: Temple University Press, 1988).

Hampton, H. Duane, *How the U.S. Cavalry Saved Our National Parks* (Bloomington: Indiana University Press, 1972).

Harrison, Laura E. Soullière, *Architecture in the Parks: National Historic Landmark Theme Study* (Washington: National Park Service, 1987).

Hart Research Associates and North Star Opinion Research, "Strong Bipartisan Support For National Parks" (Washington: National Parks Conservation Association and National Park Hospitality Association, July 2012).

Hassard, Jno. [John] R. G., "The New York Mercantile Library," *Scribner's Monthly* 1 (February, 1871): 353–367.

Hassrick, Peter H., *The Rocky Mountains: A Vision for Artists in the Nineteenth Century* (Norman: University of Oklahoma Press, 1983).

Hayden, F.V., "Preliminary Report of the United States Geological Survey of Montana and Portions of Adjacent Territories being a Fifth Annual Report of Progress" (Washington: U.S. Department of Interior, 1872).

Hayden, Ferdinand, "The Wonders of the West II: More about the Yellowstone," *Scribner's Monthly* 3 (February, 1872): 388–396.

Henry, Jeff, *The Year Yellowstone Burned: A Twenty-Five-Year Perspective* (Lanham: Rowman & Littlefield, 2015).

Hinck, Vranna Sue, "Images of the West: From Prostitutes to Polkas," *Big Sky Journal*, July 2014.

"Historic Structure Report, Historical Data Section, Old Faithful Inn, Yellowstone National Park, Wyoming" (Denver Service Center, Historic Preservation Branch, Midwest/Rocky Mountain Team, National Park Service, U.S. Department of the Interior, 1982).

http://jacksonholehistory.org/bar-bc-ranch-landscapes-of-loss/, accessed November 19, 2015.

http://quoteinvestigator.com/2014/08/29/too-crowded/, accessed October 25, 2016.

http://thedailyshow.cc.com/videos/lmoqh1/shutstorm-2013--america-sits-on-its-balls---smokey-the-bear, accessed May 28, 2015.

http://www.census.gov/population/estimates/nation/popclockest.txt, accessed November 29, 2015.

http://www.craigheadresearch.org/pika.html, accessed November 19, 2016.

http://www.nps.gov/parkhistory/online_books/grte2/hrs14.htm, accessed November 20, 2015.

http://www.nps.gov/thrb/learn/historyculture/storyofteddybear.htm, accessed November 18, 2016.

http://www.wyomingtalesandtrails.com/cody4.html, accessed November 17, 2016.

https://en.oxforddictionaries.com/definition/discover, accessed November 19, 2016.

https://irma.nps.gov/Stats/SSRSReports/Park%20Specific%20Reports/Annual%20Park%20Recreation%20Visitation%20%281904%20-%20Last%20Calendar%20Year%29?Park=YELL, accessed November 29, 2015.

https://www.nps.gov/yell/learn/historyculture/obsidiancliff.htm, accessed November 18, 2016.

http://www.yowpyowp.blogspot.com, accessed May 17, 2015.

Hyde, Anne F., *American Vision: Far Western Landscape and National Culture 1820–1920* (New York: NYU Press, 1990).

Isenberg, Andrew C., *The Destruction of the Bison: An Environmental History, 1750–1920* (Cambridge: Cambridge University Press, 2000).

Jackson, William Henry, and Howard Roscoe Driggs, *The Pioneer Photographer, Rocky Mountain Adventures with a Camera* (Yonkers-on-Hudson: World Book Company, 1929).

K[ricfalusi], John, "The Lost Ranger Smith Cartoon," January 7, 2009, http://johnkstuff.blogspot.com/2009/01/lost-ranger-smith-cartoon.html, accessed June 2, 2015.

Kensel, W. Hudson, *Dude Ranching in Yellowstone Country: Larry Larom and Valley Ranch, 1915–1969* (Norman: Arthur H. Clark Co., 2010).

Kipling, Rudyard, *American Notes* (Boston: Brown and Company, 1899).

———, *From Sea to Sea; Letters of Travel*, vol. 2 (New York: Doubleday, McClure, 1899).

Langdon, Sherman, "The New Museum Idea," *The World's Work* 12 (1906): 7711.

Langdon, William Chauncy, "America, Like England, Has Become Pageant Mad," *New York Times*, June 15, 1913, 37.

Langford, Nathaniel Pitt, *The Discovery of Yellowstone Park: Journal of the Washburn Expedition to the Yellowstone and Firehole Rivers in the Year 1870* (Text from author's 1905 edition) (Lincoln: University of Nebraska Press, 1972).

———, "The Wonders of the Yellowstone," *Scribner's Monthly* 2 (May and June, 1871): 1–16, 113–128.

Leisure Systems Inc., "Company History," http://www.jellystonefranchise.com/about/, accessed May 29, 2015.

Leopold, A. Starker, et al., "The Goal of Park Management in the United States" in *Wildlife Management in the National Parks* (Washington: National Park Service, 1963).

Lewis, Ralph H., *Museum Curatorship in the National Park Service 1904–1982* (Washington: Department of the Interior, 1993).

Loendorf, Lawrence L., and Nancy Medaris Stone, *Mountain Spirit: The Sheep Eater Indians of Yellowstone* (Salt Lake City: University of Utah Press, 2006).

Lutts, Ralph H., *The Nature Fakers: Wildlife, Science & Sentiment* (Charlottesville: University of Virginia Press, 1990).

Magoc, Chris J., *Yellowstone: The Creation and Selling of an American Landscape, 1870–1903* (Albuquerque: University of New Mexico Press, 1999).

"Mammoth Hot Spring Terraces Tour: Liberty Cap," http://mms.nps.gov/yell/features/mammothtour/librtcap.htm, accessed December 16, 2015.

Mariani, Mike, "Apocalypse Now: How Television's Boldest Sci-Fi Shows Are Tackling Contemporary Injustice," *Pacific Standard*, October 21, 2016.

Mason, Kathy S., *Natural Museums: U.S. National Parks, 1872–1916* (East Lansing: Michigan State University Press, 2004).

Mather, Stephen, "Annual Report of the Director of the National Park Service" (U.S. Department of the Interior, October 3, 1925).

McNamee, Thomas, *The Grizzly Bear* (New York: Knopf, 1984).

Mencken, H.L., *The American Language* (New York: Knopf, 1919).

Merrill, Marlene Deahl, ed., *Yellowstone and the Great West: Journals, Letters and Images from the 1871 Hayden Expedition* (Lincoln: University of Nebraska Press, 1999).

Merrill, Marlene, ed., *Seeing Yellowstone in 1871: Earliest Descriptions & Images from the Field* (Lincoln: University of Nebraska Press, 2005).

Meyer, Judith L., *The Spirit of Yellowstone: The Cultural Evolution of a National Park* (Boulder: Rowman and Littlefield, 1996).

Middleton, Arthur, "Is the Wolf a Real American Hero?" *New York Times*, March 9, 2014.

Miller, Laura, "Fresh Hell," *New Yorker*, June 14, 2010.

Miller, Michael E., "Bison selfies are a bad idea: Tourist gored in Yellowstone as another photo goes awry," *Washington Post*, July 23, 2015.

Morand, Anne, Joni L. Kinsey, and Mary Panzer, *Splendors of the American West: Thomas Moran's Art of the Grand Canyon and Yellowstone* (Seattle: University of Washington Press, 1990).

Morris, Edmund, *The Rise of Theodore Roosevelt* (New York: Modern Library, 2001).

Morrison, Micah, *Fire in Paradise: The Yellowstone Fires and the Politics of Environmentalism* (New York: HarperCollins, 1993).

Morrow, Thomas, et. al., *Hotel del Coronado* (Coronado: Hotel del Coronado, 1984).

Nabokov, Peter, and Lawrence Loendorf, *Restoring a Presence: American Indians and Yellowstone National Park* (Norman: University of Oklahoma Press, 2004).

Nash, Roderick, *Wilderness and the American Mind* (New Haven: Yale University Press, 1967; fifth edition 2014).

National Interagency Fire Center, "Federal Firefighting Costs (Suppression Only)," https://www.nifc.gov/fireInfo/fireInfo_documents/SuppCosts.pdf, accessed October 27, 2016.

Naylor, David, "The Old Faithful Inn and its Legacy: The Vernacular Transformed" PhD. dissertation, Cornell University, May 1990).

Nicholas, Liza, *Becoming Western: Stories of Culture and Identity in the Cowboy State* (Lincoln: University of Nebraska Press, 2006).

"Notes from Washington," *The Ladies' Repository: Universalist Monthly Magazine*, 48 (July 1872): 158–159.

"Old Faithful Geyser, Yellowstone National Park," Ansel Adams Photographs of National Parks and Monuments, 1941–1942, National Archives Identifier: 520017.

"Old Report Describes Photographer W. H. Jackson's Return To Yellowstone National Park At The Age Of 94," *National Parks Traveler*, August 28, 2014.

"Old West Dinner Cookout: An evening you won't soon forget," http://www.yellowstonenationalparklodges.com/things-to-do/summer-things-to-do

/wild-west-adventures/old-west-dinner-cookout/, accessed November 24, 2015.

Olsen, Jack, *Night of the Grizzlies* (New York: G.P. Putnam's Sons, 1969).

Pitts, Leonard, Jr. *Forward From this Moment: Selected Columns, 1994–2009* (Evanston: Agate Publishing, 2009).

Pritchard, James A., *Preserving Yellowstone's Natural Conditions: Science and the Perception of Nature* (Lincoln: University of Nebraska Press, 1999).

Punke, Michael, *Last Stand: George Bird Grinnell, the Battle to Save the Buffalo, and the Birth of the New West* (Washington: Smithsonian, 2007).

Pyne, Stephen J., *Fire in America: A Cultural History of Wildland and Rural Fire* (Princeton: Princeton University Press, 1982).

———, *The Northern Rockies: A Fire Survey*, To the Last Smoke, Vol. 3 (Tucson: University of Arizona Press, 2016).

Quinn, Ruth, *Weaver of Dreams: The Life and Architecture of Robert C. Reamer* (Gardiner: Leslie and Ruth Quinn, 2004).

———, "Overcoming Obscurity: The Yellowstone Architecture of Robert C. Reamer," *Yellowstone Science* 12, no. 2 (Spring 2004): 23–40.

Rasker, Ray, et. al., "Gateways to Yellowstone: Protecting the Wild Heart of Our Region's Thriving Economy" (Helena: National Parks Conservation Association, Northern Rockies office, 2006).

Reinhart, Karen, and Jeff Henry, *Yellowstone's Rebirth by Fire: Rising from the Ashes of the 1988 Wildfires* (Helena: Farcountry Press, 2008).

Righter, Robert W., *Crucible for Conservation: The Creation of Grand Teton National Park* (Boulder: Colorado Associated University Press, 1982).

Ringley, Tom, *Wranglin' Notes: A Chronicle of Eatons' Ranch* (Greybull: Pronghorn Press, 2012).

Ross-Bryant, Lynn, *Pilgrimage to the National Parks: Religion and Nature in the United States* (London: Routledge, 2013).

Rothman, Hal K., *Blazing Heritage: A History of Wildland Fire in the National Parks* (Oxford: Oxford University Press, 2007).

———, *Devils Bargains: Tourism in the Twentieth-Century American West* (Lawrence: University Press of Kansas, 1998).

———, *Neon Metropolis: How Las Vegas Started the Twenty-First Century* (London: Routledge, 2002).

———, *A Test of Adversity and Strength: Wildland Fire in the National Park System* (Washington: National Park Service, 2006).

Runte, Alfred, *National Parks: The American Experience* (Lincoln: University of Nebraska Press, 1979).

Rydell, Kiki Leigh, and Mary Shivers Culpin, *Managing the "Matchless Wonders": A History Of Administrative Development In Yellowstone National Park, 1872–1965* (Yellowstone National Park, Wyoming: National Park Service, Yellowstone Center for Resources, YCR-2006-03, 2006), 100.

Sandberg, Jeni, "History Lesson: The Aluminum Christmas Tree," https://blog.etsy.com/en/2013/history-lessons-the-aluminum-christmas-tree/, accessed May 29, 2015.

Schmidt, Carl E., *A Western Trip* (Detroit: Herold Press, c. 1904).

Schullery, Paul, *The Bears of Yellowstone* (Worland: High Plains Publishing Company, 1992).

———, *Searching for Yellowstone: Ecology and Wonder in the Last Wilderness* (Boston: Hougton Mifflin, 1997).

———, "'Buffalo' Jones and the Bison Herd in Yellowstone: Another Look," *Montana: The Magazine of Western History* 26, no. 3 (Summer 1976): 40–51.

Schullery, Paul, and Lee H. Whittlesey, *Myth and History in the Creation of Yellowstone National Park* (Lincoln: University of Nebraska Press, 2003).

Sellars, Richard West, *Preserving Nature in the National Parks: A History* (New Haven: Yale University Press, 2009).

Seton, Ernest Thompson, *The Biography of a Grizzly* (New York: Century, 1900).

———, *Krag and Johnny Bear: With Pictures* (New York: C. Scribner's Sons, 1906).

———, *Lives of the Hunted* (New York: C. Scribner's Sons, 1912).

———, *Trail of an Artist-naturalist: The Autobiography of Ernest Thompson Seton* (New York: Scribner's, 1948).

———, *Wild Animals at Home* (New York: Grosset & Dunlap, 1913).

Seton, Ernest Thompson—*see also* Thompson, Ernest Seton.

Seton, Ernest Thompson, Jeremy M. Johnston, ed., and Charles R. Preston, ed., *Wahb: The Biography of a Grizzly* (Norman: University of Oklahoma Press, 2015).

Seton, Grace Gallatin, *A Woman Tenderfoot* (New York: Doubleday, Page, 1900).

Shankland, Robert, *Steve Mather of the National Parks* (New York: Knopf. 1951, 1970).

Sholly, Dan R., with Steve M. Newman, *Guardians of Yellowstone: An Intimate Look at the Challenges of Protecting America's Foremost Wilderness Park* (New York: William Morrow and Company, 1991).

Silliman, Lee, "'As Kind and Generous a Host as Ever Lived': Howard Eaton and the Birth of Western Dude Ranching," *American West* 16 (July/ August 1979): 18–31.

Slotkin, Richard, *Gunfighter Nation: The Myth of the Frontier in Twentieth-century America* (Norman: University of Oklahoma Press, 1992).

———, *The Fatal Environment: The Myth of the Frontier in the Age of Industrialization, 1800–1890* (New York: Atheneum, 1985).

Smith, Alison, "The Sublime in Crisis: Landscape Painting after Turner," in Nigel Llewellyn and Christine Riding (eds.), *The Art of the Sublime* (London: Tate Research Publication, 2013).

Smith, Conrad, *Media and Apocalypse: News Coverage of the Yellowstone Forest Fires, Exxon Valdez Oil Spill, and Loma Prieta Earthquake (Contributions to the Study of Mass Media and Communications)* (Westport: Greenwood Press, 1992).

Smith, Jordan Fisher, *Engineering Eden: The True Story of a Violent Death, a Trial, and the Fight over Controlling Nature* (New York: Crown, 2016).

Spaulding, Jonathan, *Ansel Adams and the American Landscape: A Biography* (Oakland: University of California Press, 1998).

Standing Bear, Chief [Luther], *Land of the Spotted Eagle* (Boston: Houghton Mifflin, 1933).

Strayed, Cheryl, *Wild: From Lost to Found on the Pacific Crest Trail* (New York: Knopf Doubleday, 2012).

"Summer of Fire," *Retro Report*, September 2, 2013.

Sutter, Paul, *Driven Wild: How the Fight against Automobiles Launched the Modern Wilderness Movement* (Seattle: University of Washington Press, 2005).

Swain, Donald, *Wilderness Defender: Horace M. Albright and Conservation* (Chicago: University of Chicago Press, 1970).

Taylor, Beth, "Inside Yellowstone: Sheepeater Cliff" [video], https://www.nps.gov/media/video/view.htm?id=007BBFE1-155D-451F-6779FB37D3D5BC36, accessed November 19, 2016.

Thompson, Ernest Seton, "Elkland," *Recreation* 7 (1897): 199.

———, "Elkland II: The Beaver Pond," *Recreation* 7 (1897): 289.

———, "Mammals of the Yellowstone National Park," *Recreation* 8 (1897): 365–371.

Thompson, Ernest Seton—*see also* Seton, Ernest Thompson.

Tiffany, Russ, and Catherine Ohl, "Remembering A. Andrew Hauk," Pacific Rim Snow Sports Alliance, http://www.pacificrimalliance.org/F.PublicAffairs/SkiHistory/FWSA/AndyHauk.htm, accessed April 22, 2015.

Turner, Allan, "Hays Kirby, scion of prominent Houston family, dies," *Houston Chronicle*, Saturday, December 19, 2009.

USGS, "Questions About Supervolcanoes," http://volcanoes.usgs.gov/volcanoes/yellowstone/yellowstone_sub_page_49.html, accessed June 4, 2015.

USGS, "Steam Explosions, Earthquakes, and Volcanic Eruptions—What's in Yellowstone's Future?" http://pubs.usgs.gov/fs/2005/3024/., accessed June 4, 2015.

Vallée, Jean-Marc, dir., *Wild*, 2014.

Varley, John, "Science and the Media," *Yellowstone Science*, 17, no. 2 (2009): 16–17.

"'Wab,' Wisest of Bears, Falls Victim to Anderson's Rifle After Many Years of Defiance," *Park County Enterprise*, September 22, 1915.

Wagner, Frederic H., and Joseph L. Sax, *Wildlife Policies in the U.S. National Parks* (Washington: Island Press, 1995).

Walker, Carter G., "Eatons' Ranch," *Big Sky Journal* (Spring 2006): 112–117.

Watry, Elizabeth A., *Women in Wonderland: Lives, Legends and Legacies of Yellowstone National Park* (Helena: Riverbend Publishing, 2012).

Weber, Joe, and Selima Sultana, "Why Do So Few Minority People Visit National Parks? Visitation and the Accessibility of 'America's Best Idea,'" *Annals of the Association of American Geographers* 103, no. 3: 437–464.

Weixelman, Joseph, "The Power to Evoke Wonder: Native Americans and the Geysers of Yellowstone National Park" (Bozeman: Montana State University, 1992).

Westerling, Anthony L., et. al., "Continued warming could transform Greater Yellowstone fire regimes by mid-21st century," PNAS 108, no. 32 (June 24, 2011).

Whithorn, Doris, "Wrangling Dudes in Yellowstone," *Frontier Times*, November 1969, 18–22.

Whittlesey, Lee H., *Death in Yellowstone: Accidents and Foolhardiness in the First National Park* (Boulder: Roberts Rinehart, 1995).

———, *Gateway to Yellowstone: The Raucous Town of Cinnabar on the Montana Frontier* (Helena: TwoDot, 2015).

———, *Storytelling in Yellowstone: Horse and Buggy Tour Guides* (Albuquerque: University of New Mexico Press, 2007).

———, *Yellowstone Place Names* (Gardiner: Wonderland Publishing Company, 2006).

———, "Loss of a Sacred Shrine: How the National Park Service Anguished over Yellowstone's Campfire Myth, 1960–1980," *The George Wright Forum* 27, no. 1 (2010): 94–120.

———, "Native Americans, the Earliest Interpreters," *The George Wright Forum* 19, no. 3 (2002): 40–51.

Whittlesey, Lee H., and Paul Schullery, "The Roosevelt Arch: A Centennial History of an American Icon," *Yellowstone Science* (Summer 2003): 14–15.

Wilkins, Thurman, *Thomas Moran: Artist of the Mountains* (Norman: University of Oklahoma Press, 1998).

Wilkinson, Todd, "Bison Calf's Death Shows Dangers of People in Yellowstone," nationalgeographic.com, May 17, 2016.

———, "Fires of '88 were just a warming warning," *Jackson Hole News & Guide*, August 2013.

Wilson, Merrill Ann, "Rustic Architecture: The National Park Style," *Trends,* (July August September, 1976).

Wilton, Andrew, and Tim Barringer, *American Sublime: Landscape Painting in the United States 1820–1880* (Princeton: Princeton University Press, 2002).

Wister, Owen, "Old Yellowstone Days." *Harper's Magazine* 172 (March 1936): 471–480.

Yates, Emma Hayden Eames, *70 Miles from a Lemon* (New York: Houghton Mifflin, 1947).

Yellowstone National Park Lodges, "Services and Amenities," http://www.yellowstone nationalparklodges.com/lodging/services-and-amenities/, accessed Sept 5, 2016.

Yellowstone National Park, *Yellowstone Resources and Issues Handbook 2014* (Yellowstone National Park, WY: Yellowstone National Park, 2014).

"Yogi Bear's Big Break," http://www.dailymotion.com/video/xy25b0_yogi-bear-01 -yogi-bear-s-big-break_fun, accessed May 28, 2015.

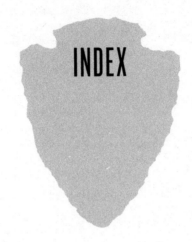

INDEX